Preventing the Next Mortgage Crisis

Preventing the Next Mortgage Crisis

The Meltdown, the Federal Response, and the Future of Housing in America

Dan Immergluck

ROWMAN & LITTLEFIELD
Lanham • Boulder • New York • London

Published by Rowman & Littlefield
A wholly owned subsidiary of The Rowman & Littlefield Publishing Group, Inc.
4501 Forbes Boulevard, Suite 200, Lanham, Maryland 20706
www.rowman.com

Unit A, Whitacre Mews, 26-34 Stannary Street, London SE11 4AB

British Library Cataloguing in Publication Information Available

Library of Congress Cataloging-in-Publication Data

Immergluck, Daniel.
Preventing the next mortgage crisis : the meltdown, the federal response, and the future of housing in America / Daniel Immergluck.
p. cm.
Includes bibliographical references and index.
ISBN 978-1-4422-5313-1 (cloth : alk. paper) -- ISBN 978-1-4422-5314-8 (electronic)
1. Mortgage loans--United States. 2. Mortgage loans--Government policy--United States. 3. Housing--United States--Finance. 4. Foreclosure--United States. 5. Subprime mortgage loans--United States. 6. Financial crises--United States--Prevention. I. Title.
HG5095.I453 2015
332.7'220973--dc23
                                                                                        2015022426

Printed in the United States of America

Contents

List of Figures

Acknowledgments

This book is primarily an effort to help inform housing and housing-finance policy in the aftermath of the U.S. mortgage crisis. It is also aimed at students of housing and urban policy who are interested in gaining a firmer grasp on the origins, effects, policy responses, and potential long-term consequences of the great U.S. mortgage crisis of the early twenty-first century. Besides all of the tumult and pain it caused for families and neighborhoods, the crisis appears to have also left in its wake a tremendous amount of confusion about its causes, whom it hit hardest, and what lessons we should learn from both the crisis itself and the responses to it. Now, almost a decade after the crisis reached national scale, policymakers are continuing to lay new pieces of the housing finance infrastructure that will shape not only individual families' access to mortgages—and so shape their housing options—but also the metropolitan fabric of the United States. The housing and neighborhood choices that are open to working-class and middle-income families will be driven, in fundamental ways, by how the housing finance system is shaped by policymakers over the next decade.

A more-than-half-century struggle to increase fairness in housing and mortgage markets is threatened to be unwound due to the parlaying of misinformation over why vulnerable families ended up in foreclosure and neighborhoods were pock-marked with vacant homes. Some parties have tried to blame the crisis on hard-working families and communities of color. Others have pointed at fair housing and community reinvestment policies—ironically, policies that have rarely been vigorously enforced. Some of this revisionism is trickling into (and sometimes, flooding into) ongoing policy debates about how the United States can create a stable and sound mortgage market. In these debates, issues of access and fairness are sometimes overlooked. Too often, as has been common in much of the history of financial regulation in the United States, there appears to be more concern for investors and financial interests than for the fate of modest- and middle-income homeowners and the neighborhoods in which they live.

This book would not have been possible without the help of a great many individuals and organizations. I was lucky enough to have the input of several national experts when writing an earlier paper that formed the basis for chapter 3. These included Frank Alexander, Kevin Byers, Phillip Comeau, Sarah Greenberg, Alan Mallach, Kathe Newman, Ira Rheingold, and Alan M. White. Of course, any errors—as well as all opinions—remain entirely my responsibility. I also want to thank the students who have taken my housing-policy class over the last decade or so. The discussions in that class—some of the best I have had in my teaching career—were critical to my developing the skeletons of this book, as well as providing fertile ground for seeding key housing research questions. I have also been aided by discussions over the effects of housing finance and urban futures with two of my PhD students, Yun Sang Lee and Elora Raymond. Their excellent work has challenged me to think in new ways about the longer-term impacts of housing finance and housing policy on cities and neighborhoods. Abram Lueders provided excellent editorial assistance; the book is clearly better than it would have been without his efforts. I also want to thank the very helpful folks at Rowman and Littlefield, including Jon Sisk, Natalie Mandziuk, and Chris Basso. Lastly, and most importantly, I want to thank my family—Lilly, Kate, and Anna—for their support and patience during this project and at all times.

List of Abbreviations

2MP Second Lien Modification Program
AEI American Enterprise Institute
AMTPA Alternative Mortgage Transaction Parity Act
ARRA American Recovery and Revitalization Act
ASF American Securitization Forum
ATR Ability to Repay
CDBG Community Development Block Grant
CDO Collateralized Debt Obligation
CFPB Consumer Financial Protection Bureau
CFTC Commodities Futures Trading Commission
CMO Collateralized Mortgage Obligation
CRA Community Reinvestment Act
DIDMCA Depository Institutions Deregulation and Monetary Control Act
EESA Emergency Economic Stabilization Act
EHLP Emergency Homeowners Loan Program
Fannie Mae Federal National Mortgage Association
FCIC Financial Crisis Inquiry Commission
FCRA Fair Credit Reporting Act
FHA Federal Housing Administration
FHFA Federal Housing Finance Agency
FIRREA Financial Institutions Reform Recovery and Enforcement Act
Freddie Mac Federal Home Loan Mortgage Corporation
FTC Federal Trade Commission
GAO Government Accountability Office
Ginnie Mae Government National Mortgage Association
GSE Government Sponsored Enterprises

H4H Hope for Homeowners
HAFA Home Affordable Foreclosure Alternatives
HAMP Home Affordable Modification Program
HARP Home Affordable Refinance Program
HERA Housing and Economic Recovery Act
HFA Housing Finance Agency
HMDA Home Mortgage Disclosure Act
HOEPA Home Ownership and Equity Protection Act
HOLA Home Owners Loan Act
HOLC Home Owners Loan Corporation
HUD Housing and Urban Development
LTV Loan-to-Value
MBS Mortgage Backed Securities
MHA Making Home Affordable
MSA Metropolitan Statistical Area
NCST National Community Stabilization Trust
NFMC National Foreclosure Mitigation Counseling
NPV Net Present Value
NRSRO Nationally Recognized Statistical Rating Organizations
NSP Neighborhood Stabilization Program
OCC Office of the Comptroller of the Currency
OECD Organization for Economic Cooperation and Development
OTS Office of Thrift Supervision
PLS Private-Label Securitization
PRA Principal Reduction Alternative
QM Qualified Mortgage
QRM Qualified Residential Mortgage
REMIC Real Estate Mortgage Investment Conduit
REO Real Estate Owned
RESPA Real Estate Settlement Procedures Act
RMBS Residential Mortgage-Backed Securities
S&L Savings and Loan
S&P Standard and Poors
SEC Securities and Exchange Commission
SIGTARP Special Inspector General for the Troubled Asset Relief Program
SMMEA Secondary Mortgage Market Enhancement Act
TARP Troubled Asset Relief Program
TILA Truth in Lending Act
UP Home Affordable Unemployment Program
VA Veterans Administration
YSP Yield Spread Premium

Introduction

The great U.S. mortgage crisis of the 2000s was a transformative event that will reverberate for decades across families, neighborhoods, and cities. It will have long-term effects on financial regulation, housing policy, and community-development planning. The crisis reversed decades of achievements in housing and community development by lowering family wealth, damaging credit histories, and scarring thousands of modest-income and minority neighborhoods with vacant homes and blight. Of course, it also triggered the global financial crisis and the Great Recession. Estimates of the total costs of the crisis have ranged widely, but generally run well into the trillions of dollars.[1]

Now, with the benefit of hindsight and years of research on various aspects of the crisis, we can examine more carefully what went wrong, and identify the factors that created a fragile housing-finance system that provided fertile ground for calamity. We can also examine the governmental response to the crisis, including who benefitted most and least from the response, and how a more effective and fair response could have been formulated. Such retrospection should improve our ability not only to reduce the probability and severity of future crises, but also to respond more effectively and fairly when the next major downturn inevitably occurs.

To reduce the incidence of future crises, we must also look at ways to build a more stable and fair housing-finance system that is less at the mercy of the booms and busts of global finance. Housing finance must be treated differently than other forms of finance because it helps determine access to stable, decent-quality, and affordable housing. In the United States, especially, it also affects the geography of housing and educational opportunities; poor access to ownership limits where families can live and attend school. Housing markets shape our communities, our neighborhoods, and our educational and economic opportunities. Like it or not, the U.S. tradition of local control and the primacy of local government in providing public services mean that the construction of local housing markets—driven in part by housing finance—drives our local political governance and the composition of our local communities.

This book looks both backward and forward at housing-finance systems in the United States, with a particular eye to the great mortgage crisis and the lessons that it offers for the future of housing and mortgage markets. It is not the only book to examine the crisis—there are now scores of such books—and it will not be the last. However, this book differs from many others due to its continuous concern for the racial, ethnic, and geographic impacts of housing-finance issues, including their impact on urban and metropolitan futures. It should be of particular interest to those concerned with urban form, neighborhood change and stability, and urban planning and policy, as well as those interested in housing and mortgage markets more generally.

THE CORE THEMES OF THE BOOK

There are six major themes of the book. The first is that the mortgage crisis was the result of a long-term shift of U.S. housing finance toward a system that was increasingly dominated by the frenzy of private global capital markets, which were drawn to U.S. housing markets by a thirty-year pattern of deregulation and privatization. U.S. mortgage markets were never primarily public-sector markets, but they have generally relied on closely supervised institutions, federal guarantees and insurance, and less volatile circuits of capital than the private-label securitization markets of the late 1990s and 2000s. The rise of private-label securitization allowed for a much more direct, less supervised connection between yield-hungry global capital and individual homeowners and homebuyers, with little governmental oversight. These investors sought places to invest that would generate higher returns than traditional mortgage markets, and when opportunities for providing higher-yielding subprime private-label securities appeared, investors rushed in and demanded more of them. The capital markets met their appetite by offering greater and greater volumes of mortgage-backed securities and collateralized debt obligations. Credit-rating agencies seized on these booming markets and provided as many AAA ratings as they could muster, allowing the pool of investors to grow even further. Some observers lay principal blame for the crisis at the foot of government housing and community reinvestment policy. However, evidence—much of it reviewed in this book—has now accumulated that overwhelmingly dismisses such arguments, and hopefully this debate can finally be put to rest.

A second major theme of the book is that the costs of the crisis go far beyond the loss of macroeconomic and financial stability, on which those within the Washington policy bubble so often focus. Macroeconomic stability is of course important, but the most acute costs of the crisis were geographically and racially concentrated in certain communities. Modest-income families and families of color suffered, on average, far more than others, as did younger families with children. Modest-income and minority neighborhoods suffered far more than more affluent communities, and recovery has lagged in these places. The costs of the crisis were clearly large enough to justify the relatively small cost of increased regulation. At the same time, policymakers should be careful that efforts to restructure housing finance do not disproportionately harm the very households and neighborhoods that bore the brunt of the crisis.

A third theme of the book is that the housing-finance system that evolved since the last quarter of the twentieth century not only was increasingly prone to collapse, but also evolved into a highly atomized, excessively complex system that was built for the production and servicing of commoditized, well-performing mortgage products. At the same time, it introduced a large segment of mortgages that were very risky and prone to high levels of default, especially when housing values were not rising. The aim of the system increasingly focused on maximizing financial returns for investors and other financial interests, yet market participants and regulators clung to low-stress assumptions and failed to consider the need for resilience to severe housing-market distress.

Another theme is that the federal response to the foreclosure crisis was slow, timid, and sometimes ineffective. The crisis began at a national scale by early 2007 and in some places it began as early as 2004 or 2005. However, while the banking industry began receiving substantial federal aid in 2008, policymakers initially only offered homeowners minor counseling initiatives. When substantive loan-modification programs were developed in 2009, they were often timid and halting and did not reach appreciable scale until 2011. By this time, the foreclosure problem had shifted significantly to the prime mortgage market, in which borrowers were more frequently white and middle-class, and many of the hardest-hit communities had already been through the ringer. Overall, the federal Home Affordable Modification Program (HAMP) never came close to its goal of reducing the mortgage payments of 3 to 4 million homeowners. The federal government's major refinancing program, the Home Affordable Refinance Program (HARP), was more successful in the long run, but it took a long time to reach its stride. Again, the fact that this program reached greater scale later in the crisis meant that the program bypassed millions of struggling homeowners in the first few years of the crisis, including many modest-income and minority homeowners. In the meantime, the Federal Reserve's quantitative easing policies brought very low interest rates to middle- and upper-income home-owners who were not in distress and could easily refinance their mortgages.

The fifth theme of the book is perhaps the most optimistic one, although a good deal of longer-term uncertainty remains. The Dodd-Frank Act passed in 2010 has largely restructured the consumer-protection regulation of mort-gages in the United States. Among its hallmarks is the creation of a high-profile Consumer Financial Protection Bureau (CFPB), a muscular agency with a primary mission of protecting homeowners and consumers against abusive and unfair financial products and enforcing stronger consumer-pro-tection laws. These include new mortgage regulations that require lenders to confirm that a borrower has the ability to repay the mortgage. Despite these and other gains, Dodd-Frank did not cure all the shortcomings of the mort-gage and financial markets, and a great deal remains undone. Moreover, regulatory gains are generally not that difficult to reverse, and foes of Dodd-Frank have continuously called for repealing various parts of the law and for reducing the power of the CFPB.

A final and key theme of the book is the continued need for a strong federal role in housing finance. Many of the proposals that have been offered for reforming housing finance since 2008 have articulated a fundamental goal of reducing the federal role—or increasing the role of private capital—in the mortgage market. Raising such an objective to the level of a fundamen-tal goal makes little sense. This is a means—a debatable one at that—and not an end. The fundamental goal of housing-finance reform should be to gener-ate sound, affordable, and fair mortgage markets. It is far from clear that measures placing private capital in the driver's seat of housing finance will achieve such a goal. I argue for a primarily public option in housing finance that utilizes private capital, but channeled through a publicly owned infra-structure. One of the key dangers of reducing the federal role in housing finance is the difficulty of pooling and cross-subsidizing borrowers, which allows a broad class of mortgage borrowers to obtain credit on similar terms and prices. Excessive privatization will lead to large levels of risk-based pricing, which would mean that those least able to afford high-cost mort-gages would be most likely to receive them.

ORGANIZATION OF THE BOOK

The book contains five core chapters and a conclusion that pulls together my findings and provides recommendations for policymakers. Chapter 1 details the formative and proximate causes of the housing crisis. While the chapter does not aim to provide a detailed history of U.S. housing finance, it explains the increasing fragility of the U.S. mortgage market in a historical context. It explains how long-term deregulation and a shift in lending from more to less regulated market segments enabled the growth of reckless mortgages funded by private-label securitization. The chapter explains how policy enabled this shift, beginning in the 1980s, and continuing into the 2000s. It also attempts to put to rest various false narratives of the crisis, including those that pin the blame on federal housing policy or those that claim that Fannie Mae and Freddie Mac had a principal, causal role in the subprime crisis.

Chapter 2 reviews the extensive literature on the household- and neighborhood-level costs of the crisis, and on the spatial concentration of subprime lending and foreclosures. The crisis resulted in a large drop in home values for many families, but the geographic concentration of the losses was disproportionately concentrated in Latino and African-American communities. Moreover, because modest-income households and households of color tended to have fewer assets in the stock market, and because home values have been slower to recover in their neighborhoods, they have tended to lose more net worth than white and more affluent households. Mortgage distress and foreclosure have also caused increased residential instability, health problems, and lower credit scores among directly affected families. However, the costs of foreclosure spread beyond the borrower's household. A good deal of empirical research has now documented that foreclosures result in lower neighborhood property values, higher levels of vacancy and blight, and neighborhood crime. Lower property values can, in turn, result in even more foreclosures, creating a vicious cycle of neighborhood decline.

In chapter 3, I review and evaluate the federal response to the foreclosure crisis. The chapter focuses particularly on the direct measures to reduce foreclosures—especially the Obama administration's Home Affordable Modification Program (HAMP)—and efforts to mitigate the negative impacts of foreclosure on local neighborhoods. The chapter also describes some of the more successful components of the policy response, including the Home Affordable Refinance Program (HARP) and later phases of the HAMP program that reduced the principal balances of loans. However, the fact that these programs reached greater scale and effectiveness after the core of the subprime crisis had passed means that many of the beneficiaries of these latter phases were not members of the communities hit hardest by the crisis.

Chapter 4 outlines the regulatory response to the crisis, focusing on various achievements contained in the Dodd-Frank Act of 2010. The act was a major milestone in regulatory reform, containing many provisions that consumer advocates had called for in recent decades. The crisis provided the critical context for Dodd-Frank, a context that allowed proponents of increased regulation to win rare victories against the financial services industry. The act was not a complete victory for regulatory advocates, however, and left many aspects of regulatory reform unfinished. Moreover, foes of regulation will almost certainly continue to try to weaken Dodd-Frank in bits and pieces.

In chapter 5, I take up the issue of the restructuring of housing finance in the United States, focusing on the future of Fannie Mae and Freddie Mac, the two government-sponsored enterprises that have been effectively controlled by the federal government since 2008. In this chapter, I adopt the uncommon position of calling for a large, permanent federal role in housing finance in the United States. Most proposals for reforming the housing-finance system have private actors handle most aspects of the mortgage-funding process, similar to the private-label securitization system that funded the subprime boom. The most common type of proposal calls for placing private securitization at the core of the funding system, but with some federal insurance and oversight over the quality of the securities and the loans backing them. Private capital would be the first-loss source of insurance, but the federal government would step in during a major collapse. Some on the political right have proposed even greater levels of privatization, in which no federal insurance is involved and the markets are left almost entirely to private-label securitizers acting on their own. The result of either partial or full privatization would include substantial risk-based pricing, so that less affluent borrowers and borrowers with even minor credit blemishes would pay much higher mortgage costs, resulting in a system where the "poor pay more" for a basic necessity like housing.

Finally, the book concludes with a synthesis of the key findings and arguments of the book followed by a variety of major policy recommendations. The book does not address all aspects of housing policy, or even of mortgage market policy, but it identifies some key policy positions that are critical for the long-term provision of stable, affordable, and fair housing markets.

Chapter One

Revisiting the Origins of the Subprime Crisis

Since the advent of the U.S. mortgage crisis, there have been hundreds of books and thousands of research reports and academic articles written on various aspects of the crisis.[1] Many of these have focused on one or more factors that contributed to the crisis. This chapter provides a summary of key forces that led to the crisis or, in some cases, to the development of a fundamentally fragile mortgage market, whose vulnerability helped enable the crisis. While some factors, such as federal policies preempting state consumer-protection laws, were near-term spurs to higher levels of subprime lending, others—such as the migration of lending activity from savings and loans (S&Ls) to less-regulated mortgage companies—led to the development of a mortgage market that was more risk-loving, less regulated, and more prone to cataclysmic failure.

RESTRUCTURING HOUSING FINANCE IN THE UNITED STATES: THE DELIBERATE SHIFT TO SECURITIZATION IN THE TWENTIETH CENTURY

As the news media attempted to explain the origins of the mortgage crisis beginning in 2007, many were introduced to the term *mortgage securitization* for the first time. However, securitization had become the dominant form of funding mortgages in the United States over more than three decades, beginning slowly in the 1970s, and then accelerating in the 1980s and 1990s. Put most simply, securitization is a process in which the funding of mortgage loans is separated from the origination (and originator) of the loans. Financial institutions bundle loans together to form isolated investment vehicles that are no longer tied to the fate of the originating lender. A key objective of securitization is to turn isolated bundles of loans into a source of cash flow for investors.

The rise of securitization as the dominant funding pathway in the U.S. mortgage market led to the widespread vertical dis-integration, or unbundling, of the mortgage market (Jacobides 2005). It enabled the origination process to be separated from the funding and servicing of the loan, resulting in what became known as the "originate-to-distribute" model of mortgage lending. Vertical dis-integration meant that more contractual relationships were now required between originators, issuers of the securities, investors that purchased the securities, credit-rating agencies, servicers, and other market participants. In the earlier originate-to-hold model used by S&Ls and banks, and still dominant in most other industrialized countries, these functions were integrated within the institution that originated, funded, and often serviced the loan. Securitization was spurred and fostered by policy changes over roughly a twenty-five-year period. As securitization structures became more complex, higher levels of risk were tolerated at the point of mortgage origination. The greater complexities and separation between sources and uses of credit also obscured the underlying characteristics of borrowers and mortgages, and increased the transactional tensions between different parties in the chain of capital.

Mortgage securitization has often been portrayed as a private-sector financial innovation. Yet, it was the Government National Mortgage Association (Ginnie Mae), the federal agency that facilitates the purchase of Federal Housing Administration (FHA) loans, that issued the first residential mortgage-backed securities (RMBS) in the early 1970s, guaranteeing interest and principal payments on pools of FHA- and Veterans Administration–insured mortgages (Geisst 1990). This first generation of RMBS was the "pass-through" security. Ginnie Mae, and the government-sponsored enterprises (GSEs), Fannie Mae and Freddie Mac, purchased loans and assembled them into pools, which diversified risk by including loans from many lenders and different regions. These agencies then issued bonds or certificates in which the cash flow generated by the loans in the pool was passed through to the investors in a pro-rata fashion. This was a fairly straightforward process that did not involve complex hierarchical structuring into different layers of risk, and thus such single-class pass-throughs were typically not classified as part of what became known as "structured finance" RMBS.

GSE securitization led to a restructuring of the lending industry. It offered greater spatial diversification of a lender's assets, and more liquidity because these diversified assets were more marketable than whole loans. Increasingly, a larger number of somewhat thinly capitalized nondepository mortgage companies were able to use independent mortgage brokers to market and bring loan applications to them for final underwriting and origination. Then, as originate-to-distribute lenders, they were able to sell off these loans to Fannie Mae or Freddie Mac (or Ginnie Mae in the case of FHA loans).

Following the growth of securitization, originate-to-hold S&Ls lost market share to mortgage companies that had gained access to inexpensive funds and were able to offer long-term, fixed-rate mortgages at competitive interest rates. Their national scope and ability to operate without brick-and-mortar facilities made them formidable competition for S&Ls, which operated local branches. In the age of securitization, the advantages of the S&L were diminished by the commoditization of residential credit.

Pass-through RMBS, though assisting in diversifying the geography- and lender-specific risks that investors would face, did little to deal with other risks facing investors, including overall market default and prepayment risks. In order to mitigate some of these problems, Freddie Mac issued the first collateralized mortgage obligation (CMO) in 1983 (Green and Wachter 2007). A CMO is a more complicated form of RMBS than a pass-through, because it allocates risk across different investors—some of whom are more willing to accept various risks than others—by structuring the security into different segments that pay back over varying schedules. CMOs and other types of structured RMBS create a hierarchy of risk by allowing some bondholders to receive their principal back before others, and some more risk-tolerant bondholders to bear losses before the holders of less risky senior bonds. These different levels of risk, which are usually accompanied by varying rates of investment return, are called "tranches" (French for *slices*) and are generally classified according to the rating they receive from the credit-rating agencies, such as AAA, AA, A, BBB, BB, B, and so on. Securitization—both of the pass-through and structured sort—provided greater liquidity to lenders that otherwise had access to relatively little capital compared to the deposits and other assets on which a bank or S&L could rely.

The eventual dominance of securitization in U.S. mortgage markets and, especially, the growth of private-label securitization beginning at the end of the twentieth century are best attributed to both active and passive federal financial deregulation in the 1980s, as well as legislation specifically supporting securitization. Active deregulation included federal efforts that allowed lenders to circumvent state consumer-protection and securities regulations. Passive deregulation included policies explicitly favoring the securitization circuit of mortgage credit over the more heavily regulated S&L and commercial bank circuit. Federal policymakers helped restructure the mortgage industry from a predominantly local to a predominantly national system, and from one in which most loans were made by more regulated depositories to one in which less regulated mortgage companies and mortgage brokers dominated. This transformation constituted not only a change in the fundamental funding mechanisms of the mortgage market but also a form of passive deregulation, in which market restructuring was not accompanied by a corresponding restructuring in the regulation and, more importantly, supervision of this newer channel of mortgage credit.

The failure of policymakers and regulatory agencies to expand regulatory supervision and enforcement to emerging lenders and new credit channels meant the path toward greater overall deregulation of the mortgage marketplace was well paved by the mid- to late 1980s. Moreover, legislators and regulators constructed policy that allowed depository institutions, especially commercial banks, to acquire or affiliate with these less regulated entities. This meant that the new financial conglomerates could conduct most of their mortgage lending through less regulated and less supervised mortgage company subsidiaries and/or affiliates, thereby minimizing regulatory oversight.

Beginning in the late 1970s and early 1980s, policymakers made it easier to operate large-scale, national mortgage-lending operations. The Depository Institutions Deregulation and Monetary Control Act (DIDMCA) of 1980 gradually abolished state usury limits on first mortgages by 1986. Then, the 1982 Alternative Mortgage Transaction Parity Act (AMTPA) overrode state laws that regulated the terms of "alternative" loans, paving the way for loan terms that became commonly employed in subprime and other high-risk loans. AMTPA also provided the growing sector of mortgage company lenders with access to federal preemption of state regulations, similar to what DIDMCA had provided to depository institutions. Moreover, these nondepositories were precisely the sort that relied especially on securitization as a means of funding their loans.

In 1981, President Reagan created the President's Commission on Housing, in part to look at housing-finance problems including unstable interest rates and the problems they caused for the mortgage market. The commission argued that all sorts of lenders and borrowers should have "unrestricted access" to money and capital markets, and that investors and originators should have "reliable ways of managing interest-rate risk" (Colton 2002, p. 11). The commission went on to recommend specific policy proposals to link broader capital markets more closely to the "underlying demand" for housing credit. These included exempting RMBS from taxation at the issuing level, having the Securities and Exchange Commission issue regulations for the streamlined self-registration of RMBS, and other regulatory changes.

Two statutes followed directly from the recommendations of the president's commission. The 1984 Secondary Mortgage Market Enhancement Act (SMMEA) facilitated non-GSE or "private-label" securitization in various ways, including exempting RMBS from state-level registration and expanding the ability of banks and thrifts to hold RMBS as assets on their balance sheets (McCoy and Renuart 2008). Structured RMBS were also directly supported by the 1986 Tax Reform Act, which created the Real Estate Mortgage Investment Conduit (REMIC), a legal structure for trusts that are used in private-label, structured RMBS. REMICs eliminated any potential double taxation of cash flows as they flowed through the securitization pathway.

In the late 1980s, changes in bank and thrift regulation supported the growth of securitization even more. The 1989 Financial Institutions Reform Recovery and Enforcement Act (FIRREA)—the S&L "bailout" bill—pushed thrifts to stop holding loans in portfolio (i.e., on their balance sheets) in order to improve their liquidity and lower their risks. Mortgages in portfolio received a 50 percent reserve requirement rating while RMBS received only 20 percent. This effectively increased the cost to lenders of holding loans in portfolio. Similar changes followed for commercial banks.

Through these means and others, federal policy sounded the death-knell for S&Ls and installed a regime of both government-sponsored and private-label securitization as the dominant sources of mortgage capital. By 1995, the GSEs and GSE mortgage RMBS accounted for 51 percent of outstanding mortgage credit, up from 10 percent in 1980 (Immergluck 2009). Banks had reached a share of 19 percent, with thrifts falling to 14 percent from a high of 58 percent in 1973 and 26 percent in 1989, the year of FIRREA. Private-label RMBS were just beginning to get started, rising from 2 percent of outstanding mortgages in 1990 to 6 percent in 1995.

THE GROWTH OF HIGH-RISK, STRUCTURED RMBS IN THE LATE 1990S AND 2000S

The deluge of media stories on the "subprime crisis" during 2007 and 2008 generated the perception that subprime lending was a phenomenon dating back no earlier than the early 2000s. Less recognized was the fact that the growth of high-risk lending did not arrive in a single explosion, but rather developed over two periods of rapid growth: one beginning in the middle 1990s, and the other beginning in the early 2000s (Howard 2013; Immergluck 2009). The first boom was marked by a surge in subprime refinance lending—loans made to existing homeowners, often with substantial equity in their homes—but slower growth in subprime home-purchase loans. Many of these loans were "cash-out" refinances, in which the outstanding debt on the home increases after the loan is made, and the loan is intended primarily for converting some of the home equity into cash. Subprime refinance loans were often made to borrowers with substantial equity in their homes, giving lenders ample opportunities to strip owners' equity away by charging excessive fees that would be added onto the loan amount.

Although subprime home-purchase loans were being made in substantial numbers before 2002, it was during the second boom in high-risk credit that subprime home-purchase loans took off (Immergluck 2009). During this second boom, both purchase and refinance loans from subprime lenders increased quite rapidly. While subprime mortgages made during the first boom did not perform well compared either to conventional prime loans or to FHA loans, the loans made during the second boom, especially during the peak of that boom from 2005 to early 2007, performed even more poorly. Some of these loans were caught in a cycle of upward-spiraling housing costs, which in turn were fueled by subprime and exotic loans that provided for much larger loan amounts per dollar of borrower income (Levitin and Wachter 2013).

Subprime lending clearly drove up prices in neighborhoods and cities during the boom, and then led to rapid price declines when the crash came. Regions with higher levels of subprime and other aggressive forms of mortgage lending experienced greater price increases during the subprime boom and greater declines in prices during the subsequent crisis (Pavlov and Wachter, 2011). Housing prices rose in the places where credit standards declined the most (Barakova, Calem, and Wachter 2012). Moreover, borrowers who received loans with high loan-to-value or payment-to-income ratios spent more on housing (Lee 2013).

In a study of regional housing prices from 1998 to 2005, researchers found that fundamental measures of demand predicted lower levels of appreciation than what actually occurred and that prediction errors were larger in areas with more subprime lending (Wheaton and Nechayev 2008). Other research has shown that home prices increased more rapidly in zip codes where denial rates declined more than what would have been expected due to borrower characteristics alone (Mian and Sufi 2008).

Structured RMBS had an important impact on mortgage markets because they peeled apart various types and degrees of risk and allocated these to different classes of investors depending on their appetite and tolerance for different sorts of risk. In this way, low-risk investors could invest in a bond that was designed to be highly secure. These AAA senior tranche bonds would provide relatively modest interest rates to investors, with lower-rated and riskier tranches earning higher interest rates. The lower-rated tranches of RMBS appealed to higher-risk investors and drew more such capital into mortgage markets. Structured securitization encouraged risk-based pricing (although how accurately the pricing matched the risk is subject to debate) rather than the traditional system of credit rationing, where essentially no institutional lender would lend to those below conservative risk thresholds. In the brave new world of private-label securitization, the more innovation employed, and the more the mortgage cash flows were repackaged, the more risk could be tolerated in home-financing transactions. However, as the risk at the origination level increased, the mortgage market became increasingly fragile. When home prices stopped rising, foreclosures spiked, imposing harm on homeowners, communities, and investors.

The growth of structured RMBS did not happen organically; it was not merely the product of private-market "innovation." In fact, U.S. mortgage and financial markets have always been heavily dependent on state and federal policy; they are, in fact, politically constructed (Gotham 2009; Immergluck 2004). The growth of the sector enabled the financial services industry and its lobbyists to push for further deregulation. These policies reflected a broader shift toward market-fundamentalist ideologies, but they were also fueled by the broader financialization of the U.S. economy (Stiglitz 2010). From 1980 to 2007, for example, the number of security broker-dealers—key actors in private-label mortgage securitizations—grew ten times as fast as the remaining economy (Shin 2009). The increased political power of the financial sector, in turn, led to further deregulation (Gotham 2009). During the 2008 federal election cycle, the financial-services lobbies contributed an estimated $475 million to political action committees and individual candidates, far more than any other industrial sector (Drum 2010). As Simon Johnson (2014) has argued, the United States' disproportionately large financial sector—at almost 10 percent of gross domestic product—has, even after the financial crisis, retained its substantial political power, including the power to block regulatory changes that might impose any major restructuring of the industry.

The weakening of consumer-protection laws (including caps on interest rates), and policies supporting structured, private-label securitization, fostered the growth of high-risk, high-cost lending, and increased the short-run returns to investors in private-label RMBS (Engel and McCoy 2011). The failure of policymakers to adapt the existing regime of regulation and enforcement to the restructured market further fed the growth of the high-risk subprime market by giving yield-hungry capital a path of least resistance to the high returns it sought.

The result of structured, private-label RMBS operating in a deregulated landscape was that subprime securitizations grew rapidly from just $35 billion in 1993 to $150 billion in 1998 (U.S. Department of Treasury and Department of Housing and Urban Development 2000). While federal policymakers overrode states' ability to regulate against abusive lending practices and products in the 1980s, they did nothing to create a new system of financial regulation—or expand the regulatory infrastructure—to adjust to the rapidly growing set of new, essentially unregulated mortgage lenders. They also drove a stake in the heart of already-struggling S&Ls, by providing their competitors with cheaper secondary market capital and relatively free reign from regulation.

Banks and S&Ls, which had traditionally utilized deposits and the Federal Home Loan Bank system for accessing lending capital, were subject to the Community Reinvestment Act, fair lending laws, and consumer-compliance regulation. A cadre of thousands of bank examiners conducted regular, proactive exams of the depositories for their compliance with these laws. At the same time, the new mortgage companies that came to dominate the subprime market were subject to little substantive regulatory infrastructure. These firms were not regularly examined by any federal agency, and state regulatory enforcement, if any existed, was often very weak. The only federal agency with explicit authority for enforcing consumer-protection laws for subprime mortgage companies was the Federal Trade Commission (FTC), an agency not at all equipped for such levels of activity. And, with the undoing of state consumer-protection laws, there were few laws on the books that state regulators or the FTC could enforce, even if they had sufficient staff and enforcement capacity. The Federal Reserve, which had the power to examine the mortgage company subsidiaries of bank holding companies, chose not to use it even as concerns over the steering of minority borrowers to subprime bank affiliates were being raised (Ip 2007; Andrews 2007).

The rise of securitization via both the GSEs and through Wall Street, and the paucity of serious regulatory restraints, meant that the geographic scope and scale of mortgage lenders increased. Interstate banking restrictions were essentially phased out by the middle of the 1990s. From 1992 to 1997, the share of mortgage loans originated by the top twenty-five lenders in the United States rose from just over 30 percent to over 50 percent, and reached 78 percent by 2002 (Apgar, Calder, and Fauth 2004; Apgar and Fishbein 2004). Some of these lenders made many of their loans through wholesale operations, using independent mortgage brokers to market loans and qualify potential borrowers. The increased scale and dominance of large lenders also occurred in the subprime market. The market share of the top five subprime lenders increased from 20 percent in 1996 to 40 percent by 2002 (Immergluck 2009). The top twenty-five subprime lenders accounted for 88 percent of the subprime market in 2002, up from 47 percent in 1996. The rapid growth of national lenders with access to broader, more robust capital markets meant that originators increasingly relied on a rapidly growing industry of mortgage brokers. The use of brokers provided these large lenders with the ability to quickly ramp up the scale of their lending operations, which was critical in their quest for all-important market share. From 1991 to 1998, the number of brokers grew at an annual rate of 14 percent (Kim-Sung and Hermanson 2003). By 2000, 30,000 mortgage-brokerage firms employed an estimated 240,000 workers and accounted for approximately 55 percent of all mortgage originations.

Originators and investors benefited from the use of mortgage brokers in several ways. The most obvious is the fact that brokers relieved originators of the need to expand or reduce staffing as lending markets ebbed and flowed. Moreover, if violations of consumer-protection or fair-lending laws occurred in the origination process, originators and investors could claim that they lacked knowledge of, or input into, any illegal or harmful actions that were carried out by the broker. Originators who did not scrutinize brokers for improper or illegal practices could gain market share by reducing brokers' compliance costs and by appealing to brokers that engaged in predatory or abusive lending practices and discrimination. An originator with strict oversight of its broker network risked losing brokers and market share.

THE ROLE OF GLOBAL CAPITAL MARKETS AND THE SEARCH FOR YIELD

A variety of forces created a surplus of global savings that, in turn, led to an excess supply of capital seeking higher returns than available in more traditional, secure investments. This meant that investors in mortgage-related securities were increasingly willing to pay a premium to invest in bonds backed by higher-risk loans. The resulting "capital-push" nature of higher-risk lending markets meant that loan originators were given an incentive to meet the appetite of Wall Street rather than respond to authentic demand from homebuyers and homeowners. Loan officers and brokers were given higher commissions to originate high-risk mortgages of various stripes (Engel and McCoy 2011; FCIC 2011). Meanwhile, credit-rating agencies that were tasked with assessing the risk of mortgage pools, and securities derived from the pools, relied on models that had not been tested in adverse housing-market and interest-rate conditions.

It became clear as early as 2003–2004 that the second high-risk lending boom was being fed by an increased appetite on the part of investors for mortgage-related securities. One key factor was the bursting of the dot-com stock market bubble over the 2000 to 2002 period. Real estate seemed to be the obvious place to put funds exiting stocks. Starting in 2000, all three major U.S. stock market indices began a two-year decline. By October 9, 2002, the Dow Jones had fallen by 38 percent from its peak and the S&P by 49 percent (Downs 2007).

The collapse of the U.S. stock market was not the only cause of the rush of capital into mortgage markets. Approximately six months before Ben Bernanke succeeded Alan Greenspan as chairman of the Federal Reserve, he gave a speech in which he described the effect of a "global saving glut" on capital flows into the United States (Bernanke 2005). In the past, more developed, industrialized countries were generally net lenders to less developed countries. However, more recently, less developed countries—including some in Asia and South America, as well as oil-exporting countries—had become net lenders to the United States, and global capital flows increased the supply and liquidity of capital in the United States (Rodrik and Subramanian 2008; Warsh 2007; Bernanke 2005). Moreover, some developed countries saw significant demographic shifts that led to higher savings rates.

Rising oil prices also played a key role, leaving oil-exporting countries with large amounts of cash reserves that were plowed back into international capital markets. In total, the net international lending to U.S. citizens, businesses, and governments increased from $120 billion in 1996, to $414 billion in 2000, and then to $666 billion in 2004 (Bernanke 2005). This constituted a sizeable increase in net U.S. borrowing from 1.5 percent of gross domestic product in 1996 to 5.75 percent by 2004. In a study of the housing markets of 18 advanced industrialized countries from 1980 to 2007, researchers found that increased levels of global liquidity had a significant impact on the occurrence of housing booms (Agnello and Schuknecht 2011).

As global capital poured into traditionally secure investments such as U.S. Treasury Fannie Mae and Freddie Mac securities, U.S. and European investors were displaced and searched for places to put their funds. Hence the resulting surge of funds into subprime private-label RMBS (Bernanke et al. 2011). Thus, issuers of these products became hungry for more loans, and increasingly less concerned about the quality of such loans. This hunger manifested itself in issuers and lenders pushing mortgage originators and brokers to serve the interests of Wall Street rather than the needs of home-buyers and homeowners.

FINANCIAL INNOVATION AND HIGH-RISK LENDING

Structured RMBS and related financial products pumped capital into subprime and high-risk lending operations. The issuance of subprime RMBS increased from $87 billion in 2001 to almost $450 billion by 2006 (Immergluck 2009). In the Alt-A market, which included low- or no-documentation loans mostly to borrowers with strong credit scores, issuance of RMBS increased from approximately $11 billion in 2001 to more than $365 billion by 2006. The combination of this explosive growth of securitization, as well as the decline of GSE issuance from 2003 to 2006, meant that the securitization of subprime and Alt-A loans together essentially equaled GSE issuance by 2006. Together with the nonagency securitization of jumbo mortgages, this meant that nonagency securitization exceeded GSE securitization ($1,033 billion to $905 billion) in 2006.

In addition to structured RMBS, a number of developments in securities markets hastened the flow of capital into high-risk mortgage markets. These included the creation of securities that were generated by cash flows from other securities. Borrowers were now even further removed from the eventual funders of their loans. In the first wave of private-label securitization, investors would invest in RMBS, which were comprised of thousands of individual mortgages. Most of these investors wanted AAA or other highly rated tranches derived from the loan pools, and they relied on the credit-rating agencies to evaluate the risks of the underlying loans and the tranches. However, relatively few investors were interested in purchasing the lower-rated, higher-risk bonds at the bottom of the credit hierarchy. What Wall Street needed was a way to increase the demand for even these undesirable tranches.

To remedy this situation, Wall Street created a new supposedly diversified, but also highly complex, security: the collateralized debt obligation, or CDO. The CDO involved additional layering between the institutional investor and the borrowers. In CDOs, lower-tranche RMBS bonds—particularly those with less than AAA ratings—were purchased and pooled with other lower-tranche RMBS bonds derived from other loan pools. Investment banks combined the cash flows from these bonds to produce a new set of CDO bonds, with senior and subordinate tranches. A large portion of the lower tranches of subprime RMBS ended up being purchased for CDOs (Cordell, Huang, and Williams 2012; FCIC 2011). By dividing the cash flow from a pool of RMBS (and potentially other CDO bonds), CDO issuers transformed the sow's ear of lower-grade bonds into what were thought to be silk purses, in the form of higher-rated CDO bonds. The values of these highly structured investments depended on investors' expectations of how well they would pay back, and that, in turn, depended on an assessment of the risks within the CDOs. What became painfully clear by mid-2007 was that the rating agencies did not have a good handle on the risks—especially in the event of a downturn in housing prices—of many private-label RMBS, yet alone most CDOs. CDOs invested $140 billion in lower-tranche (rated below AAA) RMBS in 2005, even more than the $133 billion of lower-tranche RMBS issued in that year (Mason and Rosen 2008). Thus, CDOs accounted for essentially all lower-tranche, first-order RMBS issued in 2005.

The underlying quality of CDOs deteriorated rapidly in the 2000s and shifted from multisector collateral to predominantly subprime and Alt-A RMBS (Cordell, Huang, and Williams 2012). Researchers studied a set of over seven hundred publicly traded CDOs issued between 1999 and 2007, totaling over $640 billion. Total write-downs of these CDOs reached 65 percent of their value, and most CDO bonds with less than AAA ratings were completely written off. The collateral for the 2004 CDOs was 13 percent riskier than that of 1999 CDOs, and the collateral for 2007 CDOs was 47 percent riskier than that of the 1999 CDOs.

TRANSACTIONAL TENSIONS IN COMPLEX MORTGAGE MARKETS

The vertical disintegration of mortgage markets, together with a lack of regulatory oversight, created transactional tensions between different parties in the securitization and affiliated lending process. These tensions often involved one party to a transaction using information that only it had to its advantage. In some instances, outright fraud was involved. One point of tension early in the subprime-lending process occurred between the mortgage broker and the borrower. The mortgage broker had little incentive to identify the least risky and most cost-effective loan product for the borrower. Brokers were compensated through a combination of up-front fees (some percentage of the loan amount) and something called a yield spread premium (YSP). The YSP was equivalent to a portion of the capitalized value of the difference between the interest payments that the borrower pays and a minimum base rate at which the lender will originate the loan. This arrangement rewarded brokers for placing people in loans that were priced at rates above those justified by their credit profiles. Less savvy borrowers were unlikely to understand when they were entitled to a lower interest rate. These borrowers were more vulnerable to higher rates and fees than those likely to be served by prime lenders. The YSP effectively rewarded brokers for placing borrowers in higher-cost loans, thereby exacerbating their chances of default. YSPs were often combined with prepayment penalties because originators/investors wanted to recoup the YSP in the event of the borrower selling his home or refinancing.

Mortgage brokers were frequently associated with high-risk loans and unsavory practices, especially in the subprime market. Among elderly borrowers, brokered loans were twice as likely to be subprime than nonbrokered loans (Kim-Sung and Hermanson 2003). Brokers were also more likely to assist divorced, female, and nonwhite borrowers. Sixty-two percent of older nonwhite borrowers received loans via brokers, while only 38 percent of older white borrowers did. Brokers were heavily associated with aggressive "push marketing" (FCIC 2011). In a study from the early 2000s, 56 percent of older borrowers with brokered loans reported that brokers initiated contact, while other older borrowers reported that lenders initiated contact only 24 percent of the time. Borrowers with brokered loans were generally less satisfied with their loans and were less likely to feel that they received honest information (Kim-Sung and Hermanson 2003). More generally, for subprime borrowers of any age, brokered loans were found to have higher interest rates than nonbrokered loans, even after controlling for differences in borrower and loan characteristics (Ernst, Bocian, and Li 2008).

The broker-originator relationship also exhibited substantial transactional tensions. The structure of broker compensation often did not effectively reward brokers for better performing loans or penalize them for excessive defaults. Brokers' income essentially depended on getting as many loans approved as possible, creating an incentive for brokers to falsify a borrower's income or assets, to steer them to no-documentation loans, to obtain high appraisals, and generally to downplay any apparent risk factors in applications. Brokers were much more likely than retail lenders to make low- or no-documentation loans, which turned out to be a widespread source of fraud and foreclosure. In 2005, 41 percent of brokered loans were low or no documentation, compared to 22 percent of nonbrokered loans (Golding, Green, and McManus 2008). BasePoint Analytics (2006a, 2006b), a vendor of anti-fraud software, examined a pool of 3 million mortgages and found that "the most serious fraud in mortgage lending today appears to be broker-facilitated." BasePoint also found that loan fraud was heavily concentrated in a significant, but minority share of the brokerage industry, suggesting that lenders should have been able to identify the brokers who were commonly engaged in fraud. However, if originators applied more rigorous screening to their brokered loans, they risked losing market share in the brokered-loan market.

The compensation structure of both mortgage brokers and loan officers within lending institutions rewarded aggressive, risky, and sometimes fraudulent lending. In a controlled corporate experiment regarding how loan officers were paid, researchers found that commission-based compensation schemes led to the approval of loans that would not have been approved under the prior noncommission compensation scheme (Agarwal and Ben-David 2012). The commission-based scheme also resulted in the approval of larger loan sizes and increased leverage. The commission-based scheme increased origination rates by over 30 percent, loan sizes by 15 percent, and default rates by 28 percent.

Another opportunity for transactional tensions was between the originating lender and the warehouse lender. Subprime originators often required access to short-term loans from a warehouse lender to fund loans as the need arose. Access to a warehouse lender allowed the originator to generate pools of loans large enough to sell to the RMBS issuer in bulk. The warehouse lender relied on the loans held by the originator as collateral for its short-term line of credit. Therefore, if it overestimated the quality of the originator's new loans substantially, it would have advanced funds on insufficient collateral. A number of subprime lenders who went out of business during the turbulence of 2007 did so because they lost access to their sources of warehouse credit (Ashcraft and Schuermann 2008). To maintain their lending volumes and market share, originators had incentives to understate the risks of the loans they were making when negotiating with warehouse lenders.

There was also conflict between the motives of the originating lender and the arranger/issuer of the securities. The originator had more information about the true quality of the loans that it sold than did the issuer purchasing the loans. Given this uneven information, the originator—especially if it held loans as well as sold them—had an incentive to pass off its lower-quality loans to the issuer and keep the better loans. The information that these issuers had about the loans may have lacked some crucial details that the originator knew about but might have been concealed from the issuer. Revealing these features could lower the profit the lender would earn in selling the loans. Benjamin Keys and his colleagues analyzed more than 2 million home-purchase loans originated during the 2001 to 2006 period (Keys, Mukherjee, Seru, and Vig 2010). They found that loans that were likely to be securitized defaulted at a rate of 10 to 25 percent more than similar loans (with slightly lower credit scores) that were less likely to be securitized. This result held even after controlling for a wide variety of loan, lender, and borrower characteristics. Thus, even after considering many risk factors, securitized loans were still likely to be riskier than low-documentation loans held by originators. Other researchers showed that borrowers who qualified to receive conventional loans, but were steered to higher cost or predatory loans, were more likely to receive a loan that was privately securitized (Agarwal et al. 2013).

Even when RMBS issuers had reason to suspect that the loans they were assembling for securitization might be problematic, they often appeared to ignore it, ostensibly passing the risk onto the investors in the securities. Clayton Holdings, a due-diligence firm hired by many of the largest RMBS issuers to inspect loans they were purchasing, reported to the Financial Crisis Inquiry Commission (FCIC) that high percentages of the loans that it found did not meet the issuers guidelines were "waived" into securitization pools by the issuers despite this classification. From January 2006 through June 2007, Clayton classified 28 percent of the mortgages it reviewed as not meeting issuer requirements (FCIC 2011). Of these rejected loans, 39 percent were waived into the securities pools by the issuers anyway. Their appetite for loans had become so great that they were increasingly willing to ignore their own standards. Figure 1.1 shows the percentages of loans rejected by Clayton, and the percentages of each subset that were then waived in by the issuer despite their knowing that the loans did not meet their standards.

As the subprime boom peaked, checks on the quality of underlying loans broke down severely. Adam Ashcraft and his colleagues analyzed more than three thousand subprime and Alt-A RMBS deals issued between 2001 and 2007 and found that, beginning in 2005, the standards for loans in these deals declined markedly (Ashcraft, Goldsmith-Pinkham, and Vickery 2010). One important deregulatory move that fueled the appetite for subprime loans occurred in 2004, when the Securities and Exchange Commission (SEC) relaxed the capital requirements for investment banks. The SEC reduced the minimum capital reserves of five very large investment banks, including Goldman Sachs, Lehman Brothers, Merrill Lynch, and Morgan Stanley, by 30 to 40 percent. After this change, these investment banks increased their purchase of loans that had lower credit quality but were located in zip codes with higher rates of house-price appreciation (Nadauld and Sherlund 2013). Moreover, these loans defaulted at higher rates than otherwise similar loans.

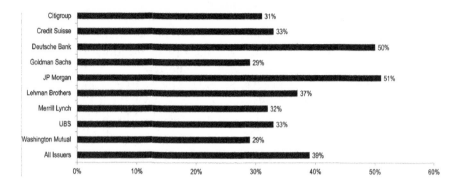

Figure 1.1.   Share of Rejected Loans (by Clayton Holdings) Waived in by Issuers, January 2006 to June 2007. *Source:* **Prepared by author from data provided by Clayton Holdings to FCIC (FCIC 2011).**

As Kathe Newman (2009) has put it, rather than simply providing homeowners and neighborhoods with access to needed credit, a good deal of policy in the latter decades of the twentieth century seemed more focused on providing global capital with access to neighborhoods and homeowners. In subprime private-label securitization, capital flowed through a large number of parties and was assessed, insured, and leveraged by additional parties, such as credit-rating agencies, bond insurers, and credit-default swap investors. Other than the borrower and the eventual investor in the RMBS or CDO products, most of the intervening parties had very little risk in the transactions. The brokers, originators, issuers, and CDO arrangers all essentially passed on risk to the next party while benefiting from large volumes of transactions. Credit-rating agencies and others played key ancillary roles while taking on little risk. Even when originators assumed some risk through warranties on the loans they sold to issuers, in which they agreed to take back certain types of nonperforming or noncompliant loans, the balance sheets of some originators were relatively thin, so the capital they risked was sometimes quite limited (Green and Wachter 2007).

THE CREDIT RATING AGENCIES

Perhaps no other parties in the securitization process have received more blame for the mortgage crisis than the three primary credit-rating agencies: Standard and Poors, Moody's, and Fitch. The private credit-rating firms, labeled Nationally Recognized Statistical Rating Organizations (NRSROs), played the role of regulator for the securitization process, a role that the SEC and bank regulators effectively delegated to these firms. Despite the special status given NRSROs, they were—and remain—subject to very little substantive regulation.

The rating firms repeatedly underestimated the underlying risk of subprime and other high-risk lending, and the risk to investors in structured finance products backed by these loans. While few U.S. companies ever achieve an AAA rating, from 2000 to 2007, Moody's rated approximately forty-five thousand mortgage-related securities as AAA (FCIC 2011). However, of the thousands of mortgage securities rated by Moody's in 2006—at the peak of the market—83 percent were later downgraded. Moreover, the agencies provided ratings that were inconsistent across different types of securities and geography (Golding, Green, and McManus 2008). Some CDOs had five-year default rates that were fifteen times greater than similarly rated corporate bonds (Mason and Rosen 2007).

The rating agencies often had too little loan-level information. The FDIC reviewed a set of twenty-four CDOs that had received a rating from one of the three major rating firms, and found the agencies only included "robust" performance data in their pre-sale reports for three of them. Moreover, models used by the rating agencies to predict defaults were based on data from periods with much smaller levels of investor and second-home properties, which are more sensitive to stalling or falling property values (Haughwout et al. 2011).

A more fundamental problem with the rating process involved conflicts of interest and perverse incentives that encouraged overoptimistic evaluations and ratings. The rating firms had an incentive to underestimate the risk of mortgage-related securities, in part because they were paid by the issuers and not by investors. Additionally, the issuer usually did not pay for the rating until the rating was obtained (Golding, Green, and McManus 2008). The credit-rating firms also played an active role in pushing back consumer regulatory initiatives by states and localities in the late 1990s and early 2000s (Immergluck 2009). Structured finance, which was mostly comprised of rating RMBS and CDOs, became an increasingly important driver of revenues for rating agencies. For example, structured finance ratings accounted for 54 percent of Moody's Investment Service revenue in 2006, up from 36 percent in 2001 (Moody's Corporation 2008; Moody's Corporation 2004). Thus, the rating firms had a clear financial incentive to keep the RMBS and CDO business as unfettered as possible.

In July of 2008, the SEC issued a report criticizing the rating agencies for their overly generous ratings of mortgage-related securities (Securities and Exchange Commission 2008). The report uncovered many emails that expressed the conflicts and looseness in the rating process. One analyst's email complained that a security "could be structured by cows and we would rate it" (Securities and Exchange Commission 2008). Another's message expressed concern that a poor rating may result in the rating agency losing the business of the issuer: "I am trying to ascertain whether we can determine at this point if we will suffer any loss of business because of our decision [on assigning separate ratings to principal and interest] and if so, how much?" (Securities and Exchange Commission 2008).

IRRATIONAL EXUBERANCE, INTERESTS, IDEOLOGY, AND THE ROLE OF THE ECONOMICS PROFESSION

Some have defended the economics profession against allegations that it should have recognized a "housing bubble," or warned more of the potential threat of stalling home-price appreciation and potential spikes in foreclosure rates (Gerardi, Foote, and Willen 2010). Such defenders have argued that the empirical evidence suggesting a housing bubble was weak, or have questioned the existence of a bubble even after prices dropped by 30 percent or more. However, others have criticized the profession, including its close ties to the real estate and finance industries, and argued that more economists should have sounded the alarm about unsustainable price appreciation and lax subprime underwriting standards (Baker 2009; Krugman 2009). Martha Starr examined the views of 153 economists quoted in twenty-four California newspapers between 2002 and 2007 (Starr 2012). She found that the preponderance of home-price trend predictions did not shift to flat or falling until 2007. The share of views suggesting that there was a bubble rose from 27 percent in 2003 to 57 percent in 2007. Moreover, there were large differences in predictions between economists who worked for the real estate industry and those who did not. Over 86 percent of economists working in the industry predicted that appreciation would continue, while just 49 percent of other economists did.

Of course, the ties between business schools, economics departments, and the financial-services sector are vast and convoluted. During their careers, economists can move among positions at universities, financial firms, and regulators, including the Federal Reserve System. Financial firms sometimes fund the academic research centers that study financial-market regulation, and many academic economists earn significant outside income consulting for financial firms and industry groups, in roles that include developing expert evidence, writing regulatory comment letters, and testifying before Congress (Carrick-Hagenbarth and Epstein 2012; Fang 2013; Kocieniewski 2013). Jessica Carrick-Hagenbarth and Gerald Epstein (2012) studied a small sample of prominent academic financial economists and found that fifteen of the nineteen economists worked in some capacity with private financial institutions, and that thirteen of these fifteen did not disclose these ties in the publications they reviewed. Moreover, eleven had published articles in the mass media, had done interviews, or testified publicly, but only three of these eleven disclosed their private financial affiliations to the media. The authors of the study found that these economists, who generally had not warned of the "increasing financing fragility and impending crisis," later developed a "basic consensus view that favors more market-based reforms and relatively less government regulation" as a means to prevent future financial crises.

SUBPRIME LENDING, EXCESSIVE LEVERAGE, AND THE FAILURE TO REGULATE

Despite evidence in the late 1990s that subprime lending—and associated predatory lending—led to high default rates, little was done to improve regulation in this market. Consumer advocates, housing counselors, and community groups testified before regulatory commissions, including a 2000 predatory-lending task force convened by the U.S. Department of Housing and Urban Development and the Department of the Treasury, as well as regional Federal Reserve hearings, about abuses in the subprime market and associated foreclosures (FCIC 2011). However, when attempts were made to regulate the subprime sector more aggressively, at the state or federal level, those efforts were largely rebuffed by aggressive industry lobbyists (Engel and McCoy 2011; Immergluck 2009). When meaningful legislation was adopted in various state capitals, including North Carolina, Georgia, New York, and other states, federal regulators stepped in to preempt state regulation to the extent they could (Immergluck 2009). Longtime Deputy Comptroller of the Currency Julie Williams delivered a lecture to states attorneys general in 2001 stating that the Office of the Comptroller of the Currency (OCC) would "quash" their efforts to control the consumer-lending practices of nationally regulated banks (FCIC 2011). Meanwhile, the credit-rating agencies and the GSEs, as well as the mortgage banking and brokerage industries, threatened states that access to credit would dry up even for lower-risk loans. In the meantime, the banking industry lobbied the Federal Reserve heavily, and the agency took very marginal steps to increase regulations on the very highest-cost loans (Bair 2012; Immergluck 2009).

By 2003, after a few years of retrenchment triggered by the Asian and Russian financial crises of the late 1990s, the subprime industry had come back with a vengeance. As foreclosures rose in regions without strong home-price appreciation, such as the industrial Midwest and some southern cities, the national foreclosure rate stayed quite low due to extremely low foreclosure rates in the hottest housing markets, including those in California, Nevada, Arizona, and Florida. As housing prices plateaued in late 2005 and 2006, foreclosure rates began to rise in those places, as troubled subprime borrowers could no longer easily sell their homes or refinance. Foreclosures began to rise nationally at a steep pace, and by early 2007, it was clear that a national foreclosure crisis had begun. Figure 1.2 shows that the national foreclosure rate for subprime loans began to rise between 2005 and 2006, and began a very steep ascent in 2007 and 2008. Meanwhile, adjustable-rate loans and property value declines in overheated markets began driving up prime foreclosure rates, although not nearly as fast as in the case of the subprime segment. By 2009 to 2010, the subprime foreclosure rate had essentially peaked, in part because the most fragile loans had been washed out of the system and no new subprime loans were being made after 2007. In the meantime, the recession and falling home values were spreading the foreclosure crisis well into the prime mortgage market, even among plain-vanilla, fixed-rate mortgages.

Subprime lending—with its predatory loan features, high interest rates, and excessive payment-to-income ratios—was the clear driver of foreclosures in the first years of the crisis. Researchers examined the effects of Illinois legislation directly banning state-defined predatory-loan features in specific zip codes in Chicago (Agarwal et al. 2013). They found that the regulations, which had a sizable negative impact on the volume of subprime lending in targeted zip codes, produced measurable declines in mortgage default rates, due in large part to the exit of some subprime lenders from

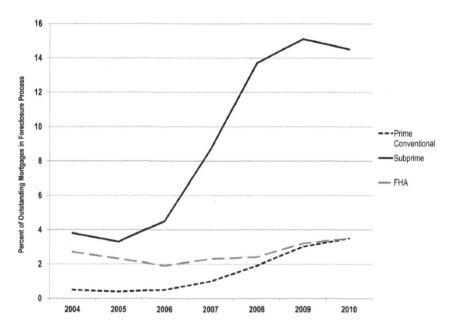

Figure 1.2.   U.S. Foreclosure Rates, 2004 through 2010. *Source:* **Prepared by author from data from the Mortgage Bankers Association National Delinquency Survey.**

these areas. More importantly, subprime borrowers' default rates declined between 18 and 26 percent due to the regulations. The research also demonstrated that loans containing state-defined predatory features had default rates that were six percentage points higher than similar loans that did not have such features.

THE PERSISTENCE OF FALSE NARRATIVES

From the beginning of the mortgage crisis, there have been competing narratives about its causes. These narratives have affected not only the short-term responses to the crisis but also debates about the restructuring of housing finance and long-term regulatory policy. The eventual emergence of any one dominant narrative—or set of aligned narratives—is likely to have profound effects on the policy debates regarding financial markets, housing markets, and other key sectors of the economy for a long time to come. The complexity of the crisis—as well as the high stakes involved in the outcomes of related policy debates—has meant that policymakers, journalists, and the general public have been offered a surplus of contributors to the crisis. These range from high gasoline prices (Cortright 2008) to local land-use regulation (O'Toole 2008). A few such phenomena may have played minor roles in exacerbating the housing boom and bust, but most were either trivial or nonfactors and serve as distractions to a core understanding of the crisis. While views on the cause of the crisis can easily be placed into more than two categories, it is useful to recognize the two dominant, opposing narratives.

The first type of narrative—which I will call the "deregulation" variety—tells the story of an under-regulated mortgage market that had become increasingly fragile, highly leveraged, and vulnerable to changes in home prices (Engel and McCoy 2011; FCIC 2011; Levitin and Wachter 2013; U.S. Department of Housing and Urban Development 2010). The case I present here clearly falls in this category. Advocates of the deregulation narrative argue that a regulatory system designed primarily for the originate-to-hold mortgage market of the mid-twentieth century suffered from decreased regulation and oversight. Federal policymakers adopted tax and securities laws that fueled private-label securitization, preempted state-level consumer-protection regulations to free up subprime lenders, and allowed RMBS issuers to increase their leverage ratios to increase the scale and profits of their operations. Federal policymakers also did nothing to modify the regulatory infrastructure to regulate the new dominant sector of nonbank mortgage companies or private-label securitization. Banks were effectively incentivized to move their lending operations to less-supervised nonbank affiliates and to originate loans via largely unregulated mortgage brokers. Even when adequate regulations were in place (and often they were not), various break-downs in the regulatory process, and cozy relations between lenders and regulators, resulted in weak enforcement.

While the evidence—including that detailed in this chapter—generally supports the deregulation narrative, an opposing family of narratives has persisted despite a lack of empirical support. These counter-narratives continue to carry a great deal of influence in policy debates as well as in the general public consciousness, despite repeated studies indicating that they have no merit. Paul Krugman (2010) and others have puzzled at what John Quiggin (2010) has called "zombie economics," or the continued diffusion and persistence of ideas that should have been discredited by the crisis. However, with a great deal at stake, those fearing greater regulation and a less financialized economy were strongly motivated to sustain narratives that furthered their policy goals. At the same time, housing policy in the United States has always been shaped by ideological, as well as interest-based, motivations (Hays 1995). Here, too, ideology has been at work, especially a form of market fundamentalism that rejects both strong regulation and efforts to reduce severe inequities in the provision of basic goods like housing.

The narrative that lies in primary opposition to the deregulation narrative—what might be called the "affordable-housing-as-cause" narrative—places the blame on two principal types of federal interventions in the mortgage market (Pinto 2010; Wallison 2011; Wallison, Pollock, and Pinto 2011). First, policies concerned with improving access to credit and homeownership to historically underserved borrowers or neighborhoods are viewed as having forced lenders to make excessively risky loans to lower-income and supposedly un-credit-worthy borrowers. These laws include the 1977 Community Reinvestment Act (CRA) and the affordable-housing goals established for the GSEs, Fannie Mae and Freddie Mac, in 1992.[2] Second, this narrative portrays the largely privatized GSEs as creatures of the political left and the dominant developers and funders of subprime loans. Key sources of this narrative have been conservative think tanks such as the American Enterprise Institute (AEI) and the Cato Institute. AEI has been a leading promoter of financial deregulation, including its sponsorship of the "Shadow Financial Regulatory Committee," (Schlesinger 2011). However, with the arrival of the mortgage and financial crises, AEI—and in particular its fellows Peter Wallison and Edward Pinto—gained new prominence as purveyors of the affordable-housing-as-cause narrative.

The affordable-housing-as-cause narrative places the primary blame for the growth of subprime lending at the door of the GSEs. Proponents of this narrative have done this partly by redefining the category of subprime lending itself. Traditionally in the United States, the term *subprime* was used to describe loans labeled "subprime" by issuers of private-label MBS, which were loans with high interest rates and/or fees, and exhibited various risk factors, such as low credit scores, prepayment penalties, low or no documentation, and hybrid-adjustable rates. Yet, in testimony to Congress, AEI's Edward Pinto offered a new definition of *subprime* that included a much broader swath of outstanding mortgages. Pinto (2010) constructed his own subprime classification to include any loan in which: (1) the borrower has a credit score below 660[3]; (2) the original loan-to-value ratio was below 90 percent; *or* (3) a nontraditional feature such as an interest-only structure is present. In doing so, he suggests loans with just *one* of these features are essentially equivalent in risk to the high-risk loans funded by private-label subprime MBS. Pinto's definition resulted in classifying 49 percent of all outstanding mortgages as of June 2008—almost 27 million loans —as "subprime" or "Alt-A." This definition of *subprime* was far more expansive than the traditional definition, which covered less than 24 percent of *originations* in 2005 and 2006 (the peak of the subprime boom), implying an even smaller percentage of *outstanding* mortgages (FCIC 2011).

In redefining *subprime*, Pinto captured far more GSE loans in his "subprime" umbrella than were captured using the more commonly accepted definition. By his measure, approximately 12 million outstanding subprime or Alt-A loans were purchased or guaranteed by the GSEs, while the traditional measure yielded a figure of less than 3 million. As the Financial Crisis Inquiry Commission (FCIC) final report argued, "The grouping of all of these loans together is misleading. . . . GSE loans with some riskier characteristics such as high loan-to-value ratios are not at all equivalent to those mortgages in securitizations labeled subprime and Alt-A by issuers" (FCIC 2011). Pinto's definition of *subprime* included many loans that were far less risky than the traditionally defined subprime segment. For example, GSE loans with credit scores below 660 had a 2008 delinquency rate of 6.2 percent, while traditionally defined subprime loans with credit scores below 660 had a 2008 delinquency rate of more than 28 percent (FCIC 2011).

In fact, during the boom in subprime lending, the role of the GSEs in the mortgage market declined due to the growth of the private-label RMBS sector. Between 2003 and 2006, Fannie Mae, Freddie Mac, and Ginnie Mae accounted for less than 28 percent of the increase in RMBS issuance and less than 14 percent of overall mortgage debt (Park 2010). As a result, Fannie and Freddie's combined net income dropped by half. As their market share and profits dropped, Fannie and Freddie were under financial pressure to enter the higher-risk segments of the mortgage market in a more robust way. They began investing in subprime RMBS, although their share of subprime RMBS investments declined after 2004.

Later direct purchases of higher-risk (but generally not subprime) loans increased, particularly Fannie Mae's purchases of Alt-A loans, many of which were low- or no-documentation mortgages to borrowers with prime credit scores. Prior to 2005, Alt-A loans represented less than 8 percent of

Fannie loan purchases, but in 2005 and 2006, that share rose to almost 19 percent (Park 2010). The share of interest-only and negative amortization loans also increased to almost 15 percent. Alt-A loans—often to borrowers with sizeable incomes and strong credit scores—accounted for 40 to 50 percent of Fannie and Freddie's total credit losses in 2008 and 2009. These were generally loans to middle- and upper-income buyers.

As the FCIC majority report described, the GSEs

> followed rather than led Wall Street and other lenders in the rush for fool's gold. They purchased the highest-rated non-GSE mortgage-backed securities and their participation in this market added to the helium, to the housing balloon, but their purchases never represented a majority of the market. (FCIC 2011)

Moreover, the loans the GSEs purchased performed much better than subprime loans. At the peak of the crisis, in the middle of 2010, Fannie Mae's seriously delinquent (ninety days plus) rate was just under 5 percent, compared to 28 percent for subprime loans (Park 2010). Even for Fannie borrowers with credit scores of less than 660, the delinquency rate was less than 14 percent, or less than half the subprime rate.

According to the affordable-housing-as-cause narrative, GSEs entered the subprime market because of explicit federal policy that established goals for the share of GSE loan purchases to low- and moderate-income people and places. As a result, this narrative frequently includes the 1977 Community Reinvestment Act as a major contributor to the crisis. Despite ample evidence that debunks these assertions, the affordable-housing-as-cause narrative has been echoed not only by conservatives, but also occasionally by some moderates, including former New York mayor Michael Bloomberg and Senator Mark Warner (D-Virginia).

The supposed role of the CRA in causing the crisis has been exhaustively debunked (Aalbers 2009; Avery and Brevoort 2011; Ding, Quercia, and Ratcliffe 2011; Foote, Gerardi, and Willen 2013; Hernandez-Murillo, Ghent, and Owyang 2012; Reid and Laderman 2011; Reid et al. 2013). Canner and Bhutta (2008) analyzed HMDA data for 2005 and 2006, during the peak of the subprime boom, finding that only 6 percent of all higher-priced loans were eligible for CRA credit. They also examined loan-performance data for borrowers in two groups of neighborhoods that were very similar except that the lending in one group received credit under the CRA. They found that the repayment performance of loans in the CRA-eligible neighborhoods was actually slightly better than the performance of those in CRA-ineligible neighborhoods. Lei Ding and his colleagues found that community reinvestment loans were approximately 70 percent less likely to default than otherwise-similar subprime loans (Ding, Quercia, and Ratcliffe 2011). Carolina

Reid and Elizabeth Laderman (2011) examined a large database of loans in California and found that CRA-eligible loans were significantly less likely to be in foreclosure than otherwise-similar loans originated by independent mortgage companies, which were not regulated by CRA. Ruben Hernandez-Murillom and his colleagues examined whether CRA may have increased subprime originations in eligible tracts or to eligible borrowers, and found no evidence of such an effect (Hernandez-Murillom, Ghent, and Owyang 2012).

The one study—by Agarwal, Benmelech, Bergman, and Seru (2012)—that appeared to bolster the conservative claim that the CRA boosted subprime lending was widely criticized and dismissed as evidence of a substantive CRA effect (Foote, Gerardi, and Willen 2013; Konczal 2012; Reid et al. 2013). The timing of the analysis used by Agarwal and his colleagues did not correspond to the actual timing of the CRA examination process (Reid et al. 2013; Foote, Gerardi, and Willen 2013). Critics also pointed out various methodological issues that led to the authors overestimating the magnitude of any the CRA effects and that, even if the authors' basic findings were accepted, the magnitudes of the finding suggest that any impact of the CRA on subprime lending was trivial, if positive at all.

Despite its lack of empirical merit, the affordable-housing-as-cause narrative persists among many U.S. policymakers and significant segments of the public. One key reason for this was that conservative media, including the *Wall Street Journal* and *Fox News*, were strong amplifiers of this message. In the pages of the *Wall Street Journal*, Peter Wallison of the American Enterprise Institute (AEI), as well as his colleague Edward Pinto, maintained this narrative in the face of daunting evidence to the contrary. Wallison, who served in the Reagan Administration when the regulatory foundation for private-label securitization was set, has been a foe of financial regulation for a long time, including opposing much of Sarbanes-Oxley, the law aimed at responding to the Enron fiasco. With the mortgage crisis, however, AEI, Wallison, and Pinto took on a major, central role as the purveyors of the affordable-housing-as-cause narrative.

Wallison, and to a lesser degree Pinto, were given prominent space in the *Wall Street Journal* to reiterate their narrative again and again. A simple examination of articles authored by these two AEI staffers reveals the frequency of this sort of coverage during and after the crisis. An analysis of all content in the *Wall Street Journal* since 1990 reveals that until 2003, these authors penned only eleven articles in the *Journal*. During the height of the mortgage boom, from 2004 to 2006, their pace picked up a little, with five articles published. However, during the peak of the crisis—from 2007 to 2011—the *Journal* published over forty articles by these two AEI staffers, all of them essentially commentary pieces. All of the articles after 2006, save for a couple, concerned the mortgage crisis or the federal response to it, with the bulk of articles suggesting that the affordable-housing goals of the GSEs and/ or the Community Reinvestment Act were a principal cause of the crisis.

As David Min (2013) has argued, deregulation, and not federal housing policy, has been the common denominator behind housing booms and busts in advanced economies. Two other countries—Spain and the UK—that saw housing booms and busts during the 2000s underwent significant deregulatory episodes leading up to the boom. Moreover, after Denmark allowed interest-only mortgages beginning in 2003, they began experiencing significant mortgage market distress. More systematically, Agnello and Schuknecht (2011) analyzed data on housing booms and busts in eighteen advanced economies (including the United States) from 1980 to 2007. They found that deregulation measures "significantly amplified the role of domestic liquidity in determining the occurrence of booms." Thus, deregulation of the mortgage market is a critical step for allowing excess capital to flood into the housing sector and create unsustainable booms.

In this chapter, I described the fundamental causes of the foreclosure crisis and reviewed the evidence on the importance of different factors. The crisis was primarily the result of an increasingly risk-loving, deregulated, and fragile mortgage market that proved attractive to global capital. It was not the result of too much government involvement in housing and housing finance. Quite the contrary, it was the culmination of three decades of the diminution of the regulation of housing finance. In the next chapter, we turn to the impacts of the crisis and to how the crisis played out in dramatic ways across both race and space in many cities.

Chapter Two

The Costs of Foreclosure and the Racialized Shape of the Crisis

The mortgage crisis brought financial pain to millions of American families. But the pain was more than just financial. It uprooted families from neighborhoods and social networks, forced kids to change schools in the middle of the year, and created strains on mental and physical health, which in turn can trigger additional financial hardship. The costs of the crisis also went well beyond impacts on borrowers and their families. We now know the crisis had much wider effects on neighborhoods, communities, and cities. Foreclosure—and mortgage distress more generally—has significant impacts on local property values, on vacancy and blight, and on the crime that can follow. As property values decline, homeowners nearby see the equity in their homes evaporate. This makes them more susceptible to foreclosure, as their homes become harder to sell and they end up with a home worth less than its outstanding mortgage ("underwater"). The impact of the foreclosure crisis, while widespread, was not uniformly or randomly distributed across homeowners around the country. Rather, subprime lending and foreclosures disproportionately affected minority homeowners and minority neighborhoods. In the first part of this chapter, I describe many of the harms that arise due to the direct and indirect effects of mortgage distress and foreclosure. However, I do not include the many broader economic effects of the crisis, which catalyzed the Great Recession and the global financial crisis. The second part describes the racial nature of the crisis, at both the household and neighborhood levels.

DIRECT HARMS TO FORECLOSED FAMILIES

Foreclosure has direct effects on families and children. Perhaps most obvious is the loss of the home itself and the need to relocate, often quickly and under stressful conditions. Of course, beyond this is the potential loss of family wealth if the family had earlier built up significant equity in the home. Even worse, the crisis spurred losses in home equity and homeownership rates in ways that were concentrated among people of color and younger families.

Figure 2.1 shows that from 2007 to 2011, the net worth of households declined substantially. Moreover, it shows that the loss of wealth varied significantly across different demographic groups. This is due to variations in losses in home values among these groups as well as the fact that stocks, which generally constitute a larger share of the household wealth of higher-income, older, and nonminority households, recovered significantly from 2008 to 2011, while home values in many places did not.

Figure 2.1 indicates that, while white and Asian families lost approximately 38 percent of their net worth from 2007 to 2011, black, Hispanic and other non-Asian minority households, as a group, lost more than 71 percent of their net worth over the same period. Many of these households were younger households, with families in the thirty-five- to fifty-four-year-old range losing far greater shares of their wealth than older households. These households lost over 60 percent of their net worth compared to less than 25 percent for those over sixty-five. Some of this is likely due to the geography and timing of home-buying among this age group, especially those purchasing homes in "boom-bust" areas, where values were boosted—temporarily—by the surge in subprime and high-risk home lending in the middle part of the decade. It also reflects the disproportionate concentration of subprime loans among homeowners of color.

The crisis pulled many families out of the dream of homeownership, and back into the rental market. Certainly, homeownership is not the best choice for all families at all times. However, as will be discussed later, in many places in the United States, and especially for families with children, responsibly financed homeownership can bring significant benefits over the available rental options. These benefits include providing a sense of stability and control, allowing for predictable housing costs, and giving families access to a wider choice of neighborhoods, including those with strong schools. Moreover, rapid declines in homeownership rates may have negative impacts on neighborhoods where homeownership provided for more stability.

While overall homeownership rates declined only moderately from their peak in late 2004 and early 2005, the decline among certain demographic groups was significantly greater. From 2005 to 2012, the homeownership rate for blacks declined by more than 5.5 percentage points, while it only declined about 2.5 percentage points for whites (Joint Center for Housing

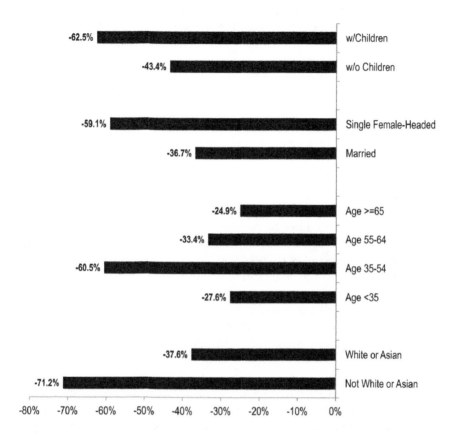

Figure 2.1.   Change in Real Net Worth, Households of Different Types, 2007 to 2011. *Source:* **Prepared by author from estimates in Pfeiffer, Danziger, and Schoeni (2013).**

Studies 2013). Consistent with the loss of wealth figures above, the homeownership rate of households aged 25 to 44 fell by almost 8.5 percent, while it stayed essentially flat for those sixty-five and older. Finally, as with the wealth figures, families with children were also hit particularly hard, with married families with children seeing homeownership decline by close to 7 percent, while married couples without children saw a decline of less than 2 percent.

In addition to the loss of wealth and ownership status, foreclosure has a direct impact on families' credit worthiness. The credit scores of prime and near-prime borrowers going through foreclosure during the early years of the mortgage crisis dropped by 170 to 200 points compared to their pre-delinquency credit scores (Brevoort and Cooper 2010). This means that they moved rapidly into becoming subprime borrowers. It generally takes many years before credit scores recover significantly, and many are likely to never recover fully. Even at seven years after a foreclosure, credit scores tend to remain fifty to seventy-five points below where they would have been before. This is despite the fact that, by this time, the foreclosure should no longer be directly considered in calculating the credit score.

Lower credit scores have critical implications for families that extend far beyond their ability to borrow. The U.S. Fair Credit Reporting Act (FCRA) allows access to credit data for a wide variety of purposes. Any firm that delivers a good or service prior to receiving payment is effectively acting as a creditor under FCRA, and is allowed to access credit reports and scores. Firms providing basic and enhanced utility services, including electricity, water, gas, phone, or cable service often use credit-bureau data. As early as 2002, TransUnion, one of the three large credit-bureau firms, reported that banks and credit unions had been overtaken as the largest users of credit data in the Philadelphia region by nonbank entities such as hospitals, telecommunication firms, and utilities (Furletti 2002).

A substantial drop in credit score, like the kind caused by a foreclosure, has the potential to create a web of barriers to employment, quality housing, and basic and affordable goods and services. For example, the bulk of auto insurers use credit-score data in underwriting new policies, although some states prohibit the use of credit data in underwriting and pricing auto insurance (Hartwig and Wilkinson 2003). In many lower-income neighborhoods, auto-insurance rates are already high, so a lower credit score may make use of a car prohibitively expensive, which in turn can hurt employment prospects. Since landlords often rely on credit scores, post-foreclosure households needing rental housing may have been excluded from the full array of housing choices they might have otherwise been able to access. Given the scarcity of affordable, decent rental housing available in many metropolitan areas, this could make quality rental housing even more difficult to obtain. Making matters worse, employers have increasingly turned to credit data in screening job applicants. In a recent survey of more than five hundred human resource managers, the Society for Human Resource Management (2012) found that 47 percent of employers used credit background checks to make hiring decisions.

Beyond direct financial and economic harm, the crisis hurt families in other ways. Among these were the effects of forced relocation on children in school. When students have to change schools, especially in the middle of a school year, it can stunt academic achievement, which can last for years (Rumberger 2002). In a study of Minneapolis during 2006 and 2007, Ryan Allen (2013) found that over 90 percent of households moved after a foreclosure, with most changing neighborhoods, and almost a third leaving the Minneapolis Public Schools District. In a similar study of students in New York City, researchers found that students in properties that went through a foreclosure were likely to move to different schools and that they tended to move to lower-performing schools (Been et al. 2011). In a study of the San Diego school system over the 2001 to 2010 period, math test scores and attendance rates of children in owner-occupied homes declined in the year after a mortgage default, and these effects persisted after controlling for a wide variety of student and school characteristics (Dastrup and Betts 2012).

While direct evidence on the effects of foreclosure on children continues to emerge, there is already a large body of literature on the effects of residential instability that can inform the costs of foreclosures to families. Heather Sandstrum and Sandra Huerta (2013) reviewed much of this literature and found that "the experience of abrupt or frequent residential moves is stressful for children since it requires them to detach themselves from what they know and adapt to new surroundings." They document the considerable evidence that chaotic environments can have very negative impacts on children, including on scholastic outcomes. One longitudinal study of children from birth through age 9 found that, after controlling for a large number of demographic characteristics, moving two or more times during the first two years of life increased the incidence of problems such as anxiety, sadness, and withdrawal at age 9 (Rumbold et al. 2012). Another study found that moving before the age of four led to increased problem behaviors at age 4, even after controlling for child and family characteristics (Taylor and Edwards 2012).

In a longitudinal study of almost five thousand children born in twenty large cities between 1998 and 2000, researchers found that children that had moved three or more times in the first five years of life had greater attention problems than those who had not moved, and this difference remained significant after controlling for a large number of demographic and household characteristics (Ziol-Guest and McKenna 2013). High levels of mobility also resulted in negative behavioral problems, and the magnitude of the effect was larger than that of any other independent variable, including race, ethnicity, parental education, family structure, and many other factors.

In particular, studies show that residential instability affects school performance adversely. One study showed that five-year-olds who had five or more moves since birth had vocabulary scores 41 percent of a standard deviation below average (Taylor and Edwards 2012). A wide variety of other studies also demonstrate that residential instability tends to result in lower grades, lower high school graduation rates, and lower adult educational attainment (Adams and Chase-Lansdale 2012; Coulton et al. 2009; Sell et al. 2010; Ziol-Guest and Kalil 2013).

When residential moves due to foreclosure result in children changing schools, school mobility increases, which can have an adverse effect on school performance. Two studies in two different cities (Chicago and Baltimore) found similar effects on academic achievement due to school transfers (Alexander et al. 1996; Temple and Reynolds 1999). For each school transfer, achievement scores declined by approximately one month of school, even after controlling for other factors. School mobility reduces reading and math achievement and increases high school dropout rates, after controlling for demographic and family characteristics (Reynolds, Chen, and Herbers 2009). Moreover, the negative effects of mobility increase with each additional move, with effects during early elementary and high school years having the largest negative impacts on learning outcomes.

Adults in a household can also suffer the physical and mental health effects of foreclosure. In some of the earliest research on the relationships between foreclosure and health, Desiree Fields and her colleagues studied eighty-eight families going through foreclosure in five cities around the country (Fields et al. 2007). They found that those going through foreclosure experience a wide range of hardships and emotional difficulties beyond the harm to their finances and credit histories. Many respondents felt shame, which sometimes discouraged them from seeking support services or even assistance from friends and family. Foreclosure harmed family stability and made it difficult to make long-term plans. In some cases, foreclosures represented a "cascading series of economic and emotional losses that interfere with people's day-to-day lives." Some respondents took on additional employment to try to resolve delinquencies. More broadly, foreclosure sometimes led to increases in "fear, tension, and stress" among family members.

Foreclosure has been found to be closely associated with poor health. Because foreclosure can be both the result of poor health (and associated expenses and loss of employment) and a potential cause, it is often difficult to determine the role that foreclosure has in generating poor physical and mental health outcomes. A study in Philadelphia found that clients of a mortgage-counseling agency who were undergoing foreclosure had higher rates of depression, hypertension, and heart disease (Pollack and Lynch 2009). Almost 37 percent of participants going through foreclosure suffered from major depression. In a study of hospital visits and foreclosures in four states, a spike in neighborhood foreclosures was associated with significant increases in unscheduled hospital visits, even after controlling for changes in unemployment, housing prices, migration, and other factors (Currie and Tekin 2011).

Longitudinal data allows for more precise measurement of the causal effects of foreclosure on physical and mental health. Dawn Alley and her colleagues examined the results of a national, longitudinal survey of adults over fifty years old during the 2006 to 2008 period (Alley et al. 2011). Controlling for a wide variety of factors, they found that delinquent borrowers were almost eight times as likely to develop elevated depression compared to nondelinquent borrowers. They also found that delinquent borrowers were almost eight times as likely to develop food insecurity, and almost nine times as likely to stop taking medicine due to cost. The elderly can also be especially adversely affected by forced relocations (Denemark and Ekstrom 1990; Smith and Ferryman 2006). Seniors are often particularly dependent on a set of social networks and relationships for their day-to-day living circumstances, and may be emotionally and psychologically less resilient to involuntary stressors and change.

COSTS TO NEIGHBORHOODS AND COMMUNITIES

Foreclosures affect more than just borrowers and lenders. They impose economic and social costs on surrounding neighborhoods and larger communities. Indirectly, as we saw during the crisis, high levels of foreclosure can also trigger major problems in national and international financial and employment markets (Levitin and Wachter 2013).

Foreclosure lowers the values of nearby homes, which in turn can result in lower property tax collections and attendant fiscal stress. Foreclosures can also lead to vacant properties that become magnets for crime, which can depress property values even more. As values decline in a neighborhood, more homeowners sink underwater, with homes worth less than their associated mortgages, making it difficult or impossible to sell a property, and forcing more homeowners into foreclosure. Thus, foreclosure creates a vicious cycle, in which foreclosures lead to value declines, which lead to more foreclosure. Foreclosure can also spur rapid neighborhood change, by forcing out long-time residents and, in some cases, allowing less-than-responsible investors to move into a neighborhood.

My colleague, Geoff Smith, and I were the first to measure the impact of foreclosures on nearby property values (Immergluck and Smith 2006a). Using data from Chicago in the late 1990s, we showed that foreclosures were associated with lower property values of nearby homes, even after controlling for a wide variety of other demographic and property characteristics, including home values in the larger surrounding neighborhood. Each additional foreclosure within an eighth of a mile was associated with declines in value of approximately 1 to 1.5 percent. In the wake of the crisis, many researchers expanded on the methods and findings of this study to examine foreclosure's effects on nearby property values, especially during the crisis period beginning in the middle 2000s. For example, Daniel Hartley (2011) examined foreclosures in Chicago over a longer period, from 1999 to 2008, and found that in high-vacancy census tracts, the effect of a foreclosure on property values within 250 feet was approximately –2 percent, while the effect in low-vacancy tracts was smaller in magnitude. These findings were roughly consistent with those of our study.

In another paper based on data from Massachusetts during 1987 to 2008, researchers found that a foreclosure within 0.05 miles lowered the price of a house by approximately 1 percent (Campbell, Giglio, and Pathak 2011). Using data from 2000 to 2005 in New York, Jenny Schuetz and her colleagues found that foreclosures also had a negative impact on home prices, but that the effect was nonlinear, so that there was little to no effect until a certain threshold of foreclosures was reached, after which the effects became more sizable (Schuetz, Ellen, and Been 2008). Brian Mikelbank (2008) also found negative effects of foreclosure on housing values in his analysis of 2006 sales in Columbus, Ohio, and found that vacant homes had an even stronger negative effect on prices than nonvacant foreclosures. John Harding and his colleagues analyzed foreclosures and property sales in seven metropolitan areas over the 1989 to 2007 period using a repeat-sales analysis, which controls for neighborhood conditions (Harding, Rosenblatt, and Yao 2009). They found that each foreclosure within three hundred feet of a property had approximately a –1 percent effect on property value, and that the effect reached its peak magnitude at the time of the foreclosure sale. In his review of the literature, Scott Frame (2010) concluded that foreclosures do have a negative impact on nearby property values, with the impact declining over time and over space.

Foreclosures have negative effects on nearby values for a number of reasons. First, they represent an increase in housing supply, and, especially if foreclosures rise quickly, they effectively create a supply shock in a neighborhood housing submarket, putting downward pressure on prices. Second, if foreclosures become a sizable share of home sales, as they often did in hard-hit neighborhoods during the crisis, their lower values put downward pressure on values by generating lower comparables in the appraisal process (especially if the most comparable sales available are those of foreclosed properties). In many hard-hit neighborhoods during the crisis, there were few comparable sales that did not involve at least one recently foreclosed property. Finally, some foreclosed homes exhibit significant blight or dilapidation that deters future homebuyers. Especially during times when homebuyer demand is already weak, having vacant, and sometimes boarded up, properties on a block can discourage the scarce active buyers from purchasing in the neighborhood. Research has shown that foreclosed homes tend to be in worse condition than owner-occupied properties. In a study of property complaints in the City of Boston from 2008 to 2012, Lauren Lambie-Hanson (2013) found that the typical single-family property was over nine times as likely to receive a complaint while in bank-ownership (after foreclosure) compared to when its previous owner was current on his or her mortgage.

One way that foreclosures can harm neighborhoods is through their effects on crime. When a foreclosure triggers vacancy, and the vacancy persists for more than a very short time, the vacant home can become a site of criminal activity. A good deal of research has explored the connection between foreclosure and crime, and most of it corroborates such an effect. The earliest study on the link between foreclosure and crime was done in Chicago around the late 1990s and early 2000s. The study found that higher levels of foreclosure in Chicago neighborhoods were associated with higher levels of violent crime, even after controlling for a large number of other neighborhood characteristics (Immergluck and Smith 2006b). A number of other studies have had similar results. In a study of New York City between 2004 and 2008, Ingrid Ellen and her coauthors concluded that foreclosures on a block led to increased crime, with violent crime increasing the most (Ellen, Lacoe, and Sharygin 2013). In a study of Indianapolis, researchers found that foreclosures led to higher neighborhood crime rates (both property and violent) during the mid- to late 2000s (Stucky, Ottensmann, and Payton 2012). Another study of Pittsburgh found that violent crimes within 250 feet of a vacant foreclosed home increased by more than 15 percent, with similar effects on property crime (Cui 2010). This study also showed that longer vacancy spells had larger effects on crime than properties that were vacant for a shorter period. Sonya Williams and her colleagues used data from Chicago over time (1998–2009) to disentangle the potential reverse causality between foreclosures and crime at the neighborhood level (Williams, Galster, and Verma 2013). They found that completed foreclosures temporally lead property crime and not vice versa, adding support to the notion that foreclosures cause crime and are not simply correlated with it for other reasons. Some other studies have attempted to measure the effect of foreclosures on crime at somewhat larger geographic levels, such as counties. However, these studies have often suffered from the substantial neighborhood-level variation in crime rates within counties, as well as some challenges in developing accurate and unbiased measures of foreclosure rates.

Foreclosures and associated vacancies also entail direct fiscal costs to local governments, including:

- increased policing due to vandalism and other crime;
- increased burdens on fire departments due to arson;
- demolition costs;
- costs of removing trash and mowing lawns for properties not being maintained;
- legal expenses;
- managing the foreclosure process, including record keeping;
- lost tax revenue if the building owner stops paying taxes;
- property tax losses due to declining values to building and nearby properties; and
- lost economic-development benefits due to decreased desirability of community for commercial/industrial development.

In a study of Chicago before the height of the mortgage crisis, Bill Apgar and Mark Duda (2005) found that these sorts of direct costs to city government sometimes exceeded $30,000 per foreclosure. On the revenue side, the fall in housing prices, often spurred or accelerated by foreclosures, led to a decline in property-tax revenue in many cities during the late 2000s. Howard Chernick and his colleagues concluded that, in cities hit hard by the foreclosure crisis, lower property values would lead to major declines in property-tax revenues (Chernick, Langley, and Reschovsky 2011). In Las Vegas, for example, they estimated a 22 percent drop in revenues, while in Modesto and Stockton, California, their estimates were in the range of 24 to 25 percent.

The Long-Term Scarring Effects of Foreclosure and Housing Distress

The accumulation of financial, social, psychological, and neighborhood effects from foreclosure may result in a long-term scarring of entire neighborhoods and communities that lasts well beyond the shorter-term effects of displacement, emotional distress, and near-term effects on property values and crime. In some communities, the foreclosure crisis triggered a longer-term destabilization of the housing market, resulting in longer-term vacancies, and longer-term declines in housing values. Many of these neighborhood-level problems are not being picked up in the often-reported rebounds in metropolitan-level housing price indices, such as the Case-Schiller index and others. These indices understate the continued slump in home values in many communities because they generally rely on measuring average changes in pairs of "repeat sales," which are inherently weighted toward those communities where regular sales of homes are more common. Because purchase activity tends to be higher in areas where home prices have rebounded more strongly—more "resilient" submarkets—the metropolitan-level indices may mask changes going on at smaller geographic levels. Indeed, as will be shown below, many neighborhoods of color and modest incomes have experienced less resilience in housing-market conditions than more affluent and white neighborhoods.

SUBPRIME LENDING AND FORECLOSURE ACROSS RACE AND SPACE

Race and the Historical Persistence of Segmented Mortgage Markets

The history of mortgage markets in the United States demonstrates that the race and ethnicity of homeowners and the racial and ethnic composition of neighborhoods are persistent and fundamental shapers of mortgage markets.

Although racial discrimination and redlining in mortgage markets became more widely discussed policy topics in the 1960s and 1970s, these problems had been recognized much earlier (Immergluck 2004a). In the early 1920s, for example, following the 1919 Chicago race riot, the Chicago Commission on Race Relations determined that blacks faced barriers in securing mortgages. Some lenders completely avoided areas where blacks lived (Hillier 2001). In the 1940s, noted economist and scholar of the American race problem Gunnar Myrdal noted that blacks faced great challenges in getting mortgages from mainstream banks. In his seminal work on housing discrimination, *Forbidden Neighbors*, the activist and planner Charles Abrams (1955) delved into the problem in more detail, noting the web of direct and referred discrimination among mortgage lenders, real estate agents, appraisers, homebuilders, and the Federal Housing Administration (FHA). Abrams also described fundamental differences in the pricing and terms of credit available to blacks compared to that available to whites, and observed effectively predatory fees on loans to blacks ranging up to 25 percent of the loan amount. Abrams called local S&Ls the "watchdogs of neighborhood purity," because they rated areas where residents had resisted minority home-seekers ineligible for home loans (Abrams 1955, p. 176). Thus, blacks wanting to buy homes were left with two alternative sources of credit: a black financial institution or some sort of informal lender who offered abusive loans at exorbitant rates. Sometimes the latter took the form of the land contract, or contract-for-deed, essentially a rent-to-own scheme that offered little protection for the "buyer" of the property and plenty of room for abuse by the seller/landlord. In a 1955–1956 study of real estate agents, most considered the land contract to be a key source of financing for black buyers (Helper 1969).

In 1961, the U.S. Civil Rights Commission reported on the "common policy of refusing to lend to Negroes who are the first purchasers in a white neighborhood" (U.S. Commission on Civil Rights 1961, p. 30). The report documented discriminatory practices, including mortgages for blacks with short-term amortization schedules and high down payments, as well as pure redlining, where lenders would simply not lend in an area. It also described the results from a 1959 Chicago survey of the 243 S&Ls in Cook County. Only twenty-one S&Ls made loans to homebuyers in a black, South Side neighborhood, and only one white-owned S&L made a home-purchase loan to a black family in a white neighborhood. The commission argued that bank and thrift regulators had the ability to reduce discrimination and redlining, but did little in the way of enforcement (U.S. Commission on Civil Rights 1961, p. 41.).

As documented by Abrams and many others, the FHA up to 1949 was a major force in promoting and institutionalizing redlining. In 1949, the FHA ruled that it would not provide insurance for mortgages on property with restrictive covenants, and that the racial composition of a neighborhood was not a consideration in determining loan eligibility. However, the agency continued to allow discriminatory lenders to participate in their programs. The agency moved from an active promoter of redlining to a complicit subsidizer and facilitator.

Things began to change somewhat in the 1960s. The Housing Act of 1968 signaled a clear turnabout of the FHA, and it began financing homes in minority neighborhoods. However, while FHA programs were being redirected toward inner-city neighborhoods, conventional lenders were not. Despite the 1968 Fair Housing Act, federal banking regulators paid little attention to the racial patterns of conventional lenders. The result was the development of a new form of dual mortgage market. Instead of minority buyers and buyers in integrating neighborhoods settling for abusive informal lenders or land-contract financing, the FHA provided the primary source of financing. Unfortunately, FHA programs that worked fairly well when borrowers had options in the conventional lending market broke down in the dual finance system (Bradford, 1979). Moreover, FHA underwriting requirements were excessively relaxed, even though 100 percent insurance was provided to lenders. Lenders were able to make loans to high-risk borrowers without bearing any of the increased risk. The results for minority neighborhoods were often devastating (Bradford 1979; Bratt 1976).

While there were some important smaller policies adopted earlier in the 1960s, the passage of Title VIII of the Civil Rights Act of 1968, known as the Fair Housing Act, was the first critical shift in federal policy with regards to the issue of access to mortgage credit. The Fair Housing Act explicitly prohibited mortgage-lending discrimination by race and was later interpreted to prohibit redlining. After the neighborhood organizing movement got more involved with these issues in the early 1970s, two critical federal laws were enacted. First, in 1975, the Home Mortgage Disclosure Act (HMDA) was passed. It required federal bank and thrift regulators to begin collecting data on home-mortgage lending by census tract for all depository institutions. Then, in 1977, the Community Reinvestment Act (CRA) was passed. The CRA, which directly addresses redlining, created an affirmative obligation for banks and thrifts to meet the credit needs of their communities. Despite differences in the enforcement of these laws, they have had a positive impact on access to mortgage credit (Immergluck 2004a). However, problems of dual mortgage markets by race and space persisted, or took on new forms.

The Racial Dynamics of Subprime Lending

In the 1990s, with the rise of the subprime market, the problems of discrimination and redlining in mortgage markets took another form. While basic access to institutional mortgage credit remained an issue for some, the rise of high-risk subprime lenders began to create wider problems in the pricing and terms of mortgage credit. Moreover, the growth of high-risk, private-label securitization meant that new sources of capital began to flow into minority neighborhoods to satisfy the appetites of yield-hungry investors (Ashton 2009; Newman 2009). A hypersegmentation of borrowers by race and neighborhood was facilitated by technology and regulation. Some of the earliest work documenting the segmentation of the mortgage market across race and space came from Chicago, the birthplace of CRA activism. This research showed that the number of subprime refinance loans made in predominantly black neighborhoods grew almost thirty-fold from 1993 to 1998, while such lending in predominantly white neighborhoods grew by just about two-fold (Immergluck and Wiles 1999). The largest lenders in predominantly black neighborhoods were specialized subprime firms while white neighborhoods were served by prime lenders. Shortly afterward, the U.S. Department of Housing and Urban Development analyzed lending patterns in the United States (and more closely in five large cities) and found that subprime lenders dominated black neighborhoods. Later analyses continued to document racially hypersegmented mortgage markets around the country (Bradford 2002; Scheessele 2002). Some researchers used multiple regression techniques to control for a variety of neighborhood characteristics to find that the racial composition of a neighborhood was a major determinant of subprime lending concentrations, even after controlling for a wide variety of other neighborhood housing and economic characteristics (Scheessele 2002; Immergluck 2004b).

Researchers during this period also found that the race of the borrower had a significant effect on the likelihood of receiving a subprime versus a prime loan, even after controlling for credit history and other variables. A study of home-purchase loans conducted by an affiliate of the Mortgage Bankers Association found that the probability of a borrower receiving a subprime loan, controlling for credit history, location, and other variables, increased by approximately one-third when the borrower was black (Pennington-Cross, Yezer, and Nichols 2000).

More recently, a great deal of additional research has documented the relationship between race and subprime lending during the 2000s subprime boom. Figure 2.2 indicates the differences among racial and ethnic groups in their propensity to receive subprime loans at the height of the subprime boom in 2006 (Avery, Brevoort and Canner 2007). For the United States as a whole, more than 53 percent of black homebuyers received subprime loans and over 52 percent of blacks taking out refinance loans received subprime loans. Moreover, black homebuyers were three times more likely to receive a subprime loan than white homebuyers. Even when these Federal Reserve researchers adjusted for differences in subprime incidence due to differences in incomes, loan sizes, metropolitan area location, sex, and the existence of a co-applicant, they still found that the adjusted rate for blacks was about 2.7 times the rate for whites. Almost half of Hispanic homebuyers in 2006 also received subprime loans. While the difference between Hispanics and whites declined somewhat more after controlling for these other factors, the adjusted differential remained two to one. Similarly, other research found that, in 2006, single black women were more than four times as likely to receive a subprime loan compared to white couples, and more than three times as likely to receive a subprime loan as single white women (Wyly and Ponder 2011).

In examining home-purchase loans originated nationally in 2006, Jacob Faber (2013) found that, after controlling for borrower income, neighborhood racial and income composition, regional and metropolitan location, and the presence of a co-applicant, blacks and Latinos were 2.4 times more likely to receive a subprime loan than similar whites. Additionally, Faber determined that higher-income blacks and Latinos were more likely to receive a subprime loan than lower-income minorities, while higher-income whites were less likely to receive subprime loans than lower-income whites. Some of this relationship may be due to higher property values associated with higher- versus lower-income minority homeowners. Moreover, higher-income whites may have been better served by prime lenders than higher-income minorities, leaving them less vulnerable to aggressive subprime lenders.

The racial patterns of subprime lending were also manifest at a spatial level, with predominantly minority neighborhoods being much more likely to see high levels of subprime loans. Tom Kingsley and Kathy Pettit (2009) found that the density of subprime loans was highest in black and Hispanic neighborhoods during the 2004 to 2006 subprime boom period. They also found that the highest subprime densities were in relatively low-poverty, but high-minority neighborhoods.

Chris Mayer and Karen Pence (2008) also focused on the spatial distribution of subprime lending in 2005 and, using loan data from the firm Loan Performance (now known as CoreLogic), they found that predominantly black and Hispanic zip codes received much higher levels of subprime lending than other areas. Even after controlling for credit scores and other economic characteristics of zip codes, they found that subprime lending at the peak of the boom was especially prevalent in predominantly minority zip codes. Paul Calem and his coauthors analyzed home loans in seven major cities in 1997 and 2002 and found that blacks were more likely than whites to receive subprime versus prime loans, even after controlling for borrower income and a variety of neighborhood characteristics including educational levels and average credit score (Calem, Hershaff, and Wachter 2010). Later, Debbie Gruenstein-Bocian and her colleagues were among the first to combine publicly available Home Mortgage Disclosure Act data (including data

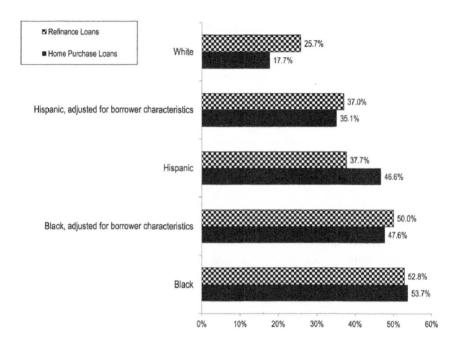

Figure 2.2. High-Cost (Subprime) Lending Incidence by Race of Borrower, 2006. *Source:* Prepared by author from data in Avery, Brevoort, and Canner (2007).

on the race and income of borrowers) with private data from a major loan-data vendor (including information on loan terms and credit quality). They found that black homebuyers were 31 percent more likely to receive a high-rate (versus a low-rate) mortgage with a prepayment penalty than white borrowers with similar characteristics (Gruenstein-Bocian, Ernst, and Li 2008).

In another paper, Gruenstein-Bocian and her colleagues found that racial disparities in receiving subprime loans during the peak of the subprime boom were actually greater among borrowers with higher credit scores (Gruenstein-Bocian et al. 2011). This was consistent with an earlier analysis by the *Wall Street Journal*, which revealed that many subprime borrowers could have qualified for prime loans based on their credit scores (Brooks and Simon 2007). These studies provided significant evidence of systematic steering of minorities toward higher-cost and riskier subprime loans. In particular, Bill Apgar and his colleagues found that the probability of receiving a subprime loan was heavily dependent on the particular lending channel through which the borrower received the loan (Apgar, Bendimerad, and Essene 2007). For example, in comparing the borrowers of a traditional, prime lending operation and a specialized subprime lender owned by the same company, a borrower receiving the loan through the subprime channel would be much more likely to receive a subprime loan (even if they could qualify for a prime loan) than an otherwise-similar borrower receiving a loan via the prime lending channel.

Researchers at the Federal Reserve Bank of Philadelphia combined data from the Home Mortgage Disclosure Act (HMDA) with data from a national proprietary data set on loan and borrower characteristics from 1999 through 2007 for three states—Pennsylvania, New Jersey, and Delaware (Smith and Hevener 2011). They found that blacks had a high probability of receiving a subprime versus a prime loan for all years of the study. They also estimated the difference in the propensity of whites and blacks to receive subprime loans due to factors other than race, including income, credit score, and neighborhood and loan characteristics, but found that the characteristics other than race explained at most only two-thirds of the higher propensity of blacks to receive subprime loans in 2005. This left one-third of the difference explained solely by race, providing substantial evidence for the existence of discriminatory forces in the mortgage market. Similar results have been obtained by researchers in other locations (Courchane 2007; Reid and Laderman 2009).

Patterns of Foreclosure by Race and Space

Minority homeowners were disproportionately impacted by foreclosures, especially in the early years of the crisis when subprime loans accounted for the bulk of the foreclosure problem. After merging Home Mortgage Disclosure Act (HMDA) data with industry data from Lender Processing Services, a major provider of loan-level data, Debbie Gruenstein-Bocian and her colleagues analyzed foreclosures between 2007 and 2009 at the height of the subprime phase of the foreclosure crisis, and estimated that owner-occupied homes accounted for approximately 80 percent of all foreclosures, and that blacks and Hispanics were disproportionately impacted (Gruenstein-Bocian, Li, and Ernst 2010). Figure 2.3 illustrates some of the findings from their study. Almost 8 percent of first mortgages to black homeowners originated between 2005 and 2008 went into foreclosure between 2007 and 2009. This compares to only 4.5 percent for white homeowners; the black foreclosure rate was 76 percent greater than the white rate.

Similarly, the foreclosure rate for Latino homeowners was 7.7 percent, or 71 percent greater than the white rate. However, because whites still accounted for a majority of borrowers during this period, whites accounted for over half of all foreclosures. Together, blacks and Hispanics accounted for about 28 percent of foreclosures, with Asians and other ethnicities accounting for the remaining portion. While the subprime crisis disproportionately affected black and Hispanic homeowners, it was not just a problem confined

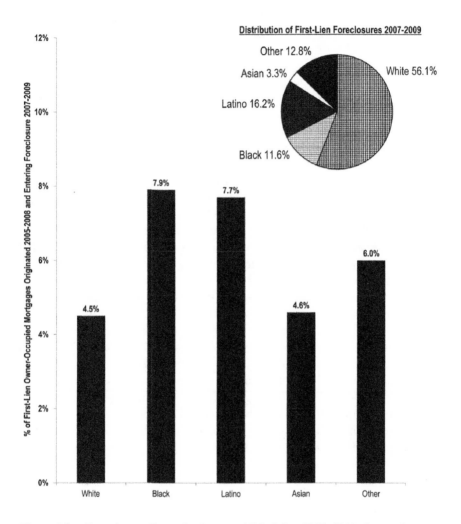

Figure 2.3. **Foreclosure Rates by Race and Ethnicity, 2007–2009, Owner-Occupied Homes.** *Source:* **Prepared by author from data in Gruenstein-Bocian, Li and Ernst (2010).**

to people of color, even at the early stages of the crisis. As foreclosures spread to the prime market, and consequently to a broader set of middle-income and majority-white communities, whites accounted for an increasing portion of all foreclosures.

During the foreclosure crisis, media reports fluctuated from describing the foreclosures as primarily affecting central city neighborhoods, to being concentrated in newer suburban or exurban areas (e.g., Farrell 2008; White-house 2007). The evidence on the intrametropolitan distribution of the crisis is more complicated than either of those simplistic narratives, since many inner-city neighborhoods and many newly developed suburban areas were both hit hard. This dichotomy was driven in large part by the opportunistic nature of the subprime boom. High-risk credit flowed wherever it could be sold, funneled, and channeled by the parties that stood to profit from it. It poured into vulnerable inner-city neighborhoods that had been starved for credit in earlier decades, and where mortgage brokers aggressively peddled home loans, including predatory refinance loans that allowed homeowners to convert hard-earned home equity into sorely needed cash, at often-exorbitant costs. It also flowed into newly developing suburban and exurban communities that offered the promise of homeownership, or sometimes larger homes, to families, but with payment burdens that were not sustainable in the event of even temporary economic hardships.

Due to differences among metropolitan areas in the geography of housing, income, and race, and due to differences in the aggressiveness of the subprime lending industry from city to city, the neighborhood distribution of foreclosures varied a good deal across metropolitan areas. The incidence and concentration of foreclosures depended not only on spatial determinants of default and foreclosure, but also especially on the geographic distribution of subprime and high-risk loans. In many older industrial metropolitan areas with traditionally weaker economies and housing markets such as Detroit and Cleveland, as well as in some cities with stronger regional economies like Atlanta and Chicago, subprime delinquencies and foreclosures had been increasing well before 2007 (Immergluck 2010a). By the first quarter of 2006, subprime delinquency rates already exceeded 12 percent in states with more troubled economies, like Michigan, Ohio, and Indiana, but also in states such as Georgia and Tennessee. Until late 2006, regions with very hot housing markets experienced low delinquency rates, with California, Arizona, and Nevada having subprime delinquency rates below 6 percent. This was partly due to the fact that borrowers struggling with their mortgages in hot markets could avoid default or foreclosure by quickly refinancing or selling their homes. By the summer of 2007, however, after appreciation had stalled in most places, delinquency and foreclosure rates accelerated in most large metropolitan areas, with steep increases in markets where housing values began to decline rapidly.

Because subprime lending was disproportionately concentrated among minority homeowners, we would expect higher levels of subprime foreclosures to occur in predominantly minority neighborhoods, which include many inner-city communities. At the same time, subprime and high-risk lending also fueled rapid growth in newer suburban and exurban communities, especially in parts of the Southwest, California, Florida, and other places (Ong and Pfeiffer 2008; Schafran and Wegman 2012). However, media reports and commentary sometimes portrayed the crisis as one exclusively centered in a new "slumburb" and neglected the fact that the crisis was also heavily concentrated in many older urban neighborhoods (Leinberger 2008).

To study neighborhood-level foreclosure patterns across a wide variety of metropolitan areas, I examined changes in the prevalence of foreclosed properties at the zip code level in seventy-five large metropolitan areas (Immergluck 2010b). Rather than measuring foreclosures by comparing foreclosures to housing units, this analysis analyzed the share of single-family properties (including townhomes and condominiums) that might have a mortgage on them that had been foreclosed on and repossessed by the lending institution. Without such careful measurement, many other estimates of foreclosure prevalence effectively assume that each housing unit equates to a "mortgageable" property, a grossly inaccurate assumption in neighborhoods with many multifamily rental units. From earlier work, I classified the metropolitan areas in the United States into three categories of foreclosure activity (Immergluck 2010a). Type 1 metros were those where housing prices had remained relatively stable and where foreclosure levels had not been large prior to the advent of the crisis in 2007. Type 2 metros were mostly older metropolitan areas where foreclosed property inventories had already reached relatively high levels before the crisis. Finally, Type 3 metros were those that had very low foreclosed property inventories before 2007, but where housing prices were declining quickly after 2006. Figure 2.4 shows the locations of the three types of metros. Type 1 metros are scattered across the country, and include most smaller metropolitan areas and many in the Great Plains and Mountain West region where the foreclosure crisis often had modest effect. Type 2 metros include most larger metros in the upper Midwest as well as some mostly larger metros in Colorado and the Southeast. Type 3 metros are clustered in California, Florida, Nevada, Las Vegas, as well as along the East Coast.

To examine how neighborhood-level patterns of foreclosure might vary across different types of metros, I used multivariate analysis to identify the contributions of different zip-code-level and metropolitan-level factors to the growth of foreclosures during the first two years of the national foreclosure crisis. The results of these analyses showed that, overall, zip codes in MSAs with falling median home values experienced greater increases in foreclosed properties from 2006 to 2008. Higher increases in unemployment also had substantial effects on the increase in foreclosures.

The prevalence of outstanding subprime mortgages in 2006 was also a strong predictor of increases in foreclosure rates. For every one percentage-point increase in the share of mortgages that were subprime, the increase in foreclosed properties over the following two years grew by more than four percentage points, a large impact. The level of junior mortgages outstanding at the end of 2006 was also positively associated with the growth in foreclo-

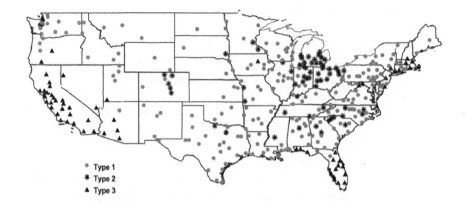

Figure 2.4. U.S. Metropolitan Areas by Foreclosure Market Type. *Source:* Prepared by author from data in Immergluck (2010a).

sures from 2006 to 2008. Another key finding was that zip codes with large amounts of recently constructed homes experienced greater increases in foreclosures. This may have been due to large shares of homes in such areas being financed during the peak of the subprime boom. At the same time, other things equal, zip codes with higher poverty rates experienced higher levels of foreclosure growth. Thus, the findings confirm the notion that the subprime foreclosure crisis was concentrated both in higher-poverty (often inner-city) neighborhoods and in many newer, sprawling communities.

Further analysis showed that the neighborhood-level patterns of foreclosures varied across the two types of metropolitan areas that experienced the brunt of the foreclosure crisis—Type 2 and Type 3. In general, Type 3 metros tended to see more of the suburbanized foreclosure patterns, especially when central city neighborhoods tended to be relatively affluent, such as in San Diego or San Francisco. The results showed that the neighborhoods with newer housing in Type 3 metros were particularly vulnerable to increases in foreclosures, which is consistent with the notion that areas receiving subprime loans near the peak of the subprime boom experienced particularly high levels of foreclosure. This occurred in Type 2 metros as well, but not to the same degree.

The Foreclosure Crisis Moves to the Suburbs

As the subprime foreclosure crisis triggered the Great Recession and mortgage and housing markets became much weaker, many homeowners with well-priced, well-structured prime home loans began to find themselves in mortgage distress. Many lost their jobs due to the recession, especially those working in industries and regions that were vulnerable to the crash of the real estate economy and, later, the broader economy. By 2009 and 2010, with housing prices and homeowner equity falling in most major metropolitan areas, millions of prime borrowers found themselves underwater on their mortgages. Any substantial economic distress, such as a job loss or a health crisis, could trigger a foreclosure. At the same time, an increasing share of subprime borrowers had already lost their homes, so the share of foreclosures associated with subprime loans began to decrease over time.

Figure 2.5 demonstrates that in three major urban counties, Fulton (Atlanta), Cuyahoga (Cleveland), and Cook (Chicago), the portion of foreclosure filings (or notices) that occurred in the suburban parts of the counties grew significantly over a relatively short period. In Fulton County, Georgia, where there are many working-class suburbs to the south of the city, the suburban share grew the most, from under 39 percent to just over 56 percent. Over the same period, the suburban share grew from 47 percent to almost 60 percent in Cuyahoga County, Ohio, and from 46 percent to 53 percent in Cook County, Illinois.

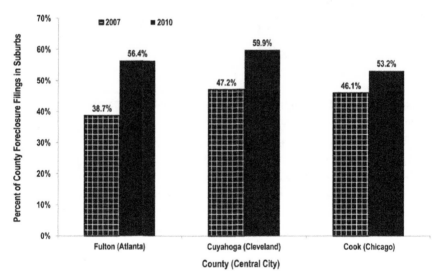

Figure 2.5.   The Suburban Share of Foreclosure Filings for Three Major Metro-politan Counties, 2007 and 2010. *Source:* **Prepared by author from data in Hexter and Schnoke (2011) and Woodstock Institute (2008; 2011), and from author's calculations of Fulton County foreclosure data.**

THE DISPROPORTIONATE LEGACY OF THE CRISIS IN
COMMUNITIES OF COLOR

Figure 2.6 analyzes data from Dreier et al. (2014), which identified the residential zip codes (those with at least five thousand residents) that had the largest percentage of underwater homeowners throughout the country as of the end of 2013. Many homes in these places had not regained sufficient value to exceed their outstanding mortgages. Figure 2.6 analyzes the median household incomes and the racial and ethnic composition of the 143 zip codes in the study where the percentage of homeowners underwater exceeded 50 percent. These are the zip codes that, under this measure at least, had the most difficult time recovering from the mortgage crisis.

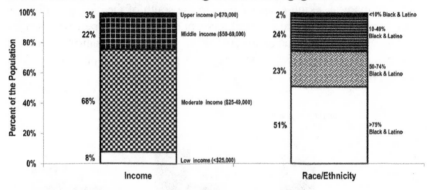

Figure 2.6. The Demographics of Majority-Underwater Zip Codes, 2013. *Source:* **Prepared by author from data in Dreier et al. (2014).**

As the left-hand bar in the figure shows, just over 75 percent these neighborhoods have median incomes below $50,000. Most of these are not the poorest neighborhoods, however. Most fall into the $25,000–$50,000 range, and might be considered either low-moderate- or moderate-income neighborhoods. As was the case with the original subprime crisis, moderate-income neighborhoods were hit particularly hard. The right-hand column in Figure 2.6 shows that the recovery has also lagged in communities of color. Approximately 75 percent of the most-impacted zip codes are majority black and Latino, with just over one half being predominantly (greater than 75 percent) black and Latino. Only 2 percent of these zip codes are predominantly white or Asian. Thus, the longer-term legacy of the crisis has followed the racial and spatial patterns of the subprime boom and its ensuing foreclosures.

This chapter examined the scope and depth of the effects of the foreclosure crisis on American households and communities. Foreclosures affect more than just the financial situations of borrowers or the balance sheets of lenders. They can affect families' sense of stability, school performance, and psychological and physical health. They also have spillover costs for neighborhoods and cities, including lower property values and associated tax revenue, vacant property, crime, and the potential to spur more foreclosures in the neighborhood.

This chapter also described the racial and geographic shape of the crisis, showing that minority households and communities were hit particularly hard by the crisis, and have recovered more slowly from it. The next chapter discusses the federal response to the crisis, and how well such efforts matched its scale and challenges.

Chapter Three

The Federal Government to the Rescue?

The Response to the Foreclosure Crisis

This chapter focuses on the federal efforts—mainly between 2007 and 2013—aimed at reducing foreclosures as well as their negative impacts on neighborhoods and communities. Most media and research-based assessments have generally described these responses as halting and inadequate, especially in light of the scale of the crisis. Of course, the magnitude of the crisis was unprecedented and policymakers faced numerous impediments—both structural and political—to a more forceful response. Nonetheless, more aggressive and impactful measures likely would have reduced the overall harm and the depth of the crisis, especially if they had been adopted in the first few years. This chapter does not address the broader, longer-term federal response to the crisis in terms of reforming mortgage-market regulation, or restructuring the housing-finance system. Later chapters address those topics in some detail.

The direct federal responses to the crisis fell into two categories: policies focused on preventing or reducing foreclosures, and policies focused on mitigating the impacts of foreclosures on neighborhoods. The first category includes major initiatives under the Bush and Obama administrations, including the creation of the National Foreclosure Mitigation Counseling program beginning in late 2007; the facilitation of the Hope Now Alliance in 2007 and the related modification programs spearheaded together with the American Securitization Forum; and the Making Home Affordable (MHA) programs, which began in 2009. The second category, which focuses on attempts to mitigate the impacts of foreclosures on local communities, includes the three phases of the Neighborhood Stabilization Program (NSP).

In the face of a number of structural and political obstacles, neither the Bush nor Obama administrations were very successful in crafting an effective and sufficiently scaled federal response. In the arena of loan-modification efforts, which were arguably the largest and most important area of response, federal initiatives suffered from an overreliance on small "carrots" and an underutilization of "sticks." While it may have been politically impossible to institute any sort of meaningful mandatory modification scheme, in which all lenders would be strictly required to modify loans en-masse, more forceful methods could have been employed to encourage servicers and investors to be more aggressive in modifying loans in meaningful and effective ways. The most important tool in this regard would have been the adoption of legislation allowing for the reduction of outstanding principal balances in bankruptcy proceedings, a measure proposed in 2007 by Senator Richard Durbin of Illinois and generally referred to as "bankruptcy cramdown." In addition, an earlier use of sanctions and penalties for loan servicers not complying with the guidelines of the Making Home Affordable programs could have encouraged more—and more effective—modifications.

Besides the failure to adopt bankruptcy cramdown legislation, there were at least three other major factors that impeded greater levels of loan modifications. One was the basic structure and dysfunction of the loan-servicing industry, which was never designed for large-scale modification operations. The industry was fundamentally designed to service performing loans and had a low-margin structure that did not provide incentives for meaningful modifications. Another obstacle was a set of competing goals and objectives held by federal agencies. While the Treasury Department was seeking to promote payment-reducing loan modifications, the conservator of Fannie Mae and Freddie Mac, the Federal Housing Finance Agency (FHFA), had different goals. The FHFA, which was charged with "conserving" the assets of the firms, was resistant to moves that might require the firms to take large-scale, short-term write-downs on their balance sheets. Even if such modifications might increase long-term returns by improving loan performance or the broader housing market, the pressures to conserve agency assets in the short run, as well as the ideological predisposition of agency leadership, worked against a long-term perspective. Another key factor was a political climate in which there was a good deal of opposition to using federal resources to assist distressed homeowners. Neither the Obama nor the Bush administrations made sustained efforts to convince the public that helping distressed homeowners was the right or sensible thing to do. Instead of confronting the calls for horizontal "fairness" (i.e., why should my neighbor get a principal reduction and not me?) by pointing out the damage that foreclosures and negative equity were doing to the country as a whole, leaders often chose to fashion marginal solutions that skirted these difficult issues.

The Neighborhood Stabilization Programs, a key part of the federal response to the neighborhood effects of foreclosure, also faced significant challenges. First, the level of funding under these programs was very modest in relation to the volume and flow of foreclosed properties. Second, the narrowness of NSP legislation, especially of NSP 1, made it difficult for localities to respond effectively to the evolving nature of the foreclosed and vacant property problem. The nature of property records in many states made it difficult for localities to identify those in control of the properties, and in the case of privately securitized mortgages, the complexities of ownership often made negotiating with lenders extremely difficult. In some places, as NSP 1 was just getting underway in early 2009, many bank-owned properties, especially lower-valued ones in the types of neighborhoods targeted by the program, were being sold off quickly to private investors. Although later incarnations of NSP increased flexibility, localities would have benefitted from a more robust and responsive source of funding to tackle the vacant property problem. Other problems that NSP recipients faced included their frequently limited experience in acquiring and rehabilitating vacant single-family homes, and the cumbersome nature of the legacy systems of funding and oversight that the U.S. Department of Housing and Urban Development used to deploy NSP monies.

Overall, this examination of the federal response to the foreclosure crisis suggests three broad lessons. First, many of the policy responses and programs were tentative, incremental, and marginal. The response often nibbled the edges of the core problems, especially in the first few years of the crisis. Perhaps this was to be expected, as problems of widespread negative homeowner equity and large-scale unemployment deepened the crisis. However, if the resources and energy devoted to the response had been more focused and aggressive earlier on, the response might have reached greater scale more quickly and attenuated the crisis in a more fundamental way.

A second lesson is that some programs were excessively engineered to avoid particular potential problems, but this sometimes made them clumsier and more difficult to implement at scale. In the NSP arena, for example, federal policymakers were so concerned with potential local malfeasance related to NSP funds that they developed burdensome administrative procedures that made it difficult to reach scale quickly. In the loan-modification arena, moral hazard was a constant concern. Servicers and others argued that more aggressive loan-modification programs, especially those involving principal reduction, would encourage borrowers to default to take advantage of such programs. However, there was little evidence that mortgage delinquencies would increase substantially because of such initiatives. Moreover, there are at least two other responses to such concerns. First, as William

Dudley (2012) and others have argued, programs can be, and have been, efficiently designed to discourage such activity. Second, even where concern over moral hazard is warranted, the possibility of some moral hazard may be more than compensated for by the positive outcomes of an initiative.

A third lesson is that, because policy interventions took some time to become stronger, the more effective responses benefitted households and communities impacted more heavily in the latter stages of the overall crisis. Because the crisis began as a subprime mortgage crisis, which was dispro-portionately concentrated among minority and lower-income families and neighborhoods, they received effectively less assistance from the govern-ment than did middle-income homeowners and communities that experi-enced more distress during the latter part of the crisis. The earlier stages of the crisis began in more vulnerable, majority-minority communities, and by the time that federal interventions became more effective, generally after 2010, they arrived too late for many hard-hit communities. By this time, the national crisis had reached another stage, where mortgage distress and fore-closures had shifted substantially into the prime mortgage market, where they affected more moderate- and middle-income—often less-minority—communities. By 2011, many inner-city and predominantly minority neigh-borhoods hit hardest by the crisis, while still struggling, had moved past their peak levels of foreclosure. Meanwhile, many families had already been dis-placed, and many properties—often sitting vacant—were sold off by lenders to private investors (Immergluck 2012).

This chapter describes the major federal foreclosure-prevention initiatives since the beginning of the crisis. These efforts include loan-modification programs as well as complementary initiatives such as housing-counseling resources aimed at keeping people in their homes. There is also some discus-sion of important proposals that were not adopted or implemented. Because there was a significant change in approach to foreclosure prevention in the transition from the Bush to Obama administrations, the programs are distin-guished by the administration in which they began.

I focus heavily on the outcomes of the Obama foreclosure-prevention initiatives, not only because they were more ambitious than the Bush initia-tives, but also because a large portion of the crisis played out during Obama's first term. Data on program performance and outputs are presented when available. The aim here is not to provide in-depth evaluations of every specif-ic program. Rather, I rely primarily on existing reports to make my assess-ments. The goal here is to ascertain some of the key factors that may have limited the greater overall scale and impact of the broader effort.

This chapter then shifts to the federal Neighborhood Stabilization Pro-grams, including NSP 1, NSP 2, and NSP 3. These programs constitute the principal federal response aimed at mitigating the neighborhood and commu-nity effects of foreclosures. More attention is given to NSP 1, primarily because more is known about the program's implementation at this point. The NSP programs are less difficult to describe than the larger set of foreclosure-prevention programs, although the detailed mechanics of their operations are not necessarily less complicated. I conclude with a discussion of broader lessons learned from the federal response, in both the foreclosure-prevention and mitigation arenas.

Figure 3.1 indicates the key federal responses to the U.S. foreclosure crisis. It also indicates some events that had particular influence on the crisis and the policy response. It does this against a plot of the share of mortgages entering the foreclosure process during the period. The scale of the crisis was vast. There were 55 to 60 million mortgages outstanding at the height of the housing boom, and by the beginning of 2009, 5 percent of outstanding mortgages (3 million) were entering foreclosure per year. From March 2009, when the Obama-era MHA program was announced, through the middle of 2011, there were well over 5 million foreclosure starts on owner-occupied homes (Immergluck 2013). While not all of these resulted in lost homes, this figure is a conservative indicator of the number of households in severe financial distress and at imminent risk of losing their homes during this period.

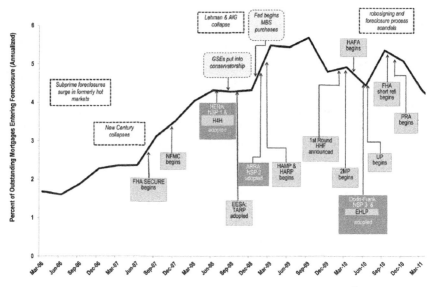

Figure 3.1. Federal Policies Responding to the Foreclosure Crisis [1]

FORECLOSURE-PREVENTION POLICIES

While there is no clear start date for the U.S. foreclosure crisis, many would point to late 2006 or early 2007, when foreclosures began to grow rapidly in many regions that had previously seen low foreclosure rates, especially the "sand states" of Arizona, California, Florida, and Nevada. One of the largest subprime lenders, New Century, went bankrupt in the spring of 2007. In late spring and early summer, Federal Reserve Board chairman Ben Bernanke and U.S. Department of Housing and Urban Development (HUD) secretary Alphonso Jackson called for federal funding for foreclosure-prevention counseling (Joint Economic Committee 2007). And in August of 2007, the Federal Housing Administration (FHA) announced its FHA Secure program, which would refinance delinquent homeowners into more affordable loans to reduce foreclosures. While FHA refinances surged in 2008, due in part to the decline in credit from other lenders, by April of 2008, fewer than 1,800 borrowers with delinquent mortgages were served through FHA Secure (Swarns 2008).

In October, as the subprime crisis was making national headlines, Senator Richard Durbin (D-IL) introduced the Helping Families Save Their Homes in Bankruptcy Act (U.S. Senate 2007). The bill would have allowed bankruptcy judges to reduce the balance due on owner-occupied home loans. When borrowers file for bankruptcy under chapter 13, the court can modify certain debts, including reducing the balances owed ("cramming down") to the fair market value of the property or other collateral securing the loan. However, this authority does not extend to loans secured by owner-occupied residences. Bankruptcy judges can modify the balance due on a vacation home or an investment property, but not on a primary residence. The Durbin bill would have removed the primary-residence exclusion on a temporary basis, which would have provided relief for those filing bankruptcy, and given investors in mortgage-backed securities (MBS) and servicers an incentive to modify loans voluntarily before the borrower might file bankruptcy. Opponents to the Durbin bill, including much of the lending and securities industries as well as the Bush Administration, argued that the proposal would raise mortgage rates substantially. However, Adam Levitin and Joshua Goodman (2008) estimated that mortgage cramdown would result in at most an increase of only 0.05 to 0.15 percentage points in mortgage rates. Industry lobbyists successfully blocked the bill.

The Bush Administration, in part to offer an alternative to the Durbin bill, announced the Hope Now Alliance in October of 2007 (Hope Now Alliance 2007). The Alliance included banks, lender and investor trade associations, the NeighborWorks network, and other organizations. Hope Now offered foreclosure-prevention counseling to homeowners via a 1-800 number. Rejecting calls for stronger interventions, the administration also announced an effort to promote "streamlined" voluntary loan modifications for a subset of subprime mortgages (American Securitization Forum 2007). This proposal was developed primarily by the American Securitization Forum (ASF), a trade group of structured finance investors. The plan was criticized by many consumer advocates in part because it was entirely voluntary on the part of servicers and investors, and because it carved out a narrow segment of at-risk borrowers as eligible for assistance (Said and Zito 2007). Estimates of the proportion of subprime borrowers who would fit the program's eligibility requirements fell in the range of 3 to 12 percent (Immergluck 2009).

To complement the Hope Now initiative, the National Foreclosure Mitigation Counseling (NFMC) program began in December. Over five rounds of funding through 2011, NFMC provided more than $500 million to counsel homeowners in or at risk of foreclosure via the NeighborWorks network. NFMC counselors became key advocates for borrowers applying for loan modifications during Bush- and Obama-era loan-modification initiatives.

NFMC was a bright spot among the Bush Administration's programs. As of early 2010, it had supported the counseling of over 1 million homeowners. A congressionally mandated evaluation of the program found that it significantly reduced foreclosures among counseled homeowners. Researchers at the Urban Institute found that the odds of counseled homeowners curing their foreclosure were 70 percent greater than if they had not received NFMC counseling (Mayer et al. 2010).[2]

By the summer of 2008, with the economy faltering and a national election approaching, there was more political pressure to address the foreclosure crisis. Due to losses on some of their investments in subprime mortgage-backed securities, it became increasingly apparent that the government-sponsored enterprises (GSEs), Fannie Mae and Freddie Mac, would need federal assistance. The stock price of the GSEs had been falling, leaving the firms even more highly leveraged than they had been. Moreover, in July 2008, the Housing and Economic Recovery Act (HERA) was enacted (U.S. House of Representatives 2008). HERA was a complex piece of legislation that created a new regulator for the GSEs that could, if necessary, place the GSEs under direct government control in a "conservatorship" (Weiss et al. 2008). HERA also contained tax breaks for residential builders, a complicated first-time homebuyers tax credit (which was later simplified), and funding for local government and nonprofit acquisition of foreclosed properties, later called the "Neighborhood Stabilization Program."

HERA's principal foreclosure-prevention program was the $300 billion Hope for Homeowners (H4H) program, run by the FHA, which was intended to refinance distressed borrowers out of unaffordable mortgages and into smaller, more affordable, fixed-rate loans. The program required borrowers to share at least 50 percent of any equity gain with the FHA upon sale of the home. The program did not address the prevalence of junior mortgages among distressed borrowers, since junior lenders can hold up the refinancing process. H4H failed to get any traction. Even after HUD eased the requirements for lenders and borrowers, and tried to make it easier to compensate junior lenders for releasing their liens, only 340 loans were made through the H4H program in fiscal year 2010 (U.S. Department of Housing and Urban Development 2011a).

After HERA was passed in July 2008, housing prices continued to fall rapidly in many regions, and foreclosures continued to increase and spread to the near-prime and prime sectors. By early September, Treasury Secretary Paulson announced that he would provide financing to the GSEs and direct the Federal Housing Finance Agency (FHFA), the new GSE regulator, to place both firms in conservatorship, wiping out GSE stockholders and giving the FHFA substantial operational control of both companies. After further turmoil in U.S. and global financial markets, including the fall of Lehman Brothers and near collapse of the insurance firm AIG, Secretary Paulson introduced a $700 billion proposal to establish the Troubled Asset Relief Program (TARP). The proposal had been prepared earlier for the eventuality that the crisis might become significantly worse (Nocera 2008). In early October, after significant Congressional gymnastics, the Emergency Economic Stabilization Act (EESA), which authorized TARP, became law. TARP was originally portrayed as an effort to purchase mortgages or mortgage-backed securities from financial institutions to rid them of bad assets. By mid-October, after the United Kingdom initiated its own equity injections into banks, the Treasury Department directed TARP funds to be used to buy preferred stock in mostly larger financial institutions. The Bush Administration decided against using TARP funds to assist struggling homeowners directly, despite provisions in the bill that gave it the authority to do so.

In late 2008, even before taking office, the Obama Administration sought to draw down the second half of the TARP funds. Larry Summers, the incoming director of the National Economic Council, wrote a letter to Congress stating that the new administration would use $50-$100 billion of TARP funds for foreclosure mitigation (Summers 2009). The letter also suggested that the new administration would seek to change bankruptcy laws to permit cram-downs of primary-residence loans.

Obama-Era Foreclosure-Prevention Policy

One of the earliest domestic policy priorities of the Obama Administration was to create a more forceful foreclosure-prevention initiative. The Bush-era Hope Now initiative had been widely criticized as inadequate and ineffective, and the ASF/Hope Now modification initiative was responsible for only approximately 9 percent of loan modifications in the first six months of 2008, a figure that dropped to 2 percent in the latter half of the year (Fitch Ratings 2009). The bulk of these modifications were the servicers' private, proprietary modifications, which often did not involve substantial reductions in payments, and sometimes actually resulted in increased payments. Because many modifications during the early part of the crisis did not lower mortgage payments, let alone the outstanding principal, the portion of modifications that redefaulted within just six months ranged from 34 to 51 percent (Agarwal et al. 2010).[3] While loan modifications that reduced mortgage payments grew in 2008, many interventions still focused on very short-term forbearance, which reduced payments for as little as one month or did not reduce payments at all.

In March 2009, as the foreclosure crisis deepened, the Obama Administration aimed to assist 7 to 9 million homeowners by introducing the Making Home Affordable (MHA) initiative (U.S. Department of the Treasury 2009). Initially, MHA consisted of two key components. The Home Affordable Refinancing Program (HARP) provided for expanded loan refinancing through the GSEs. The GSEs had traditionally not made loans for more than 80 percent of the value of the home unless private mortgage insurance insured the value above this level. Because an increasing number of homeowners were underwater (with home values less than outstanding loan amounts), they were unable to refinance their loans during a time of historically low interest rates. Refinancing would allow homeowners to reduce their loan payments, thereby reducing their foreclosure risk.[4] Under HARP, the maximum loan-to-value (LTV) limit for refinance loans increased to 105 percent, and then to 125 percent a few months later. In late 2011, the maximum LTV for borrowers refinancing into fixed-rate loans was removed altogether. The administration suggested that HARP would refinance 4 to 5 million homeowners into lower-cost loans (U.S. Department of the Treasury 2009).

The Home Affordable Modification Program (HAMP) was another high-profile component of MHA. In HAMP, which was funded by TARP funds, borrowers at imminent risk of foreclosure could apply for a loan modification that would reduce mortgage payments. HAMP was intended to encourage the modification of loans in cases where reducing mortgage payments would make more sense from the perspective of the lender than foreclosure.

HAMP was a complex program in which mortgages were modified in two basic steps. First, lenders/investors lowered monthly mortgage payments to the point where they were equal to 38 percent of monthly gross income. Second, the costs of further reducing the loan payments to 31 percent of monthly income were shared between the lenders/investors and the federal government.[5] In June of 2012, a modified "Tier 2" HAMP was introduced in which borrowers with lower debt-to-income ratios could qualify for a modification, as well as some owners of rental properties. Under the HAMP program, servicers could (but were not required to) reduce principal owed. Another MHA program described below, the Principal Reduction Alternative (PRA), was introduced later to encourage this.

After meeting other eligibility requirements, HAMP applications were evaluated by using a standardized net present value (NPV) test that compared the net present value to the lender/investor of modifying the loan to the status quo of no modification. The NPV test used specified inputs to compare the two alternative cash flows and discounted them to current dollars. If the NPV of the cash flow expected from modifying a loan was greater than the NPV of the cash flow expected from foreclosing, the servicer had to modify the loan. The logic of the NPV test was that servicers should modify loans when it made sense from the perspective of the lender/investor. Loan-modification programs, while billed in the media as focused on aiding distressed borrowers, were also a component of a broader strategy of lender-loss mitigation. A key argument in favor of loan modifications was that lenders/investors often lost more on a foreclosure than they would if the loan had been appropriately modified (White 2009). When servicers foreclosed, lenders/investors generally recovered well under half of the loan amount, with loss severity ratios typically running over 60 percent for subprime loans, and as much as 50 percent for prime loans. [6]

The NPV test was conducted solely from the perspective of the lender/investor and not that of the borrower—or society. It did not take into account the negative spillovers that foreclosures have on surrounding neighborhoods or communities, or the feedback effects that those spillovers can have on other borrowers' loan performance. Moreover, since the servicer had some ability to influence the implementation of the NPV analysis, if the servicer did not benefit from the modification process, then it may have had a vested interest in skewing the results toward a "do not modify" result.

All HAMP borrowers were placed in trial modifications for a period that was supposed to last three months, although almost 20 percent of trial modifications lasted longer than six months in practice (SIGTARP 2011). During the trial period, HAMP borrowers had to make at least three payments at the modified payment level. After transitioning to "permanent" modifications, the terms of the loan remained fixed for at least five years, after which interest rates could increase at 1 percent per year back up to market rate, if the borrower received a below-market interest rate during the modification period.

A fundamental proposition behind HAMP was that resistance from servicers and lenders/investors to modifications would be diminished with small incentive payments and a standardized protocol for evaluating and implementing modifications. The design of the program rested on the notion that a rational set of procedures and incentives could be layered on the existing loan-servicing system, and that the industry would respond well to this overlay. However, HAMP did not fundamentally alter the locus of decision-making or address some fundamental barriers and blockages to modifying massive numbers of distressed borrowers in a quick and fair way.

Another key feature of HAMP, one that followed from the Bush-era Hope Now efforts, was that it did not impose strong modification requirements on servicers. Even when some steps in the process supposedly triggered modification, there were many ways that the complex HAMP procedures allowed servicers or lenders/investors to limit loan modifications. Moreover, servicers controlled many key inputs or assessments in the HAMP modification process.

In introducing HAMP, the administration suggested that it would be complemented by adopting the bankruptcy mortgage-modification provisions similar to those proposed in the 2007 Durbin bill (U.S. Department of the Treasury 2009). Such a bill would have provided the stick needed to get lenders to the modification table, while the incentives to servicers in HAMP provided the carrot. A bankruptcy mortgage-modification bill passed in the House, but failed in the Senate. Instead of fighting for the bankruptcy bill, the administration argued that HAMP could reach its goals without bankruptcy modification (Lillis 2009). As a result, the key Obama-era foreclosure-prevention strategy, while more focused, ambitious, and structured than the Bush-era Hope Now initiative, relied on the carrots of small incentive payments without the stick of bankruptcy modification. The Obama Administration projected that the MHA programs would help 7–9 million homeowners, with HAMP assisting 3–4 million of those (U.S. Department of the Treasury 2009). These ambitious and widely publicized goals would become a significant problem for the administration.

The MHA initiative was soon expanded by adding supportive programs aimed at a variety of barriers to foreclosure prevention, and at creating opportunities for "soft landings," using short sales, deeds-in-lieu of foreclosure, and relocation assistance when keeping a homeowner in a home did not appear to be feasible.[7] The second lien-modification program (referred to as "2MP"), which focused on eliminating or modifying junior mortgages, was one of these programs. When a borrower's first-lien mortgage was modified under HAMP, servicers participating in 2MP had to offer to modify the borrower's junior mortgage. As in HAMP, servicers followed specified protocols that resulted in either extinguishing the junior mortgage, or reducing it partially and modifying the terms of the remaining portion. Servicers received incentive payments to execute 2MP modifications. Although the program was announced in the spring of 2009, it did not begin operating until the spring of 2010 (SIGTARP 2011). Moreover, despite the large percentage of junior mortgages in the housing market, fewer than thirty-five thousand 2MP transactions occurred in the fifteen months after implementation. Even by December 2013, the 2MP program only reached a level of just under 80,000 active modifications (U.S. Department of the Treasury 2013).

Until the latter part of 2010, HAMP did not address severely underwater borrowers. Without realigning loan balances with property values, underwater borrowers had less motivation to maintain ownership of the house, especially if it meant defaulting on other debts or creating severe strains on household finances. This was one reason why allowing bankruptcy judges to modify loan balances would have provided a strong complement to any large-scale loan-modification effort. Without the threat of bankruptcy modification, servicers and investors had little incentive to make substantive and sustainable loan modifications in large enough numbers to put a major dent in foreclosure volumes. The Treasury Department's response to this problem was the Principal Reduction Alternative (PRA) program, which did not get going until late in 2010 (SIGTARP 2011). PRA gave servicers additional incentives beyond those in HAMP to reduce principal; it also gave incentives to loan investors. However, PRA did not require servicers to reduce principal, even when doing so provided greater benefits to investors than other forms of modification. As a result, only about 5 percent of HAMP permanent modifications included principal reduction through 2011 (U.S. Government Accountability Office 2012).

Another MHA foreclosure-prevention program was the Home Affordable Foreclosure Alternatives (HAFA) program. Rules for HAFA were issued in late 2009, and the program began in the spring of 2010 (SIGTARP 2011). HAFA was aimed at encouraging short sales and deeds-in-lieu of foreclosure as a preferable alternative to foreclosure. In many states, borrowers engaging in these types of transactions were still liable for the unpaid balance on the loans through deficiency judgments. As a result, these transactions were less advantageous to borrowers than they appeared. One component of HAFA was a requirement that participating lenders/investors waive any rights to pursue deficiency judgments. HAFA provided for incentives to servicers and borrowers to execute short sales or deeds-in-lieu of foreclosure. Servicers were given a $1,500 incentive for executed HAFA transactions, and homeowners were given $3,000 in relocation assistance. However, many servicers and lender/investors were reluctant to give up the ability to pursue deficiency judgments after a short sale or deed-in-lieu of foreclosure, at least where they were allowed to pursue them by state law. Indeed, the ten largest servicers participating in HAMP reported that, as of May 2011, they had completed over 112,000 short sales and deeds-in-lieu for HAMP borrowers whose modifications had failed, more than ten times the volume of all HAFA transactions. However, the HAFA program did catch on later, especially as the housing market rebounded in many places, and short sales became more common. Total HAFA transactions grew to 101,000 by the end of 2012 and to 258,000 by the end of 2013. However, these transactions, the bulk of which were short sales, were heavily concentrated in California (40 percent) and Florida (16 percent). The geographic concentration of HAFA short sales (vs. other short sales) was most likely influenced by state deficiency laws. In states where deficiency judgments were generally allowed, servicers and loan investors may have been much less likely to cooperate with the HAFA program, where borrowers had to be released from any potential deficiency judgments.

One TARP-funded initiative that took a very different approach from HAMP and its affiliated MHA programs was the Hardest Hit Fund (HHF), which provided funds to state housing-finance agencies (HFAs), which in turn designed and implemented detailed foreclosure-prevention programs in their states, subject to Treasury Department approval (Immergluck 2010; SIGTARP 2012). HHF was billed as an effort to promote innovative approaches to reducing foreclosures in ways that could be customized to regional housing-market and economic conditions. Beginning in February 2010, the HHF program allocated over $7.6 billion to HFAs via four rounds of funding. The criteria for funding and the eligible uses of funds changed in each round. The first round provided $1.5 billion to the five states (Arizona, California, Florida, Michigan, and Nevada) where home values dropped by at least 20 percent from their peak. Initially, the Treasury Department appeared open to a wide variety of uses for the funds in this round, as long as they were aimed at reducing foreclosures or mitigating their impacts on households. In a second round a couple of months later, $600 million in funds were allocated to five more states. This time, states with high percentages of people living in high-unemployment counties were selected, including North Carolina, Ohio, Oregon, Rhode Island, and South Carolina. The eligible uses for this round of funds were similar to those of the first round. In August 2010, a third round of HHF funds, amounting to another $2 billion, was allocated to states with unemployment rates above the national rate. This amounted to seventeen states plus Washington, DC, including all of the previously funded states except for Arizona. This third round of funds was directed toward programs to assist the unemployed in paying their mortgages. Finally, just before the Treasury Department's authority to allocate TARP funds ended at the end of September, an additional $3.5 billion was allocated to existing HHF states to be used in existing HHF programs.

By using a wholesale, block-grant-like approach, the HHF programs were intended to provide for localized innovations in foreclosure-prevention and loan-modification programs. However, even though the EESA gave the Treasury Department broad discretion in designing foreclosure-prevention programs such as HAMP and HHF, the flexibility of the Treasury Department in responding to the states' HHF proposals was, in practice, limited (Immergluck 2010). For example, proposals to utilize HHF funds to support legal assistance to borrowers were rejected. In addition, servicers and the GSEs resisted some HHF state plans to implement principal-reduction programs, even when such reductions would be subsidized one-for-one with HHF dollars. As in the case of HAMP, the Treasury Department did little to push servicers or the GSEs to participate in principal-reduction programs.

Unemployment increased in 2009 and 2010, and became an important driver of foreclosures. In March of 2010, the Treasury Department introduced the Home Affordable Unemployment Program, known as "UP" (SIGTARP 2011). Under UP, HAMP borrowers received partial forbearance of their mortgage payments for a period of three months. After hearing complaints that a three-month forbearance period would not be of much use in an economy where unemployment spells were averaging over six months in many parts of the country, the administration increased the period to twelve months. However, the GSEs refused to participate in the UP program, making it available only for borrowers with non-GSE loans. The UP program was complemented by HHF programs aimed at helping unemployed borrowers pay their mortgages, as well as a newer program aimed at unemployed borrowers in states not funded via HHF. In the 2010 Dodd-Frank regulatory reform bill, Congress allocated $1 billion to fund the Emergency Homeowners Loan Program (EHLP), a mortgage-payment assistance program aimed at helping unemployed homeowners pay their mortgages. EHLP was designated for use only in the thirty-two states where HHF funds were not available. However, it took until the summer of 2011 for the administration to get the program launched with GSE support (Prior 2011). When it ended in late 2011, EHLP had helped fewer than twelve thousand homeowners instead of the projected thirty thousand (U.S. House of Representatives 2012).

Examining the Results of Obama-Era Foreclosure-Prevention Efforts

Figure 3.2 provides activity numbers for the Obama Administration's principal foreclosure-prevention program, HAMP, through the end of 2013. Determining how many borrowers received substantive assistance is not a completely straightforward or objective task. For example, over 2.1 million borrowers entered a HAMP trial by the end of 2013, and the Treasury Department has argued that this is a reasonable measure of the number of households assisted, because households made reduced mortgage payments during the trial periods. Others, notably the special inspector general for the Troubled Asset Relief Program (SIGTARP), have disagreed, arguing that only sustainable, permanent modifications should be considered meaningful assistance. The SIGTARP has even argued that many borrowers applying to TARP and either not qualifying for a trial or having their modification cancelled may actually have been harmed by HAMP (SIGTARP 2011).

If one uses the number of permanent modifications that remain active (plus any loans that have been paid off) as a metric of successfully assisted homeowners, then HAMP had reached 950,000 successful first-lien modifications by the end of 2013—a far cry from the goal set originally in 2009 of 3–4 million modifications by the end of 2012. MHA activity also included

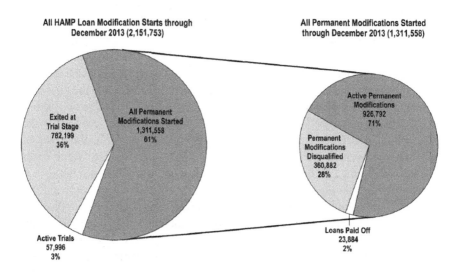

Figure 3.2.   HAMP First-Lien Loan-Modification Activity through December 2013. *Note:* Does not include approximately 26,000 FHA-HAMP modification starts.

79,891 2MP active modifications, 37,873 UP forbearance plan starts, and 258,444 HAFA short sales or deed-in-lieu transactions. (It is important to note that some of these transactions assisted the same borrowers that had received HAMP modifications.) While the 2MP and UP figures were somewhat underwhelming, the HAFA program began to achieve more significant scale in 2012 and 2013, especially as the demand for owner-occupied homes improved in some parts of the country.

One key concern among critics of the HAMP program was the scarcity of principal-reduction modifications, even when millions of homeowners were seriously underwater. Of the 930,000 or so active permanent modifications at of the end of 2013, fewer than 113,000 had principal reductions under the PRA program, with an average principal reduction of 32 percent. Another 36,510 HAMP loans included some (generally a smaller level) of principal reduction outside of the PRA program. This means that only 16 percent of HAMP modifications through the end of 2013 involved principal reduction. By the end of 2013, among non-GSE loans, principal reduction was occurring at a higher rate than it had during earlier periods of the program. However, an increasing share of distressed loans over time was now made of GSE loans, due in part to the spread of the mortgage crisis over time from the subprime to the prime market. Therefore, the FHFA's refusal to allow GSEs to reduce principal meant that most of the loan modifications didn't include principal reduction.

In addition to HAMP, the HARP program was the other major piece of the original Obama response to the foreclosure crisis. It was introduced in 2009 with a goal of refinancing 4–5 million homeowners with loan-to-value ratios exceeding 80 percent. HARP got off to a slow start in the first three years of its existence. About 1 million HARP loans had been made through December 2011, despite the fact that the Federal Reserve Board estimates that approximately 4 million borrowers were eligible (Duke 2011). Furthermore, approximately 91 percent of these loans had loan-to-value ratios between 80 and 105 percent, the original HARP guidelines. Only about 90,000 HARP borrowers were significantly underwater (with loan-to-value ratios between 105 and 125 percent). The Federal Reserve suggested a number of "frictions" that might have kept HARP from reaching more borrowers. First, the GSEs charged higher upfront fees for refinancing loans with higher risk factors, including higher loan-to-value ratios. Such fees may have limited the benefits of refinancing through HARP. Second, as the GSEs became more risk-averse during the mortgage crisis, they began aggressively requiring originating lenders to repurchase loans that violated GSE guidelines. This made lenders generally more risk averse, especially in the case of loans with any higher-risk features, including high loan-to-value ratios. In addition, some second mortgage holders were refusing to agree to refinance the senior loans, even though this would likely reduce the risk on their junior loans.

In order to address some of these barriers to greater utilization of HARP, the GSEs and the FHFA agreed to a number of changes in HARP (labeled "HARP 2.0") that took effect in December 2011. These included relaxing repurchase requirements and eliminating the maximum loan-to-value ratio for borrowers refinancing into fixed-rate loans. Figure 3.3 shows that these changes made a clear positive impact on HARP volume, which increased markedly as early as January 2012. HARP volume in the first six months of 2012 exceeded the total volume for all of 2012. Figure 3.3 shows that much of the initial increase was in 80–125 percent LTV loans. For those loans at least, it was not raising the LTV ceiling that made the difference, but the other changes, like relaxing repurchase requirements when loans defaulted. Increasing the LTV limits clearly did have some impact, however, as the number of refinances with LTVs above 125 percent grew fairly quickly and reached over 80,000 by the third quarter of 2012. Loans refinanced through HARP performed at markedly better rates than loans that were eligible for HARP but did not go through the program. For example, only 5.7 percent of HARP refinances in June of 2009 were delinquent for more than 90 days through the end of 2013, compared to 12.5 percent of HARP-eligible GSE loans that did not go through the program (U.S. Department of the Treasury 2013). Thus, HARP reduced the foreclosure rate among these loans by more than half. However, the fact that it took more than two years before the changes in HARP 2.0 were implemented, combined with the fact that HARP resulted in a major reduction in foreclosure rates, begs the question of how many more households could have been helped if these changes had been implemented earlier in the crisis.

Still, HARP was the bright spot of the Obama Administration's response to the foreclosure crisis. The program refinanced more than 3 million borrowers through 2013, including almost 2.6 million owner-occupied properties, with the rest being second homes and investor properties (U.S. Department of the Treasury 2013). HARP, while still falling short of its stated 4–5 million refinances by the end of 2012, achieved significantly greater volume than HAMP, and was closer to reaching its goals. However, the beneficiaries of HARP were GSE borrowers, who were less spatially and racially concentrated compared to subprime borrowers. HAMP was aimed more at subprime borrowers (at least early on), and because it was less effective, the federal response to the crisis was less effective at helping many of the most vulnerable families and neighborhoods.

The federal foreclosure-prevention response, while purportedly aimed at many modest-income and minority homeowners, turned out to be, in effect, tilted toward helping many prime borrowers, more of whom were middle-class, white homeowners. From the perspective of saving the housing market as a whole, the efforts no doubt helped, and they certainly helped millions of homeowners who were financially distressed. At the same time, it is also the case that many millions of subprime borrowers—who were disproportionate-

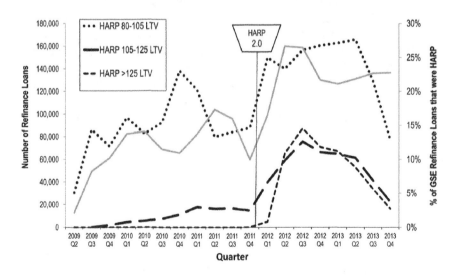

Figure 3.3. HARP Refinance Activity 2009–2013. *Source:* Prepared by author from data in Federal Housing Finance Agency Refinance Reports, March 2012 and Fourth Quarter 2013.

ly people of color and residents of low- and moderate-income neighbor-hoods—fell through the very large cracks in the federal response, especially in the first few years of the crisis.

While not as central as HAMP or HARP, the Hardest Hit Fund (HHF) was also a component of the Obama Administration's response to the crisis. While some states were not able to begin their programs until late 2010 or later, HHF reached scale much more slowly than HAMP. From February 2010, when the first round of HHF began, to December 2011, only $217 million (or 3.2 percent) of the $7.6 billion had been expended (SIGTARP 2012). Although the expected timeline for the full expenditure of these funds went through 2017, these first two years still represented approximately 24 percent of the full program period. (Again, some states effectively started their programs later than others did.) What was also clear from the HHF allocations through December 2011 was that the bulk of the funds had been spent on unemployment assistance and loan-reinstatement programs, two initiatives that were clearly spelled out by the Treasury Department as likely uses of the funds early in the program. More ambitious or creative initiatives, including principal-reduction programs and funding for rental-housing tran-sitions, received much less actual funding, with only 436 borrowers receiving principal reduction and 72 receiving transitional assistance during this initial period. While the actual distribution of unemployment expenditures had reached 5.2 percent of the six-year allocation after 24 percent of the program period had elapsed, principal reduction expenditures had reached only 0.7 percent of the six-year allocations, and transitional assistance expenditures had reached only 0.6 percent of the planned allocations. This was particularly disappointing, because HHF funds were viewed as a promising source of funds for principal reductions and transitional assistance, and were allocated heavily to states likely to need such assistance.

The SIGTARP (2012) found that loan servicers and the GSEs were strongly resistant to principal-reduction programs, even when such reduc-tions would be subsidized on a one-for-one basis. Overall, the slow pace of HHF implementation was attributed to the lack of participation by the major servicers. Initially, lender participation was dominated by local financial in-stitutions, often servicing their own loans. The individual HFAs had little assistance from the Treasury Department to negotiate participation and pro-gram design with the servicers. The Treasury Department failed to use its considerable leverage to bring servicers to the table quickly.

By September 2013, the states had increased their HHF activities signifi-cantly, disbursing $2 billion in funds to assist over 140,000 homeowners (U.S. Department of the Treasury 2013). However, this still represented less than 30 percent of the total $7.6 billion available under the program. By this point, it was clear that the foreclosure crisis (while not at all over) was abating somewhat. As was the case with HAMP and HARP, the slow rollout of HHF meant that the families and households hit hardest by the initial subprime crisis were left out by the time the programs reached scale.

Structural Obstacles in Loan-Modification Efforts

The Obama Administration foreclosure-prevention initiative suffered from many flaws in design and implementation. Most of these concern HAMP and the other HAMP-like programs (PRA, 2MP, UP). Some are also relevant to the HARP and HHF programs.

Small Carrots and Few Sticks

A key design premise of HAMP and related MHA programs was that servicers could be induced to modify large numbers of mortgages through two principal vehicles. First, a standardized protocol sanctioned by the federal government would speed modifications and potentially shield servicers from fears of legal action from investors. Second, servicers would be given incentive payments to perform modifications and would receive additional payments as modified loans continued to perform. These incentives, however, were modest.[8] MHA programs frequently did not provide a substantial disincentive to proceed with foreclosure, or a system in which servicers were actively held accountable for processing modifications in a timely manner. In the first few years of the programs, lenders often proceeded with legal foreclosure process even after the borrower had entered into the loan-modification process, a procedure known as "dual-tracking." When the Obama Administration announced HAMP, it originally recommended a promising disincentive to foreclose: allowing bankruptcy judges to reduce the principal on mortgages on owner-occupied properties. If servicers and investors faced such a threat of modification via the courts, they would have been more likely to reduce principal voluntarily and modify loans more aggressively.

The Treasury Department rarely employed sanctions against servicers, especially in the first two years of HAMP. Despite many early complaints about servicer actions, the department did not sanction any servicers for noncompliance with HAMP rules until mid-2011. In earlier statements, the agency claimed that it did not have the power to assess such penalties. However, in June of 2011, the department issued a release stating that it was "withholding financial incentives" for three of the largest servicers in the HAMP program, Bank of America, J.P. Morgan Chase, and Wells Fargo Bank (U.S. Department of the Treasury 2011b). This sanction, which itself was very limited, was the first in the program after two years of numerous complaints about major servicers and disappointing results.

Substantial variation in HAMP-servicer performance may reflect the limited success that the Treasury had in getting all servicers to implement HAMP aggressively. For trial modifications begun after June 1, 2010, the conversion rate from trial to permanent modifications ranged from 62 percent to 88 percent among the largest servicers.[9] Although some of this may have been due to differences in the risk of borrowers entering trials, some of the servicers that specialized in subprime loans, such as Ocwen, had relatively high conversion rates. In addition, some of the smaller servicers were more aggressive in implementing principal reductions than were some of the larger servicers. Researchers found that, even after accounting for a wide variety of loan and borrower characteristics, modification behavior varied significantly by servicer (Agarwal et al. 2010). This might be explained by differences in the organizational cultures, or other characteristics, of the servicers.

There were numerous reports of servicer problems in handling loan-modification requests (Kiel and Pierce 2010). In late 2010, the U.S. Government Accountability Office (2011) conducted a survey of almost four hundred housing counselors involved in the National Foreclosure Mitigation Counseling program, which was federally funded and managed through the NeighborWorks organization. The survey asked respondents to list the three most common reasons why borrowers contacted them about the HAMP program. The most common top response (59 percent) was that servicers claimed to have lost HAMP application information. Another top reason (37 percent) was that borrowers had difficulty contacting the servicer. Overall, 75 percent of counselors characterized borrowers' experiences with HAMP as "negative" or "very negative," with 33 percent falling into the "very negative" category. Moreover, 86 percent of counselors reported that it typically took four months or longer to receive a decision about a HAMP trial modification after the time the borrower requested it. More than 45 percent reported that it typically took seven months or more.

A lack of "sticks" was not just a problem with HAMP. In the case of the HHF program, several states designed initiatives that included subsidized principal-reduction programs, in which HHF funds would match principal reductions from the servicers on a one-to-one basis. However, the large servicers, as well as the GSEs, resisted these programs (Immergluck 2010; SIGTARP 2012). Initially, the Treasury Department encouraged states to develop such programs in their HHF plans, but after receiving significant pushback from servicers and the GSEs, the department recommended against such initiatives, although several states persisted (Weise 2010). In later rounds of the HHF, the Treasury Department reportedly told states that they should get servicer "buy-in" before proposing a particular program to the Treasury Department to be funded with HHF funds (Immergluck 2010).

Fundamentally, the MHA programs were designed around the systems and the preferences of the servicing industry. Instead of being driven by the needs of borrowers, the programs were shaped by the demands and perceived limitations of financial institutions. Certainly, some consideration to such concerns was merited. However, the federal response was generally tilted toward the preferences of servicers and investors, and away from the interests of borrowers and communities.

A Servicing Industry Built for Foreclosure, Not Modification

The single-family mortgage-servicing business developed as a large-scale, "low-touch" industry built around volume and speed (Jacobides 2005; Levitin and Twomey 2011). Servicing industry structures, policies and procedures, and organizational cultures could not be turned on a dime. More specifically, the servicing business was designed in some ways to make money on foreclosures, not to work against them. Overlaying modest incentives and incremental policy changes on top of such an entrenched system was not sufficient to immediately alter the industry's response to delinquency and default in a fundamental way. There were a number of structural reasons why servicers tended to favor foreclosure over loan modification and why servicers did not always act in the best interests of lenders/investors or borrowers, including accounting rules, private-label securitization structures, fee structures, and staffing issues (Levitin and Twomey 2011; Thompson 2009).[10] The last two may have been among the most important obstacles to successful modifications. Servicing contracts allowed servicers to retain many of the fees charged to delinquent homeowners. Servicers captured these loan-level fees when the borrower repaid the arrearage, or collected them from the proceeds of the foreclosure sale before the investors were paid. More fundamentally, servicing delinquent or defaulted loans was substantially more expensive than servicing performing loans, so servicers often favored foreclosure and liquidation over modification to eliminate the more cost-intensive portions of their portfolios.

Servicers had difficulty (or resisted) gearing up quickly for massive numbers of loan modifications. Speedy mobilization by servicers would have required heavy fixed costs, including new staff and infrastructure, plus outside costs such as property valuation, credit reports, and financing costs (Thompson 2009). Traditional servicing was a low-margin business that depended on repetition, speed, and few deviations from regular practice. Loan modifications, on the other hand, were more complex, involved more human intervention and judgment, and required a more complex regime of detailed policies and procedures. Minor changes in per-loan costs could wreak havoc on a servicer's bottom line, so they were reluctant to deviate from routine protocols. The crisis required large, performing-loan servicers to act like nimble and responsive default servicers. However, incrementalism and a failure to recognize the depth and length of the crisis impeded such a response.

A Political Climate Hostile to Helping Borrowers

The MHA was introduced in March of 2009, just after the second round of TARP funds was released and during a time when the Great Recession was peaking. Public backlash against the TARP program had been building. Many commentators portrayed the subprime crisis as one caused principally by the decisions of irresponsible homebuyers and homeowners (e.g., Percelay 2007; Tamny 2008). Anecdotes of reckless borrowers using home equity loans to buy expensive television sets or go on extravagant vacations were ubiquitous. The early outlines of HAMP spurred CNBC reporter Rick Santelli's now-famous "losers' mortgages" rant on the floor of the Chicago Mercantile Exchange in February of 2009 (Stolberg 2009). Santelli's "losers" were people who made greedy, selfish, and stupid decisions that brought them to financial ruin.

In this climate, it became difficult for policymakers to propose bolder approaches to reducing foreclosures and, especially, to propose large-scale principal-reduction programs (Kashkari 2011; Zandi 2012). This problem grew more significant when Republicans took over the House in 2010, as Republicans called for dismantling HAMP, the Neighborhood Stabilization Program, and other policies responding to the foreclosure crisis (Chaddock 2011). Instead of confronting the early public resistance to programs such as HAMP, the Obama Administration tried to work around such resistance, attempting to shape its rhetoric in a way that accommodated, rather than challenged, those who blamed the crisis on "irresponsible borrowers." As the election year of 2012 approached, the administration appeared to take its attention away from HAMP and focus more on HARP and other refinancing proposals to assist what were portrayed by some as more "deserving" borrowers, especially those current on their (mostly prime) loans but having difficulty refinancing into lower interest rates.

Mixed Signals from Federal Policymakers and the GSEs

As the foreclosure crisis spread from the subprime to the prime mortgage market in 2009 and 2010, more foreclosures were on loans owned by the GSEs. Given that the firms were under federal conservatorship, this presented federal policymakers with the ability to exercise more control over loan modifications and to reduce principal balances where appropriate. However, the agency in charge of the GSEs, the independent Federal Housing Finance Agency (FHFA), was charged with "conserving" the short-term assets of the firms and was resistant to moves, including principal-reduction and unemployment-forbearance programs, that might require the firms to take short-term write-downs on their mortgage assets (Weise 2010; Timiraos 2011). Even if such modifications increased long-term returns by improving loan performance and the broader housing economy, the more immediate pressures to "conserve assets" worked against a long-term perspective (Dudley 2012). In late 2010, the Obama Administration made one short-lived attempt to replace the holdover director of the FHFA, Edward DeMarco, with someone expected to be friendlier to principal reduction and aggressive assistance to distressed borrowers (Timiraos 2011). However, after meeting some initial resistance in the Senate, the administration backed off, even though DeMarco continued to block key measures aimed at preventing foreclosures.

MITIGATING NEIGHBORHOOD EFFECTS: THE NEIGHBORHOOD-STABILIZATION PROGRAMS

While the largest set of federal responses to the foreclosure crisis were focused on preventing foreclosures, another set of responses focused on addressing the negative effects that foreclosed, vacant properties can have on neighborhoods. The Neighborhood Stabilization Programs (NSPs) were a set of three different programs aimed at the acquisition and reuse of vacant, foreclosed residential properties. The three programs were referred to as NSP 1 (authorized by HERA), NSP 2 (authorized by the 2009 American Recovery and Revitalization Act [ARRA]), and NSP 3 (authorized by the 2010 Dodd-Frank Wall Street Reform and Consumer Protection Act). While the precise details of eligible uses varied among the three programs, funds were generally able to be used for five principal purposes: (1) the acquisition and rehabilitation of abandoned or foreclosed homes; (2) financing mechanisms such as down-payment assistance programs (to purchase foreclosed homes); (3) the land-banking of properties; (4) the demolition of blighted properties; and (5) the redevelopment of demolished or vacant properties.

In NSP 1, Congress gave HUD two months to develop a formula for allocating $3.9 billion across existing Community Development Block Grant (CDBG) entitlement communities as well as states. States receiving funds could devote resources to purchasing foreclosed homes, or redistribute the money to localities. HERA required that each state receive a minimum allocation of 0.5 percent of total NSP 1 funds ($19 million). HUD allocated the bulk of the funds by developing a formula that relied on indirect data sources to indicate foreclosure prevalence. If HUD's formula resulted in a CDBG community receiving an allocation of less than $2 million, the locality was not awarded a direct grant and the sum was rolled into the overall state grant. Among the 1,201 CDGB-eligible state and local governments, HUD made more than three hundred direct grants (U.S. Department of Housing and Urban Development 2008). The local government NSP recipients received awards up to $62.2 million (Miami–Dade County), with a median award of $4.3 million.

As of October 2010, when the vast majority of NSP 1 funds had been obligated, the allocations broke out as follows: 66 percent of funds were obligated toward acquisition and rehabilitation; 11 percent for the construction of new housing; 6 percent toward homeownership assistance; 5 percent for demolition; and 4 percent for land-banking and other activities, leaving 9 percent for administrative costs (U.S. Government Accountability Office 2010).

The NSP 1 program was criticized by community-development experts for a number of reasons (Newberger 2010; Mallach 2009). One complaint was that the eighteen-month timeline to obligate NSP funds was too short to develop and execute complex local redevelopment programs.[11] As a result, many NSP 1 recipients obligated a large percentage of their grant funds within the last three months of the eighteen-month period. Given the complexity and challenges of implementing NSP 1, it is not surprising that a large percentage of recipients had not obligated a large portion of their funds at the fifteen-month mark. While the eighteen-month deadline was consistent with the urgency intended in HERA, it may not have been the best strategy for making the most effective use of resources.

One byproduct of the need to obligate substantial amounts of funding in the last few months of the NSP 1 period was that some localities changed their NSP strategies as they neared the deadline for obligating funds. An example is that some localities shifted away from plans that focused on acquiring single-family homes toward purchasing foreclosed multifamily apartment buildings (Korte 2010). This may have been one of the rare forays that some of these localities had made into the redevelopment of multifamily rental housing.

Another criticism of NSP 1 was that Congress required localities to capture any earnings they might receive from the program, although these requirements were eliminated in later phases of the program. The statute also required that local recipients purchase foreclosed properties from lenders or loan servicers at discounts of 5 to 15 percent below appraised value, a practice that was difficult to implement during a time of highly volatile property values. This policy could also make it difficult for NSP 1 recipients to compete with speculative investors or bulk purchasers who might pay more. (This requirement was later modified to only a 1 percent discount.) It also prohibited recipients from selling properties for prices that exceeded the sum of their acquisition and redevelopment costs, meaning that a local government could not use profits from one property to subsidize the redevelopment of another property that might be sold at a loss. Successful vacant property reclamation initiatives have utilized such cross-subsidization tactics to increase scale and overall impact (Paul 2008).

NSP 1 allowed only 10 percent for administrative costs. Given that most local governments had little infrastructure for acquiring and redeveloping foreclosed homes, this modest allocation was insufficient to enable many to develop capacity in this area. In NSP 2, the shortage of administrative resources was partly rectified in some places by the inclusion of dedicated technical-assistance funding.

At the time of NSP 1 implementation, most local governments did not have established land banks that could accept properties, erase back taxes, and hold properties until redevelopment plans were implemented or housing markets recovered (Alexander 2011). While HERA encouraged the use of local land banks, it did not establish any form of national land bank for localities without such entities, nor did it provide start-up funding or technical assistance for such endeavors.

Many NSP localities faced two key problems in acquiring real estate–owned (REO) properties. First, identifying the party that actually controlled the sale of the property was often complicated. The quality and consistency of foreclosure and property records data vary widely. In some places, even when data were available, identifying the appropriate party to contact to try to acquire the property was very difficult. Property records, for example, might list the name of the institution where the mortgage was held in a trust, but not the loan servicer responsible for the management and sale of the property.

Second, many foreclosed properties, especially in the earlier stages of the crisis, were embedded in complex private-label securities, where the servicer was acting as an agent for the owners of the property. Yet the actual beneficial owners of the foreclosed property were effectively a set of diffuse investors in the mortgage-backed securities. Thus, servicers handling such properties were often difficult to work with when localities were trying to purchase properties, and were sometimes reluctant to accept prices that were substantially less than the outstanding loan balances. In early 2009, a hedge-fund investor in subprime-mortgage-backed securities filed suit against a servicer, accusing it of selling REO at prices that were too low (Buhl 2009). This may have made servicers more reluctant to cut REO prices in some cases.

Another key challenge for NSP efforts in some cities was the appetite that investors had for foreclosed properties in late 2008 and early 2009 (Immergluck 2012; Coulton et al. 2008). Some NSP recipients reported that servicers (or their realtors) did not want to work with the cumbersome NSP process when they could sell quickly to an investor purchasing a home with cash (Newberger 2010; U.S. Government Accountability Office 2010). Research in Atlanta and Cleveland found that about the time that NSP 1 was being implemented, sales of foreclosed properties by lenders, especially lower-value properties, were accelerating rapidly (Coulton et al. 2008; Immergluck 2012). Thus, many properties that might be targeted for strategic acquisitions by NSP efforts fell into the hands of investors before they could be acquired with NSP funds.

For properties selling for well under $100,000, and especially for those selling for well under $50,000, servicers having to liquidate thousands of homes often had little patience for buyers who needed to get appraisals and environmental reviews before completing an acquisition. For NSP efforts focusing on specific blocks or neighborhoods, losing properties to investors was particularly problematic. If these properties remained vacant, or were not rehabilitated sufficiently, they could be impediments to the revitalization of the targeted area.

One response to the investor-competition problem was the introduction of "first-look" programs developed by the National Community Stabilization Trust (NCST) in cooperation with the GSEs, some of the large national loan servicers, and the FHA. In a first-look program, a lender or servicer agrees to offer local governments—and sometimes NSP recipients in particular—a chance to purchase foreclosed properties before offering these homes for sale on the open market. In 2010, a "National First-look Program" was sponsored by NCST and HUD. NSP grantees were notified when an REO property owned by the GSEs, the FHA, or some large banks became available in an NSP-targeted area. NSP recipients then had twenty-four to forty-eight hours to express interest in a specific property (U.S. Department of Housing and Urban Development 2010a). The first-look period lasted five to twelve business days, during which the NSP recipient conducted inspections and estimated repair costs. The NSP recipient had to commit to purchasing the home by the end of the first-look period, or the property would be put up for sale on the open market.

In early 2009, as ARRA was being drafted, a second phase of NSP (NSP 2) was designed as a competitive rather than formula-funded program, in part to address the issue of grantee capacity (U.S. House of Representatives 2009). This was a major change in the approach of NSP, because it allowed for the concentration of resources in particular markets based not only on need, but also on the ability of local actors to come together to create a strong plan. Besides the competitive funding approach, the $2 billion NSP 2 program also provided $50 million in technical-assistance funding that could be used to help both NSP 1 and NSP 2 recipients. NSP 2 also encouraged nonprofits and consortia of nonprofit and/or local governments to apply for funding.

While NSP 2 addressed some of the problems identified with NSP 1, it also introduced some additional challenges. One change was that any NSP 2 redevelopment had to be focused only on housing uses, while NSP 1 had allowed redevelopment for uses other than housing. Given the oversupply of housing and the dilapidated nature of many homes in some communities, such a constraint may have precluded some sound redevelopment plans that were aimed at converting excess housing to other more needed uses in a neighborhood. Another challenge was that NSP 2, like NSP 1, relied on an existing infrastructure of federal-local intergovernmental funding regulations and requirements.

NSP 3, which was included in the Dodd-Frank Wall Street Reform and Consumer Protection Act of 2010, was funded at $1 billion, with $20 million set aside for technical assistance (U.S. House of Representatives 2010). NSP 3 returned to a formula-based funding approach similar to NSP 1, although with some focus on areas with high unemployment rates.

As of January 2014, HUD reported that the combined NSP programs were estimated to have resulted in the construction or rehabilitation of over sixty-one thousand housing units by March of 2013 and the demolition or clearance of twenty-three thousand housing units, as well as providing homeownership-financing assistance to seventeen thousand units (U.S. Department of Housing and Urban Development and U.S. Department of Treasury 2014). This suggests that HUD's 100,000 estimate appears not to be widely off the mark.

Key Lessons for Neighborhood-Stabilization Policy Design

While there have no doubt been many successes from the various NSP programs, there are a few major lessons that can be gleaned from the NSP experience.

NSP Funding Was Small in Relation to the Flow of Foreclosed Properties in the United States

Given the scale of the problem in many metropolitan areas, NSP funds alone were unlikely to make a substantial dent in the vacant property problem. The volume of foreclosed properties held by lenders, investors, and government agencies at any one time ebbed and flowed, but conservative estimates tended to fluctuate between 550,000 and 720,000 properties between 2007 and 2012.[12] Given that properties are continuously entering and exiting lender ownership, the number of foreclosed properties flowing into communities during the life of the NSP programs will certainly be on the order of magnitude of several million properties.

By contrast, HUD's estimate in 2011 of how many homes had been directly affected by all three NSP programs was on the order of 100,000 properties (U.S. Department of Housing and Urban Development 2011b). Thus, the NSP programs, even if highly effective, were very limited in scale compared to the aggregate flow of foreclosed properties.

The Narrow NSP Legislation, and the Resulting Rules,
Constrained Localities from Being Responsive to Local Market Conditions

The narrow focus of the NSP programs on purchasing lender-owned properties for redevelopment and reoccupancy hamstrung local governments and
NSP recipients from making the most effective use of NSP dollars over time.
While NSP 1 was rolling out, banks in some cities rapidly sold off properties,
especially lower-value properties in the lower-income neighborhoods targeted by NSP (Coulton et al. 2008; Immergluck 2012; Newberger 2010). By
the time NSP recipients in these cities were beginning to acquire properties,
many key strategic properties were already in the hands of investors. [13] A
more robust and adaptive approach would have involved providing funds to
local intermediaries and redevelopment organizations to purchase and redevelop not just foreclosed properties, but vacant properties more generally, or
to engage in proactive activities to control properties and keep them occupied
before the foreclosure process was completed. While some administrative
rule changes nudged the programs in this direction, such incremental move-
ments often came after substantial NSP dollars had already been committed.
Moreover, it remains unclear how effective such changes were in allowing
for more creative and efficient uses of program dollars.

Most Localities Had Little Experience Addressing Foreclosed or Vacant
Properties

Despite the mismatch between the flow of foreclosed properties and the
funding of NSP programs, funding levels were sometimes large compared to
the existing capacity of local governments to acquire and redevelop foreclosed properties. The formula-funding approach of NSP 1 meant that many
localities with little experience in dealing with vacant or foreclosed properties were thrust into addressing a very challenging problem with limited
resources and little established capacity. Moreover, many of the localities hit
hardest by the foreclosure crisis—especially in the sand-state suburbs and
exurbs of California, Florida, Arizona, and Nevada—were especially inexpe-
rienced in community development and in dealing with troubled properties.
In some ways, the older industrial cities of the Midwest and Northeast had at
least been familiar with these sorts of problems, having struggled in the past
with depopulation, foreclosures, and vacancies. Even for these cities, however, the scale, complexity, and pace of the foreclosure crisis were often overwhelming, especially as new foreclosures mounted during 2009 and beyond.

NSP Programs Were Constrained by Cumbersome Legacy Systems of Funding and Oversight

NSP programs utilized CDBG and HOME funding systems to distribute funding and monitor performance. Many federal rules from these programs were imposed on NSP funds. This made the programs more cumbersome than they might have been, and made it difficult to be entrepreneurial. At the beginning of NSP 1, there were anecdotal reports of recipients being told that they should be very careful in implementing the program because HUD's investigators would be keeping a close eye on compliance.

BROADER LESSONS LEARNED FROM CRISIS-BASED POLICYMAKING

Notwithstanding the important programmatic lessons learned from HAMP, NSP, and other policy responses to the foreclosure crisis described above, there are at least three broader lessons that can be drawn from the federal response. First, many responses, especially loan-modification efforts, were tentative, incremental, and marginal. Moreover, they did not accumulate to a sizeable response, particularly in the first two to three years of the crisis when intervention would have been most promising. Due to the nature of housing price and foreclosure cycles, it would have been easier to have a material impact on foreclosures if a more forceful response came much sooner, before job losses and housing depreciation accelerated. Even after policy initiatives were announced, it could take over a year to launch them. The political hostility to helping "undeserving" homeowners, the dysfunctional nature of the mortgage industry, and the difficulty of working with Congress all contributed to this problem.

Second, some programs were so engineered to anticipate or prevent certain types of problems that the fundamental efficacy of the programs was negatively affected. Concerns about foreclosure-prevention programs often centered on issues of moral hazard or "undeserving borrowers." In the case of NSP, the concerns centered on inappropriate use of funds or some other types of malfeasance. The heavy focus on these issues affected the fundamental design of the policy responses in ways that sometimes limited program effectiveness, and made it difficult to reach scale. In the loan-modification arena, lenders and economists argued that by offering advantageous loan modifications to defaulting borrowers, some programs might encourage others to default. Yet any evidence that delinquencies would increase substantially due to aggressive modifications was thin. In an occasionally cited paper, Chris Mayer and his colleagues found that after a major settlement was announced in which delinquent Countrywide borrowers were unilaterally offered aggressive loan modifications, the proportion of borrowers going from being current to being sixty days delinquent only increased by 13 percent (Mayer et al. 2011). This amount of moral hazard could be easily compensated for by the benefits of reduced foreclosures. Fitch Ratings (2012), one of the major credit-rating agencies, found that after the announcement of the national attorneys general settlement with large servicers, which included large targets for principal-reducing loan modifications, the percentage of loans entering delinquency actually declined somewhat.

As William Dudley (2012) has argued, programs can be, and have been, designed to avoid moral hazard problems. Two such approaches were "earned forgiveness" and "shared appreciation." In the former, a portion of principal is put in "forbearance" (that is, temporarily eliminated), but each year some portion of the forbearance is converted to permanent principal reduction. In this way, borrowers are not motivated to receive a modification solely to sell their home. In a shared-appreciation structure, some portion of the principal is reduced, but if the house is sold for more than the new loan amount in later years, some portion of any profit is shared with the lender. Both of these structures reduce the debt burden in the near term, while reducing the incentive to default for those who are able to afford their existing loans.

Even where concern over moral hazard was warranted, the benefits of going forward with an initiative were likely to outweigh the negatives. Yet a full analysis of the likely benefits and costs of some important proposals did not seem to be terribly important. Rather, often-vague rhetoric about moral hazard contributed to the cumbersome and ineffective design of the FHA Hope for Homeowners program and to continual resistance to principal-reduction proposals.

A third broad lesson from the crisis is that, because policy interventions took quite a while to mature, and became more effective after the first few years of the crisis, the more effective responses benefitted households and communities impacted more heavily in the latter stages of the crisis. By 2010, the national crisis had reached another stage, where mortgage distress and foreclosures had shifted substantially into the prime mortgage market, where they affected more middle-income—and often white—homeowners and neighborhoods.

The policy efforts deployed by the Bush and Obama administrations—especially the loan-modification programs—were no match for the nature, scale, and depth of the foreclosure problem. Without the stick of bankruptcy cramdown, servicers and lenders/investors were able to drag their feet. Bankruptcy is a critical economic relief valve used by entrepreneurs and corporate America in the face of catastrophic losses, allowing markets to reset when needed. Yet, in the face of the largest financial crisis since the Great Depression, this key tool was unavailable to the typical U.S. homeowner, at least when it concerned their largest source of debt. Massive federal intervention successfully rescued the automobile and financial-services industries, while many homeowners were left with ineffectual programs when it came to addressing their mortgage problems.

While there may have not been a politically viable policy that would have compelled servicers to make mandatory modifications on existing mortgages as some called for, federal policy could certainly have been more forceful. The Treasury Department might have used aggressive servicer sanctions earlier in the implementation of its modification programs. Periodic servicer report cards and occasional jawboning by cabinet secretaries were clearly not sufficient to get servicers to respond aggressively enough to the crisis (Braucher 2010).

As suggested above, the policy responses to the crisis suffered from many problems of design and implementation that could have been avoided. More forceful approaches that did not yield so readily to the desires of the financial services industry would likely have proven more effective. At the point early in the crisis when aggressive intervention had the best chances of substantially slowing foreclosures, weak, voluntary efforts delivered little relief to distressed homeowners. When proposals to create more promising responses met strong resistance from the financial-services industry, they were typically not supported by congressional policymakers, federal bank regulators, or the Bush or Obama administrations.

Notwithstanding issues of political will, many policy responses were confounded by a host of dysfunctions and misaligned incentives in the mortgage-servicing and -securitization industries. If the nation is to be prepared for any future surge in foreclosures, the mortgage market must be reformed in ways that will allow it to respond to economic and housing-market shocks, and work for the interests of homeowners, communities, and the broader economy. Relying on financial-market expertise during the foreclosure crisis was essential. However, allowing the financial sector, after receiving unprecedented federal support, to dictate the boundaries of federal policy was a recipe for a timid and fundamentally insufficient response.

The next chapter addresses another aspect of the policy response to the crisis—one that continues to play out. It discusses federal efforts to improve consumer protection and other forms of regulation in the mortgage market and the efforts to ensure that a crisis of this magnitude never happens again.

Chapter Four

Regulating the Mortgage Market

PRE-CRISIS ATTEMPTS TO TAME SUBPRIME AND RECKLESS LENDING

Other books have detailed the efforts to rein in reckless lending before the mortgage crisis of the 2000s (Engel and McCoy 2011; Immergluck 2009). However, it is important to review the broad strokes of such efforts to understand the nature and magnitude of the post-crisis regulatory initiatives. Many consumer advocates and state regulators made serious attempts to improve the regulation of mortgage markets, but they often saw their efforts overwhelmed by fierce resistance from industry opponents and by federal moves to preempt state regulations.

The first significant federal attempt to constrain subprime lending actually occurred at the beginning of the first subprime surge in the 1990s. The 1994 Home Ownership and Equity Protection Act (HOEPA) required certain protections for borrowers when loans exceeded a specified interest rate or fee threshold. The law also gave the Federal Reserve the authority to declare some practices on loans under this threshold unfair or deceptive, expanding the potential scope of the law (U.S. Department of Housing and Urban Development 2010). However, HOEPA proved to be ineffectual in slowing the growth of subprime and predatory lending in the late 1990s and early 2000s, partially due to the Federal Reserve's failure to use the authority it was given by the statute.

During the first boom in subprime loans in the late 1990s, consumer advocates found some initial success at the state level. In 1999, North Carolina adopted the first comprehensive state anti-predatory lending legislation. The bill followed the threshold approach of HOEPA, but set the triggers significantly lower so that the law would capture a much larger portion of subprime loans. By 2003, more than 30 states had passed predatory lending statutes, and by the beginning of 2007, only seven states had no statutes restricting prepayment penalties, balloon payments, or predatory practices or terms (Bostic et al. 2008). However, there was great variation in the sorts of loans these statutes covered and the extent to which the laws banned various practices or products.

At the federal level, a number of bills were introduced in the early 2000s that aimed at increasing the regulation of subprime mortgages, but none were adopted. In May 2000, House Banking Committee Chairman Jim Leach (R-IA) chastised the Federal Reserve Board for not using its regulatory authority under HOEPA to act on the issue. Leach asked, "Is the Federal Reserve AWOL? That is a question that I think demands a response" (Leach 2000). The board, however, still failed to use its broader powers to expand the impact of the law in a substantial way.

Besides some very marginal changes to HOEPA rules in 2001, federal policymakers made no substantive changes in regulations aimed at curbing the growth of risky lending practices. In early 2004, the GAO issued a report calling for stronger regulatory supervision in the subprime market, including giving the Federal Reserve more power to conduct regular examinations of lenders affiliated with banks through bank holding-company structures (U.S. General Accounting Office 2004). Earlier in 2000, Federal Reserve Board Governor Edward Gramlich urged Fed chair Alan Greenspan to direct examiners to examine the lending of bank-affiliated mortgage companies on a pilot basis, but the recommendation was rebuffed (Andrews 2007).

As states began to adopt predatory-lending regulations in 2000, lenders turned to Washington to override state laws, arguing that state laws were creating a "patchwork" of regulation that made it difficult for lenders and secondary market firms to operate national lending operations. Federal regulators had a vested interest in preempting state consumer-protection laws. If a regulator has the power to override state rules, banks may change their charters to fall under its authority, creating a "competition in laxity" among regulators competing for power and revenue (Scott 1977). Demonstrating the importance of preemption to the value of a charter type, a banking attorney asked the *American Banker*, "Why would you want a national charter but for the preemption authority?" (Davenport 2003).

In 2003, the Office of Thrift Supervision (OTS), which regulated savings and loans, preempted key provisions of the State of Georgia's predatory-lending law, and a week later it preempted a similar New York State law (Blackwell 2003). The Office of the Comptroller of the Currency (OCC), the regulator of national banks, followed quickly. It had earlier issued a letter to national banks in November of 2002 asserting its jurisdiction over all state regulators and asked banks to inform it if a state regulator may have asserted its authority over a national bank. It was not long before National City Bank of Cleveland, which had a subprime unit, requested that the OCC preempt the Georgia law. In the summer of 2003, the OCC obliged and suggested that it would preempt all similar state laws.

In addition to deregulating markets on the loan-origination side, federal policymakers continued to accommodate the financial-services industry on the capital markets/securities side in ways that induced more risk in the mortgage market. Perhaps the most prominent example was the explicit move to prevent the regulation of credit default swaps in the late 1990s. Earlier in the decade, some in Congress proposed increasing regulation of financial derivatives, partly because the Commodities Futures Trading Commission (CFTC), under the direction of Wendy Gramm, wife of Senator Phil Gramm—a strong proponent of mortgage-market and financial-services deregulation—had explicitly exempted some derivatives from regulation (Lipton and Labaton 2008). In the late 1990s, under Brooksley Born, the CFTC switched course and recommended increased regulation of derivatives such as credit default swaps. However, her recommendation was opposed by key Treasury Department officials, including Lawrence Summers, as well as by Fed chairman Alan Greenspan and Arthur Levitt Jr., the head of the Securities and Exchange Commission (SEC). Their opposition to regulation was reinforced by Congress when it passed the Commodity Futures Modernization Act in 2000, further protecting derivatives from increased regulation.

Another securities policy decision that had a direct impact on the volume of subprime lending was the SEC's 2004 relaxation of capital requirements for investment banks. The SEC reduced the minimum capital reserves of several very large investment banks, including Goldman Sachs, Lehman Brothers, Merrill Lynch, and Morgan Stanley, by 30 to 40 percent (Nadauld and Sherlund 2009).

THE REGULATORY RESPONSE TO THE CRISIS

As the U.S. mortgage crisis catalyzed the global financial crisis of 2008 and the U.S. presidential election approached, housing policy and mortgage regulation were no longer topics relegated to technocratic policy networks, and had become the subject of front pages and political talk radio. Given the public anger over the crisis, it seemed that strong steps toward increased financial regulation were inevitable. In addition, the crisis had caused some in government, the media, and policy circles to question the entire neoliberal paradigm of deregulation and unfettered capital flows. In September of 2008, Republican presidential nominee John McCain, who had earlier described himself as "fundamentally a deregulator," blamed the financial crisis on "failed regulation, reckless management and a casino culture on Wall Street" (Davis 2008; Kranish and Stockman 2008). Even Alan Greenspan, considered among the key champions of financial deregulation, admitted to Congress in October of 2008 that he had "made a mistake in presuming that the self-interests of organizations, specifically banks and others, were such as that they were best capable of protecting their own shareholders and their equity in the firms" (Irwin and Paley 2008).

With an apparent reawakening to the need for regulation and the problems of unbridled financial markets, as well as the election of President Obama, the prospects for a long-term, fundamental shift toward stronger regulation seemed promising. The Obama campaign had outlined six principles for financial regulatory reform, including: consolidating regulatory agencies, in part to reduce competition in laxity; establishing stronger capital and liquidity requirements for financial institutions; expanding a meaningful federal regulatory umbrella over lightly regulated lenders; increasing penalties for predatory lending and market manipulation; creating a new oversight committee to monitor systemic risks; and providing shareholders with more say on executive compensation and board membership (Calmes et al. 2008).

Despite the favorable political headwinds for strengthening financial regulation, the direction that the administration would take was initially unclear. Besides the appointment of the New York Federal Reserve president Timothy Geithner as treasury secretary and Lawrence Summers as director of the National Economic Council, Obama also appointed Cass Sunstein as head of the Office of Information and Regulatory Affairs. Sunstein was a well-known proponent of "paternalistic libertarianism," including various schemes to encourage better choices without resorting to proscriptive regulation (Thaler and Sunstein 2008). Early appointments like these gave those favoring stronger, proscriptive regulations cause for concern. At the same time, the administration appointed Michael Barr as assistant treasury secretary for financial institutions in the Treasury Department. Barr had written extensively on financial regulation and was considered sympathetic to the need for increased regulation. In the spring of 2009, the administration also established a new Office of Consumer Protection and appointed consumer advocate Eric Stein of the Center for Responsible Lending as deputy assistant secretary for consumer protection (U.S. Department of the Treasury 2010).

The Treasury Department issued its Plan for Regulatory Reform in June 2009. The plan contained five key components: increased regulation of institutions that pose systemic risk to the broader financial system; improved market discipline and transparency; the establishment of a Consumer Financial Protection Agency—eventually ending up as the Consumer Financial Protection Bureau (CFPB)—and various other measures aimed at improving consumer protection and reducing risky lending; new resolution powers so that distressed institutions could be wound down without posing systemic risks; and raising the bar for international regulatory standards and coordination (U.S. Department of the Treasury 2009). The creation of the CFPB, a concept first proposed by Elizabeth Warren (2007), was among the most contentious parts of the plan. The proposal called for consolidating both the ability to issue regulations and the supervision of essentially all sorts of consumer lenders regardless of their charter type (U.S. Department of the Treasury 2009). The CFPB was originally proposed as an independent agency with "broad jurisdiction" that could collect data from financial institutions and conduct regular examinations. This would effectively mean that nondepository financial institutions would be subject to routine supervision by a federal regulator for the first time. The plan would strip rule-making authority from the Federal Reserve on mortgage and consumer-finance regulations, a significant step given the Federal Reserve's tepid moves under HOEPA. The plan proposed that the CFPB's rules would act as a "floor, not a ceiling" vis-à-vis state regulations, so that states would have the ability to adopt and enforce regulations that were stricter than federal law. This effectively would end federal preemption in the consumer-finance arena, a proposal that sparked heated resistance among industry groups. The plan would also require lenders to prominently offer lower-risk, "plain-vanilla" mortgage products, such as thirty-year, fixed-rate mortgages, when offering loans to potential borrows.

The plan also called for moving Community Reinvestment Act (CRA) enforcement to the new agency and away from the federal bank regulators. Some lower-income community advocates were happy with this proposal, because they expected the CFPB would be a stronger implementer of CRA than the four banking regulators, who were seen as too friendly with the banks they regulated. In the largest banks, regulatory staff were often physically located at the offices of the bank itself, giving more cause for concerns about excessive coziness with the regulated entities. At the same time, other nonprofit organizations—often those who benefitted from existing CRA regulations that encouraged banks to invest in nonprofit financial intermediaries—were less keen on shifting CRA responsibility away from the bank regulators. After all, a new agency could shift CRA priorities in ways that could disrupt the incentives that encouraged banks to invest in their institutions.

The Plan for Regulatory Reform also called for issuers of mortgage-backed securities to have more "skin in the game" by retaining ownership of a modest but nontrivial proportion of mortgages they fund. By calling for reduced leverage ratios of institutions issuing securities and higher fees on firms posing significant systemic risks, the plan could potentially reduce the appetite of investment banks and others for high-risk loans.

Many portions of the plan were met with stiff resistance from industry groups and members of Congress. The U.S. Chamber of Commerce and most of the financial services groups lobbied heavily against the CFPB, for example. They launched www.stoptheCFPA.com and placed ads against the proposed agency in radio and print media (U.S. Chamber of Commerce 2010). Opponents attempted to weaken what became the Dodd-Frank Wall Street Reform and Consumer Protection Act (Dodd-Frank Act) in several ways, including exempting various types of lenders—including small banks and auto lenders—from the regulatory purview of the CFPB. One unsuccessful attempt to weaken the agency was aimed at making the agency a bipartisan-governed commission, in which there would be no strong centralized authority in the form of a presidentially appointed director. Opponents were more successful in deleting a requirement from the original bill that would have required all mortgage lenders to offer a "plain-vanilla" mortgage product (e.g., a thirty-year, fixed-rate mortgage) to customers alongside any other product.

In the first round of compromises in the House of Representatives, forty-seven amendments had been offered to the Dodd-Frank Act—mostly aimed at weakening the legislation. Of these, about half were passed (Kirsch and Mayer 2013, p. 86). These compromises allowed Barney Frank, the Democratic leader of the House Financial Services Committee, to bring along his more conservative Democratic colleagues and pass the bill out of committee in October 2009 on a mostly party-line vote. Due to its ability to draw in large campaign contributions from the financial industry, the House Financial Services Committee is generally a popular committee among conservative Democrats—including members of the Blue Dog and New Democratic caucuses. In 2009 and 2010, 40 percent of the committee were members of one or both of these two caucuses (Kirsch and Mayer 2013, p. 83).

One effort to weaken the Dodd-Frank Act concerned the critical issue of federal preemption of state consumer-protection laws. One of the reasons that state consumer-protection laws were limited in their ability to restrain the subprime industry was the aggressive use of preemption powers by federal banking regulators. Without preemption, when federal regulators or Congress move toward weaker regulations, state regulators can pick up the slack and protect their citizens with their own state laws. However, as we saw in the early 2000s, federal regulators were able to preempt stronger state laws for national banks and even their affiliated mortgage companies. The administration's plan called for an end to federal preemption of state consumer-protection laws. Regulations created by the CFPB would serve as a regulatory "floor" and not a "ceiling," so that states could create stronger consumer-protection laws if they chose to. Industry advocates fought hard to retain the ability of federal regulators to preempt state laws, perhaps because they could more efficiently focus their lobbying resources in Washington rather than fighting grassroots groups throughout the country on their own turf.

Industry advocates enlisted conservative Democrats in their fight to retain federal preemption and weaken the regulatory power of the Dodd-Frank bill.

In particular, the fight for preemption was led by Melissa Bean of suburban Chicago, a young member of Congress. As Larry Kirsch and Rob Mayer (2013) suggest, this may have been a poor choice, because in picking a Chicago-area Democrat, they picked a fight with a very well-organized constituency that could isolate the congresswoman on predatory lending, an issue that was well known in Chicago and Illinois. Moreover, Illinois had an attorney general, Lisa Madigan, who had been instrumental in passing state laws aimed at reining in predatory lending. Even Barack Obama, when he was a state senator in Illinois, had fought for improved state regulation of predatory lending, only to see federal regulators preempt such efforts. With the assistance of Attorney General Madigan, a slew of consumer advocacy organizations in Illinois put pressure on Bean back in Chicago over her support for preemption (Kirsch and Mayer 2013, pp. 130–132). While Bean did not change her position, she was clearly weakened, and the eventual form of preemption that did survive Dodd-Frank was notably weaker than what had been possible before the law.

The financial industry also argued strongly against issuers having to retain even very small portions of the principal value of their securitizations. Originally, the administration's plan had called for issuers of all mortgage-backed and other securities to retain a small percentage of the value of each security as what is called "risk retention." The concept of issuers holding back a bit of the securitization to share in its risk was not a new concept. In fact, this was frequently standard practice, although the risk-retention portion was generally referred to as the "equity tranche" of the securitization. In the structure of many mortgage-backed securities, the equity tranche was retained by the issuer and was repaid after all the other bondholders in the hierarchy of bondholders were paid. In this way, the issuer had an interest in structuring high-quality securitizations with expectations of low loan losses. However, in practice, the equity tranches became extremely small, or issuers were able to sell off or hedge against the tranches, thereby negating their incentive-aligning effects.

Requiring that MBS issuers retain a modest portion (e.g., 5 percent) of the total securitization is expected to moderate the impact on the risk that issuers will tolerate in the underlying pool of mortgages. Critics contended that requiring risk retention would debilitate private-label securitization markets, because many issuers would not be in a position to carry such risk over a substantial period. This, in fact, may have been the case for many thinly capitalized and overly leveraged issuers during the subprime boom, but proponents of risk retention would argue that this is exactly the point. Risk retention at a meaningful level would force a restructuring of the securitization market, a restructuring that was arguably warranted given the role of private-label securities in funding the worst excesses of the subprime boom. Moreover, the plan called for not allowing issuers to sell off or hedge against these risk-retention tranches, so that the incentives of issuers would be better aligned with those of the investors in the MBS.

As a way to make risk retention more acceptable to the financial-services industry, the eventual Dodd-Frank Act included an exemption for certain types of mortgages from risk-retention requirements. "Qualified residential mortgages," or QRMs, would be exempt from risk-retention requirements. Rather than specify the details of which mortgages would qualify for exemption from risk retention, the act delegated that decision to federal banking regulators. The promulgation of QRM regulations and the associated debate will be discussed later in this chapter.

Initially, the administration's proposals faced even more difficulty in the Senate, where key Democrats on the Senate Banking Committee were resistant to many key parts of the plan, including limiting federal preemption and creating the CFPB (Paletta 2010). Senate banking chair Christopher Dodd (D-CT) attempted to break negotiations into substantive components, with pairs of Democratic and Republican committee members negotiating on each part. Dodd found little common ground on consumer protection with the ranking Republican member of the committee, Richard Shelby (R-AL), but then began negotiating with Senator Robert Corker (R-TN). Corker not only rejected an independent CFPB but also rejected Dodd's offer to put the agency within the Treasury Department and insisted it could only be housed within the Federal Reserve, which had declined to take aggressive action during the subprime boom. Upon hearing of the plan to transform the new agency into a division of the Federal Reserve, House Financial Services chair Barney Frank was quoted as saying, "It's almost a bad joke. I was very disappointed" (Kaper 2010a). Even more importantly, the Dodd proposal, as it was initially presented, would exclude a wide swath of nonbank financial institutions (Kaper 2010b).

The debate over financial regulatory reform reached its climax in the spring and summer of 2010. Many of the original proposals had been watered down significantly and some parts of the financial-services sector were either exempted from new rule making, or protected from being regulated by the new consumer-protection agency, which ended up as a bureau within the Federal Reserve. However, when it was finally passed, the Dodd-Frank Wall Street Reform and Consumer Protection Act ("Dodd-Frank Act") was stronger than many consumer advocates had expected during earlier stages of the congressional debate, at least with respect to its consumer-protection provisions. One key improvement in the bill was the independence it granted to the CFPB. While the CFPB was still technically contained within the Federal Reserve Board System, its budget was determined as a specified portion of the overall Federal Reserve budget, and the director was appointed by the president, not by the Federal Reserve. This independent funding source turned out to be an important strength of the CFPB, as the agency's congressional opponents continually introduced bills to reign in the agency. If the agency had been funded by Congress, its opponents could have much more easily weakened it through restricting its budget, as later occurred with the Commodities Futures Trading Commission. In fact, since Dodd-Frank passed, opponents of the CFPB have repeatedly offered legislative proposals to pull the agency's budget out of the Federal Reserve and turn budgetary authority over to Congress.

One reason that the Dodd-Frank Act ended up somewhat stronger than expected was the fact that, in April 2010, the SEC formally charged Goldman Sachs with fraud surrounding subprime mortgage securitizations (U.S. Securities and Exchange Commission 2010). The SEC charged that the firm had sold complex subprime mortgage-related securities to investors without making it known that the composition of the securities had been chosen with the help of a hedge fund that held a short position on the subprime market. Thus, the selection of the assets comprising the securities was partly directed by a party that stood to gain if the value of subprime securities plummeted.

This high-profile move by the SEC and the highly publicized congressional hearings that followed, together with a variety of similar investigations and enforcement actions around the same time, temporarily shifted the political environment in favor of stronger regulation. The final bill included language calling for tighter rules requiring lenders to assure that borrowers had the "ability to repay" their mortgages and for regulators to collect new data from lenders on mortgage pricing and terms.

At the same time, other measures to strengthen regulation or limit risk did not make it into the final legislation or were watered down. One of the most important compromises was on the issue of federal preemption. While the final bill did end preemption of state regulations for mortgage-company affiliates of banks, and made it more difficult for federal regulators to issue blanket preemptions of state regulations, it retained some ability of regulatory agencies to preempt specific components of state laws. Other significant dilutions of the bill included the exemption of various sorts of lenders from the supervision of the CFPB and the ability of other regulators, collectively, to veto the CFPB's rule making.

Dodd-Frank: A Major Achievement in Consumer Protection in Mortgage Markets

Despite the significant successes of Dodd-Frank opponents to weaken the bill, the act's passage in July of 2010 represented the "most important change in consumer protection laws since the late 1960s" (National Consumer Law Center 2010). Besides creating the CFPB and instituting a risk-retention requirement for mortgage securitization, the law laid the groundwork for the consumer-protection landscape of mortgage and other forms of consumer lending and loan servicing, the reforming of the mortgage- and asset-backed securities markets, and increasing the amount of information that lenders would be required to provide under the Home Mortgage Disclosure Act.

As with most areas of complex regulation, the Dodd-Frank Act did not specify the precise parameters of most rules. This would have been impossible with such a wide-reaching law. Rather, the law authorized various federal agencies to propose and adopt new regulations to implement different components of the law. The act required the promulgation of over 350 new rules and regulations by many federal agencies, ranging from the new CFPB to the Federal Reserve and the SEC. The law moved most of the responsibility for issuing consumer-protection rules and regulations in the mortgage and consumer-finance arena from the Federal Reserve to the new CFPB. The intent was that an agency whose principal mission was to protect consumers was the best place to originate such rules and regulations. The Federal Reserve System is governed partly by the heads of twelve Federal Reserve banks, and while it has significant regulatory duties, safety and soundness of the financial system—and not consumer protection—is its primary charge.

Dodd-Frank made dozens of important changes to the Truth in Lending Act (TILA), the Real Estate Settlement Procedures Act (RESPA), the Fair Credit Reporting Act (FCRA), and other consumer-protection laws (National Consumer Law Center 2010). For example, with TILA, the act raised the dollar limit for class-action lawsuits from $500,000 to $1,000,000. In a major victory for consumer advocates, the act effectively banned yield spread premiums (YSPs) and other compensation to mortgage brokers that are based on the terms of a consumer loan (including mortgages) other than the loan amount. YSPs provided an incentive for mortgage brokers to steer borrowers into more expensive loans than they might otherwise qualify for, because the originating lender would increase the fee to the broker as the interest rate paid by the borrower increased. Dodd-Frank also instructed the CFPB to promulgate additional rules to restrict the steering of borrowers into more expensive or less advantageous loans.

A key component of Dodd-Frank required mortgage lenders to determine and document that a borrower can afford the proposed loan. The act provided an incentive for responsible lending in this area by giving lenders some protection from litigation. Namely, the lender is assumed to comply with the law's ability-to-repay (ATR) requirements if the loan follows specific guidelines. Loans qualifying for these protections, termed *qualified mortgages*, cannot include negative amortization, balloon payments, or high fees. The full determinants of qualified mortgages were left, appropriately, to the rule-making process, where extensive public comment could be entertained.

Dodd-Frank expanded the coverage of the 1994 Home Ownership and Equity Protection Act (HOEPA) by expanding the fees included in calculating the triggers for HOEPA protections, and lowering these triggers. It also gave the CFPB the authority to define a new category of "abusive" financial practices that "materially" interfere with a consumer's ability to understand a financial product or service, or takes "unreasonable" advantage of a consumer in a financial transaction.

One lower-profile provision of the Dodd-Frank Act may be as important as many of the highly contested provisions. The law called for a significant expansion and restructuring of the data collected under the Home Mortgage Disclosure Act (HMDA) of 1975. HMDA was adopted due to concerns over redlining and urban disinvestment, and was a precursor to the 1977 Community Reinvestment Act (Immergluck 2004). In the 1989 savings and loan bailout bill, HMDA was amended significantly to provide disclosure of loan-level data, including the race and income of mortgage applicants, and the eventual outcome of the application. Later in the 2000s, due to concerns over loan-pricing discrimination, HMDA regulations were modified so that some limited pricing data on high-cost loans began to be collected. However, the data continued to lack some critical underwriting and pricing information, limiting its usefulness in detecting potential lending discrimination, redlining, and abusive behavior, as well as in allowing lenders, researchers, and community groups to assess the credit needs of local communities. Dodd-Frank added several new HMDA data fields, including the age and credit score of the borrower, and additional data on loan terms, fees, and interest rates. It also gave the CFPB authority to collect and report "such other information as the Bureau may require" (Consumer Financial Protection Bureau 2014). Additional data points out that the CFPB, as of this writing, is considering requiring the inclusion of the combined loan-to-value ratio of a loan, the number of housing units in the property, the debt-to-income ratio, and other data. The statute recognized possible tensions between the need for additional HMDA fields and potential privacy concerns. To address these tensions, the CFPB may release certain fields in ways that lump the precise numerical responses into broader categories, or suppress some fields from public disclosure. All changes to HMDA, just as with other regulatory changes called for in Dodd-Frank, will be proposed in standard rule-making procedures, with public (including industry) comment periods. Responses to such comments will be incorporated into the final rules. Many lay observers are unaware of the degree of advocacy and lobbying that occurs in the rule-making process, assuming incorrectly that advocacy is focused only on the legislative arena. In fact, the rules implemented under Dodd-Frank have already generated tens of thousands of formal comments during the years following the statute's enactment. HMDA rulemaking will be no exception. To the extent possible, disclosure of data to the public, in particular, is likely to be fiercely opposed by many industry advocates, just as it has been in prior phases of HMDA rule-making (Immergluck 2004).

Again, from the perspective of those favoring a stronger regulatory regime, the Dodd-Frank Act had significant shortcomings, many of which have been detailed elsewhere (Blinder 2013; Johnson 2011; Stiglitz 2012). Some of its biggest deficiencies were in the area of overall financial stability, including failing to break up very large financial institutions, weak regulation of the credit-rating agencies (discussed more below), and the failure to reestablish the walls between commercial and investment banking operations that existed up until the 1980s, when federal regulators began to weaken Glass-Steagall barriers. These failures caused many to doubt the significance of Dodd-Frank as meaningful regulatory reform. On the consumer-protection side, however, the law contained many major victories for advocates of stronger regulation, and was generally viewed by consumer advocates as a major step forward (National Consumer Law Center 2010).

Notwithstanding the significant achievement of passing Dodd-Frank, the law's adoption was only the first step in a long process of reforming lending regulation. In many cases, the devil was in the details of implementing the statute, through both the rulemaking that remained, as well as the on-the-ground enforcement of such rules. It will take a decade, if not more, to judge the full impact of the act on consumer protection and mortgage markets. Some of the debates will continue to be revisited regularly over the next ten to twenty years at least. Some industry advocates have already attempted—and will continue to work—to weaken the impact of some of these measures through lobbying on the rule-making side, as well as in Congress. Advocates of stronger prudential regulation, consumer protection, and community reinvestment and fair lending will likely wage an uphill battle to counteract such lobbying. As memories of the 2000s subprime crisis fade, these advocates may lose much of the limited political advantage they had in 2009 and 2010.

Resisting Dodd-Frank and the CFPB

The Dodd-Frank Act called for hundreds of regulations to be issued and the adequate staffing and resources to implement them. Both the regulations themselves and the resources to enforce them have been the source of significant industry and congressional opposition. The election of a Republican majority in the House and the weakening of the Democratic majority in the Senate in the fall of 2010 led to significant congressional pressure to undo some of the act. Numerous hearings were held to question the operations of the CFPB, the "unintended consequences" of various regulations, and other purported problems with the law. While President Obama promised to veto any major legislative reversals, incremental or even radical weakening of Dodd-Frank remains a continual threat in both the legislative and rulemaking arenas.

The highest-profile opposition to Dodd-Frank came early in the form of opposition to the new CFPB and its key champion, Elizabeth Warren. Warren, a Harvard Law School professor, had led the Congressional Oversight Panel for the Troubled Asset Relief Program, and was the most commonly mentioned potential nominee for the director of the new agency. Rather than appointing her as CFPB director in September 2010, however, President Obama named her as a special advisor to the Secretary of the Treasury on the CFPB. Some observers suggested that this was because appointing Warren might engender too much hostility from Congress (Villafranco and McPartland 2010). Warren was charged with "standing up" the new agency by July 2011, when it would officially take over many of its regulatory duties. Warren brought in a number of prominent academics, state regulators, and industry experts to lead various parts of the agency, including Pat McCoy from the University of Connecticut, Richard Cordray, the former Ohio attorney general, and Raj Date, a former banker and founder of the Cambridge-Winter Center, a think tank. The CFPB also pulled in veterans of existing federal regulators, including the Federal Reserve, the Federal Trade Commission, and the Federal Deposit Insurance Commission.

Though highly popular among those who thirsted for a tougher approach to Wall Street, Warren became a lightning rod for those resistant to increased regulation. Even before Republicans took control of the House in January 2011, Spencer Bauchus (R-Alabama) and Judy Biggert (R-Illinois) asked the inspector generals of the Federal Reserve and the Treasury Department to begin investigations of the CFPB (Villafranco and McPartland 2010).

In May of 2011, forty-four Republican Senators signed a letter to President Obama stating that they would not vote to confirm a director of the CFPB until the agency was restructured into a five-member commission (Applebaum 2011; Hamilton and Pachkowski 2011). Various opponents of the CFPB made it clear that, even if the Administration appointed someone other than Warren as director, they would still oppose any appointee until the agency was "restructured" to their liking. Thus, these opponents admitted to using the confirmation process to try to undo the creation and design of an agency authorized by Dodd-Frank. They did not have the wherewithal to restructure the agency via legislation, so they resorted to using the confirmation process as a way to try to weaken the agency as much as they could.

Despite broad support among supporters of the CFPB for Warren as director, in July 2011, just before the deadline for the transition of rule making and regulation to the CFPB, President Obama announced that Richard Cordray, the CFPB's director of enforcement, would be nominated as director of the agency (Appelbaum 2011). In some progressive circles, this choice was seen as capitulation to anti-CFPB forces, and a move toward weakening the agency before it had gotten off the ground. Those familiar with Cordray's strong record on consumer regulation as Ohio's attorney general, however, were somewhat less dismayed. While they would have been happy to see Warren as director, they did not view Cordray as a weak-kneed compromise.

Resistance to Dodd-Frank was not limited to the structure of the CFPB or to Elizabeth Warren. The law's vast coverage engendered fierce resistance. The statute called for hundreds of rules to be written, in areas ranging from consumer protection to asset-backed securities and credit default swaps (Villafranco and McPartland 2010). Many agencies beyond the CFPB were charged with promulgating rules, including the banking regulators, the Commodities Future Trading Commission, and the SEC. At every step of the way, vested interests lined up to resist the new rules, or to try to shape them to their advantage.

The House Financial Services Committee, under Republican control after the 2010 midterm elections, took the lead on attempting to rein in the CFPB in any way that it could. Bills were proposed and hearings held on efforts to curtail key regulations called for by Dodd-Frank, including the vital requirement that lenders ensure that borrowers have the ability to repay their mortgages. However, the committee did not stop there. It offered bills such as the "CFPB Slush Fund Elimination Act of 2013," which would eliminate the Bureau's Civil Penalty Fund, and require the agency to transfer any fines it collects back the U.S. Treasury (Housingwire 2014). Another proposed bill would repeal the CFPB's authority to prohibit or regulate the use of arbitration clauses in consumer-product contracts, a significant provision of Dodd-Frank. Yet another proposal was aimed at prohibiting the CFPB from including its enforcement attorneys in its examination processes, and minimizing the amount of time that field examiners could take to issue their reports. Over time, the CFPB's opponents had given up on a general repeal of Dodd-Frank or dissolution of the agency. However, they had now begun to throw dozens of deregulatory proposals at the wall, with the hope that a few of them might stick. And if more than a few stuck, they might effectively be able to defang the agency. As Representative Carolyn Maloney (D-NY) was quoted as saying, "It's like death by a thousand cuts for the CFPB" (Housingwire 2014). This bombardment strategy was also effective in attracting campaign contributions and the support of various financial industry interests. By offering many narrowly crafted bills, opponents of the agency and of Dodd-Frank could appeal to many different lobbying and trade groups.

Many of the largest banks banded together to fight new regulations aimed at "too big to fail" problems, in which large and complex financial institutions benefit from notions that, if they take on excessive risks and things go badly, they will nonetheless be bailed out by taxpayers due to their systemic importance to the broader economy. Many critics felt that Dodd-Frank did not go far enough in this respect, but others, such as Sheila Bair, former director of the Federal Deposit Insurance Corporation, felt that the law gave regulators the tools they needed to take over important institutions in the event of future crises (Bair 2013). Following Dodd-Frank's enactment, a number of large institutions banded together to form a "rapid response" strategy, including hiring a number of former Bush and Obama administration officials, to respond to criticisms that large banks should be broken up or required to hold more capital (Solomon, Sidel, and Lucchetti 2013).

One area of rulemaking that met a good deal of bank resistance was the so-called Volker rule, which was intended to limit the types of investments that banks can make with their own funds, which are backed by federal deposit insurance. In October 2011, regulators offered an almost three-hundred-page proposed rule, seeking comment on more than 380 questions (Patterson and Solomon 2013). The regulators received more than eighteen thousand letters commenting on the proposed rules, predominantly from banks and trade groups. Almost three years after draft rules were first proposed, regulators finalized the Volker rule regulations in March 2014.

Another way that opponents of stronger regulation fought the implementation of Dodd-Frank was through limiting the enforcement capabilities of regulators. One notable example was the Commodities Futures Trading Commission (CFTC), which was charged by Dodd-Frank with regulating so-called clearinghouses through which many financial derivatives—including credit default swaps—are traded. Credit default swaps are a form of insurance that compensates investors when the insured investment performs poorly. Through a clearinghouse, an investor engages in a swap transaction with a counterparty that receives payment from the investor in exchange for a promise of a payment should the investment suffer losses. The size of the swaps market was estimated at roughly half a trillion dollars in 2013 (Binham and Schafer 2013). However, the Obama Administration's funding requests for the CFTC to staff up adequately to enforce regulations were rebuffed in Congress. In 2013, Gary Gensler, the chair of the CFTC, estimated that the agency needed to increase its staff by almost 50 percent to regulate the exchanges (Binham and Schafer 2013).

While the Volker rule, staffing at the SEC, and other efforts to limit overall risky behavior by banks did not directly concern mortgage regulation, they were likely to have a serious effect on the supply and quality of mortgage credit. If mortgage markets allow for the resurrection of high-risk, high-cost subprime lending again, inadequate regulation of capital markets means that high-risk capital will once again flood the most vulnerable parts of the housing market.

In some ways, the widespread public support for the CFPB and its chief advocate, Elizabeth Warren, resulted in the successful implementation of many consumer-protection regulations and the survival—so far—of a vigorous CFPB. Warren, Cordray, and other officials at the CFPB were able to convince a broad part of the general public of the relevance and importance of stronger consumer-protection regulations. Unfortunately, the complexity and opacity of regulations in the broader securities and capital markets—and the greater challenges in mobilizing public opinion in support of such rules—have benefited the opponents of regulation and made it more difficult for meaningful regulatory initiatives to prevail.

Mission Not Accomplished: Regulating the Credit-Rating Agencies

One of the culprits that shouldered a great deal of the blame for the crisis was the credit-rating system, led by the firms Standard and Poors, Moody's, and Fitch Ratings. As explained in chapter 1, the credit-rating "agencies" (which are in fact private, profit-seeking firms) constituted a government-sanctioned oligopoly that provided AAA ratings to many mortgage-backed securities and collateralized debt obligations that later were revealed to be inherently risky and had to be downgraded to junk status during the crisis. Critics found many faults with the ratings industry, including a system in which ratings firms were paid by the issuers of the securities that they were rating. Thus, if a rating firm was tempted to give a security a low rating, it would risk losing that issuer's business in the future. Rating firms' profits were closely tied to the share of the booming mortgage-securitization industry that they were able to capture, so incentives to go soft on these ratings were strong (Immergluck 2009). The firms would sometimes provide guidance to the issuers on how to engineer a security to maximize its rating, and not necessarily by reducing the underlying riskiness of the loans. Another major problem with credit ratings was that the firms were generally exempt from lawsuits over the quality of their ratings, hiding behind claims that they were similar to journalists exercising their free-speech rights.

Despite wide consensus on the innacuracy and dysfunction of the bond-rating business, especially in the mortgage industry, advocates for reforming the industry and increasing regulations were significantly stymied during the development of Dodd-Frank. In May of 2010, the Senate approved a measure offered by Senator Al Franken (D-MN) to address the conflict of interest presented in the issuer-pays model of credit-rating compensation (Herszenhorn 2010). Franken's proposal would have created a ratings board overseen by the SEC that would end the issuer-pays conflicts and rating shopping that issuers could engage in by randomly or systemically matching ratings agencies with specific issuances. This process would decouple the issuer from the choice of rating agency, effectively ending the problem of ratings shopping and inflated credit ratings.

After its approval in the Senate, the Franken Amendment was effectively neutered in conference committee by giving regulators a major "out" from implementing the law (Herszenhorn 2010). The final statute made it possible for the SEC to adopt Franken's proposed system, but allowed the agency to avoid implementing the system if it recommended alternatives after a required study. The SEC took until December of 2012 to finally issue the study, which recommended still more deliberation—a "roundtable" discussion that took place in May of 2013, almost four years after Dodd-Frank was enacted (Neumann 2013).

As early as 2013, it became clear that the problem of rating shopping and rating inflation had not been solved. The *New York Times* reported that after Standard and Poors (S&P) discovered that its mortgage-backed securities unit was losing money in the summer of 2012, pressure built at the firm to relax standards in order to regain market share (Popper 2013). Within a few months, S&P modified its standards to allow analysts to give bonds higher ratings. After this, its market share skyrocketed. From 2010 until November of 2012 when the standards were eased, S&P rated just two of the eleven (18 percent) mortgage-bond deals issued during this period. Of the twenty-nine deals rated after the November change, up through September 2013, S&P rated twenty (69 percent) of them. For the two bond deals that S&P rated before relaxing its standards, its projections for expected losses were among the three highest of the nineteen ratings on all eleven bonds. After the standards change, S&P's loss projections dropped significantly, so that when other firms rated a bond as well as S&P, S&P's loss projections were typically the lowest. Of the twenty ratings S&P performed after November 2012, nineteen were also rated by other firms. In sixteen of these cases, S&P projected losses lower than those projected by all other firms. These patterns were suggestive of a major easing of S&P standards aimed at gaining market share. An industry expert was quoted by the *Times* in claiming that the increase in S&P market share was "largely a function" of the revised rating standards (Popper 2013). This is evidence of a continued "competition in laxity"—driven by efforts to gain and retain market share—among the rating firms similar to that which contributed to the mortgage crisis.

Perhaps in response to the *New York Times* stories and other complaints about the agency's inaction, the SEC revised its proposed credit-agency rules when finalizing them in August 2014. The SEC increased its requirements for disclosure of the models used for deriving ratings and established rules for attempting to segregate marketing and sales staff from rating analysts and to prevent marketing pressure from influencing the ratings process (U.S. Securities and Exchange Commission 2014). However, the new rules did not fundamentally change how ratings firms were compensated or selected by securities issuers and so did not get at the heart of the conflict-of-interest problem (Better Markets 2014; Dayen 2014).

In a failure to fulfill the intent and direction of Dodd-Frank, the SEC effectively blocked implementation of the statute's explicit call to end the protection that the rating agencies enjoyed from the potential legal liability that brokers, auditors, and other financial advisory firms faced. Dodd-Frank ended this exemption, referred to as "Rule 436(g)" (U.S. Securities and Exchange Commission 2010b). This rule had meant that firms rating a bond or security were not considered "experts," and thus were more difficult to sue for shoddy analysis compared to an auditor or other expert advisor. (Ratings agencies could still be sued for fraudulent activity, as evidenced by fraud-based lawsuits by state attorneys general and the Department of Justice in years following the crisis.) Yet analysis and expert advice were precisely what the firms were selling when they rated securities. This protection from greater liability allowed rating firms to have their cake and eat it too by selling expert services without being held accountable the way other experts were. Dodd-Frank contained a provision that should have ended the 436(g) exception and forced the agencies to stand by their work.

The credit rating firms balked, however, and immediately claimed that they would no longer rate securities without the 436(g) exemption. In a "no-action" letter on the day the new legislation was to go into effect (July 22, 2010), the SEC capitulated immediately, stating that it would "not recommend enforcement action to the Commission" at least until January 24, 2011 (Securities and Exchange Commission 2010b). Then, in November of 2010, the SEC issued another letter, stating that its decision to not enforce this provision of Dodd-Frank would remain in effect indefinitely. In kowtowing to the credit-rating firms and acting in opposition to an enacted statute, the SEC followed the tradition of other governmental agencies that have been bullied into submission by the rating firms. In the early 2000s, when states attempted to regulate subprime mortgage lending, the rating agencies sometimes issued statements that they would no longer rate securities containing loans in the affected states. States crumbled in the face of the rating agencies, just as the SEC did here (Immergluck 2009).

In addition to these clear shortcomings, Dodd-Frank has, at least to this point, failed to make a meaningful dent in the credit-ratings oligopoly. One chief way that the law was supposed to facilitate greater competition was by reducing federal reliance on the use of "Nationally Recognized Statistical Rating Organizations" (NRSROs), a small group of firms led by the big three, Standard and Poors, Moody's, and Fitch Ratings. By eliminating the legally specified reliance on these firms, the logic went, the market would open up to renewed competition from smaller rating firms (Novick, Chavers, and Rosenblum 2013). Unfortunately, the government designation of NRSROs was not the only effective barrier to entry that supported the ratings oligopoly, so it remains unclear how substantial an effect the movement away from specifying the use of NRSROs will have on the industry. The historical dominance of these firms and their reputational—and political—power cannot be easily undone. This may explain why Dodd-Frank, and the resulting regulations, has had so little effect on the practices of these financial crisis culprits. Stronger actions are likely needed to rein in the power of the big credit-rating firms.

From Disclosure-Based to Proscriptive Regulation: QM and QRM

Prior to Dodd-Frank, the paradigm for consumer-protection regulation in the mortgage market was based almost entirely on the concept that regulations should focus on providing a borrower with disclosure of the terms and conditions of a loan. The logic of relying primarily on disclosure-based regulations is that once a consumer is informed of the details of the loan—details that can run dozens of pages in documentation—he or she will be empowered to make a wise financial decision. Offering disclosure as the principal means of regulation can effectively crowd out calls for firmer proscriptive regulation, in which certain loan terms or features are either banned or seriously discouraged. Those opposing "paternalistic" regulation often prefer relying on disclosure, while those favoring stronger proscriptive measures argue that relying on disclosure alone is not sufficient to address the complex world of consumer finance, where lenders have many incentives to steer customers to risky or unsuitable products.

While Dodd-Frank included many measures aimed at reducing the proliferation of abusive, high-cost, and risky mortgage products, two key measures went significantly further than previous regulatory efforts had gone. First, the legislation authorized the CFPB to issue regulations that would compel lenders to consider borrowers' ability to repay (ATR) a loan in their underwriting decisions. The statute effectively banned the use of no-documentation loans and discouraged risky features such as balloon payments and negative amortization structures. One key part of the ATR regulations opened lenders to potential litigation if they did not go through reasonable steps to ensure that borrowers had an ability to repay their loans. In order to provide lenders with a broad pathway for originating fairly standard, lower-risk loans, the statute also provided that the CFPB would define a "qualified mortgage" (QM), which would generally be presumed to meet the ATR requirements. The QM definition would lay out a series of specified loan features that, if present, would constitute a non-QM loan, and thus place a greater burden on the lender to prove that it had confirmed the borrower's ability to repay. These features included risk-inducing terms such as high debt-to-income ratios.

According to the ATR regulations issued by the CFPB in early 2013, lenders were required to consider eight specified underwriting characteristcs, including income and assets, employment status, monthly payments for all mortgages, current other debt obligations and alimony or child support obligations, monthly debt-to-income ratios, and credit history. One way that lenders can be sure to meet the ATR requirements is to make a QM loan that meets various criteria specified by the CFPB (Consumer Financial Protection Bureau 2013). Most low-cost, QM loans would enjoy "safe harbor" protection from potential legal challenges regarding the ATR requirements of Dodd-Frank. A smaller subset of higher-priced loans that met the QM guidelines would enjoy a "rebuttable presumption" that they met the ATR standard. While not offering as much protection from litigation as the safe harbor, meeting the rebuttable-presumption standards shifts the burden onto the borrower to demonstrate why the loan did not meet ATR requirements.

According to the final regulations issed by the CFPB, QM loans generally include those where:

- there are no negative-amortization, interest-only, or balloon-payment features;
- the term does not extend beyond thirty years;
- points and fees, excluding "discount points," are no more than 3 percent of the loan amount (higher for small loans);
- the total "back-end" debt-to-income ratio is no more than 43 percent;
- for adjustable-rate loans, the debt-to-income ratio is calculated based on the maximum payment that could occur over the first five years of the loan;
- income and assets must be documented; and
- most loans (not those containing features prohibited in the Dodd-Frank statute) meeting the underwriting requirements of the GSEs (while under conservatorship) or other government agencies such as the FHA or the VA would be classified as QM loans, for a temporary period lasting up to seven years.

While some argued that the QM process and the use of a 43 percent debt-to-income ratio would exclude many credit-worthy borrowers from the credit market, the evidence generally did not support such claims. First, it is important to point out that not meeting QM guidelines does not mean that a loan will not be made, merely that there is a greater burden on the originator to ensure that the loan meets the ability-to-repay criteria specified in the regulations. Many opponents of the QM standard—including the Republican leader of the House Financial Services Committee in 2014—implied in their arguments that not meeting QM guidelines is equivalent to being shut out of all credit markets (Henserling 2014).

Not meeting QM guidelines might add some cost to underwriting by requiring more work to ensure that the borrower has the ability to repay the loan, but those costs should be quite marginal. Moreover, the need to document such capacity should generate demand for data and technology useful for making such loans in a responsible manner. In fact, the major mortgage lenders announced in late 2013 that they would be making non-QM loans and other firms had announced plans to begin operations specializing in non-QM loans (Timiraos 2013).

Second, in looking at actual mortgage data from 1997 to 2003, even if lenders did not change their behavior to adapt to the new QM standards, only 8 percent of mortgages would not have complied with the ability-to-repay (ATR) rule, even when not including the temporary GSE-qualifying provisions of the regulations (Hoskins 2014). It is important to keep in mind that this period included a significant amount of subprime lending, because it included the first subprime boom of the late 1990s as well as the first year or so of the second boom. Moreover, at least 70 percent of loans originated during this period would have achieved "permanent" QM status (meaning that these loans do not have to be GSE-approvable loans to meet QM standards) with another 22 percent meeting ATR requirements but not permanent QM status. Again, these figures are not adjusted for the likely changes in lending behavior that would almost certainly occur in the face of the QM and ATR requirements. While some fraction of the 8 percent of non-ATR loans might not have been made at all, others would have been made for smaller amounts or at lower costs in order to meet ATR requirements. Similarly, some loans would have been modified to meet QM standards.

The available analyses on ATR and QM coverage are conservative, because they do not consider lender response to the new regulations. That is, the presence of the QM standard will encourage lenders to shift loans into the QM "bucket" by changing the size and terms of the loans. A borrower seeking to pay $400,000 for a house with a loan that yields a debt-to-income ratio of 45 percent could be encouraged by a lender offering QM loans either to put more money down on the house, to purchase a smaller home, or to negotiate a slightly lower price for the home, all of which might be desireable outcomes. They might also be able to lower their debt-to-income ratio by first reducing their nonmortgage debt in some way, and then coming back to the housing market when their debt burden is a bit more manageable. Alternatively, the borrower could seek a loan from a non-QM lender (perhaps the same lender who offered the QM loan), but that lender would have to be more careful in ensuring that the borrower could repay the loan.

In order to assure concerned parties that the QM standard would not overly constrain credit during a time of housing-market recovery, the CFPB also included a "temporary" provision—one that could last as long as seven years—that any loan meeting the underwriting requirements of Fannie Mae or Freddie Mac, while they were under federal conservatorship, would qualify as a QM loan. Moreover, the Federal Housing Administration and the Veterans Administration mortgage programs established their own QM standards, effectively creating a QM channel for loans insured or guaranteed by those agencies. Thus, even if a loan had a feature otherwise excluded from the QM standard, if it is eligible to be bought by Fannie Mae or Freddie Mac, it qualifies as a QM loan. After this temporary provision expires, the regular QM guidelines will apply to all mortgages, regardless of whether they meet GSE standards.

A separate component of Dodd-Frank required securitizers to retain at least 5 percent of the value of a loan pool when issuing mortgage-backed securities (Federal Reserve Board of Governors 2013). This risk-retention requirement was intended to give issuers of mortgage-backed securities more "skin in the game," so that they had a long-term interest in the performance of the loans that were being securitized. This should help to align the interests of the issuers with those of the investors, and thus reduce the incentives for issuers to pass off risky bonds to investors who had less information about the underlying loans than they had. However, real estate and finance-industry advocates worried that this would somehow gum up the private-label securitization machine that had proved so lucrative, and had provided ample liquidity and credit access to lenders, including many of the riskiest ones. They managed to have their congressional advocates create a class of loans that would be excluded from the risk-retention requirement, presumably because they would be so safe that no such requirements were needed. This class of mortgage is called the "qualified residential mortgage" (QRM), and its features are prescribed, jointly, by a group of six federal financial regulators.

Notice the somewhat-tortured logic of the QRM provision in Dodd-Frank. It suggests that risk retention is not needed for a group of safe, low-risk loans. However, if this group of loans is very safe, then retaining a small fraction of their worth when issuing securities backed by them would not seem so onerous. Yes, the issuer would need to hold this asset on their balance sheet, but presumably this is a highly secure asset, so holding a very small portion of it should not be very detrimental to an organization's balance sheet. And nondepository lenders who claim they have no capacity to hold debt are not likely to be the issuers of the securities themselves. Rather, it is the Wall Street firm that will have to retain the 5 percent, and these firms should be well-capitalized investment firms. Indeed, most of the major issuers are now also large commercial banks.

A key problem with the QRM provision was that it could create a stigmatized class of loans—non-QRM loans—that would be relatively more expensive to make than QRM loans, at least for lenders that depended on securitization as a primary means to fund their lending operations. If all loans were subject to risk retention, as had been originally proposed in the earlier versions of Dodd-Frank, then risk-retention would not introduce a stigmatizing effect to any one class of loans. In some sense, QM had already created two classes of loans—QM and non-QM—although the QM definition was very broad and would allow for the bulk of loans to meet the QM safe harbor or rebuttable presumption standards. Adding a QRM exception from risk-retention that was significantly narrower than the QM definition would create a narrower class of loans with no stigma, thus exposing a much larger class of borrowers and loans. This would likely relegate them to a more expensive, and potentially more abusive, part of the mortgage market.

It was not clear that the QRM provision in Dodd-Frank made sense or was necessary. Very low-risk loans should be easily securitized and the risk-retention piece should pose little burden to issuers of mortgage-backed securities with adequate capital structures. One problem introduced by the QRM provision is that when a class of loans is created that is perceived as *relatively* more costly to the securitization market, higher-quality, lower-cost capital will avoid that market, and higher-risk investors—demanding higher returns—will be left to serve the non-QRM market. This fuels greater risk-based (and thus pricing) segmentation of mortgage markets that puts borrowers who qualify for a QM loan—but not quite for a QRM loan—at a significant disadvantage in the mortgage market. The issue of housing-finance structures that fuel segmented markets—and higher financing costs for those least able to pay them—will be discussed more in the next chapter. However, QRM provides yet another way in which segmentation might be inadvertently encouraged.

As of this writing, it seems likely that the QRM provision in Dodd-Frank will not have as much impact as it might have. After issuing an early QRM definition that was significantly narrower than the QM definition, so that many loans—especially those with down payments below 20 percent—would be classified as non-QRM even though they met QM standards, regulators received many comments from those concerned about the stigmatization of a broad swath of the mortgage market (see Reid and Quercia 2013 for an example). In revising the proposal, regulators settled on a primary option of aligning the definitions of QRM and QM, so that all QM mortgages would be exempted from risk retention. While arguably not consistent with some of the legislative intent of the QRM amendment to Dodd-Frank, I would argue that risk retention should apply either to all mortgages equally, or to only the very highest-risk loans, which are essentially those outside the QM definition.

The next chapter will address the fundamental structure of U.S. mortgage markets going forward. Of particular concern is the extent to which mortgage markets may become much more highly segmented by price and quality. While discussions of the restructuring of Fannie Mae and Freddie Mac have often focused on issues of broader financial stability and the need to bring more private-sector capital into housing finance, many have missed the the critical implications that such policies will have for the future of families, neighborhoods, and cities in metropolitan America.

Chapter Five

The Housing Finance Debate

Although the United States has established a new set of regulations to protect borrowers and reduce the opportunities for excessively risky mortgage products, the long-term architecture of the housing-finance system remains uncertain. Since Fannie Mae and Freddie Mac were placed in federal conservatorship in 2008, there have been several rounds of debate over reforming the basic funding structure for U.S. mortgage markets. This chapter engages in this debate. However, I start by discussing why housing finance is important to families and neighborhoods in the United States. I reframe the "homeownership versus rental" debate into one about how to provide the best housing opportunities to moderate and middle-income households and neighborhoods, and the role of housing finance in that process. Rather than oversimplify the debate into an "ownership is better" versus "renting is better" dichotomy, I examine the legal, economic, and spatial context of housing tenure and focus on goals of maintaining affordable and sustainable homeownership options while also supporting affordable rental alternatives.

The chapter then delves into the impact that housing finance can have on affordable homeownership, and on neighborhoods and cities. To help inform the debate over the future federal role in housing markets, I review the historical development of mortgage markets in the United States since the early twentieth century and the importance of a federal role in maintaining stable and sound markets. I then turn to the current debate over the future of housing finance, reviewing some of the primary proposals that have been put forth, as well as articulating a proposal that has received short shrift in the policy debate.

WHY HOUSING FINANCE MATTERS TO HOUSEHOLDS AND NEIGHBORHOODS

In the debate over the proper role of government in U.S. mortgage markets, some key arguments have centered on the desirability of homeownership versus rental housing (Gyourko 2009; Randazzo 2010). If homeownership is not more beneficial than renting, some argue, what is the justification for a federal role in mortgage markets? However, this question is overly simplistic. Households are usually not presented with a simple, other-things-held-constant choice between homeownership and renting. Rather, some rental options are generally good, just as some homeownership options are generally good. At a specific point in the life of a family, at a specific place, one form of tenure may make more sense than the other. Housing is a bundle of services and amenities—along with a location and community—that a family chooses at a particular time.

Housing—and housing tenure—options are embedded in a complex set of legal, economic, and social contexts and constraints. For example, if a family is seeking a home and neighborhood in which it can lay down deep roots, it may value security of tenure and stability over the ability to relocate quickly with little financial risk. In many cities in the United States, tenant-protection ordinances are weak and quality rental options are scarce. A home financed with an affordable, fixed-rate mortgage may offer greater stability and a sense of control that may benefit such a family. Factors like short-term leases, landlord-friendly eviction laws, and potential gentrification pressures may work against the stability of rental options.

However, if homeownership can only be financed with expensive, adjustable-rate financing, ownership may not be such a good option, even for a family seeking to put down roots. High financing costs and risk will reduce housing stability and affordability, and make equity gains from homeownership less likely. Moreover, if the rental market is more renter-friendly, offers greater tenant protections, and provides greater stability, the balance will also tip toward renting.

At the national level, tenant protections and the quality of rental housing vary tremendously, and other advanced economies typically have higher levels of subsidized or alternative-tenure housing, such as cooperatives (Andrews, Sanchez, and Johansson 2011). When opponents to a significant federal role in mortgage markets argue that other well-off countries have substantially lower homeownership rates than the United States, they tend to ignore these key differences (Min 2013).

In the United States, due to a complex cultural and policy history, the vast majority of families are either renters or homeowners, and the vast majority of families live in privately owned, unsubsidized housing units. Publicly or socially owned rental housing is a very small fraction (less than 6 percent) of the housing market, and only about 4 percent of the population receives housing allowances (Andrews, Sanchez, and Johansson 2011). Housing allowances in the United States, in the form of vouchers, are available only to quite poor households, and are not an entitlement, so most eligible households do not receive vouchers. Moreover, in most parts of the United States, the private rental market is largely unregulated compared to other industrialized countries, with no rent control and minimal tenant-protection regulations. Researchers from the Organization for Economic Cooperation and Development (OECD) have developed an index describing landlord-tenant regulations (Andrews, Sanchez, and Johansson 2011). As shown in figure 5.1, of the thirty-two countries in the study, the United States ranked last in terms of tenant protection. On this criterion alone, the rental market is the United States is not at all comparable to rental markets in countries such as Sweden, France, Spain, Italy, or Germany (which ranked first, fifth, sixth, seventh, and ninth in the OECD ranking, respectively).

In comparative international studies of housing markets and policies, researchers sometimes classify countries as having rental markets that are predominantly "dualist" or "unitary" (Kemeny 2006; O'Sullivan and De Decker 2007). Dualist systems are dominated by private, less regulated rental markets, with a smaller, tightly controlled public or social rental sector. These systems are generally found in countries with stronger market-fundamentalist tendencies. Unitary rental systems include a framework of stronger rental

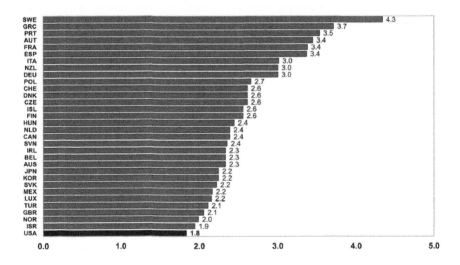

Figure 5.1. Tenant Protection Levels in Private Rental Markets in OECD Countries, 2009. *Source:* Prepared by author from data in Andrews, Sanchez and Johansson (2011).

regulation, and their larger social rental sectors subject private landlords to significant competition with nonprofit and public-sector landlords, putting downward pressure on rents. These differences tend to make rental housing relatively more attractive than ownership in unitary systems as compared to dualist systems. Perhaps more so than in any other industrialized country, the rental market in the United States is firmly in the dualist camp, where owner-occupied housing exhibits a diverse set of advantages over rental housing.

The adverse conditions, legal context, and spatial availability of rental housing in many U.S. cities create a context in which many households are likely to prefer ownership to renting. These contexts are created more by state and local planning and policies than by particular federal policies. Thus, efforts to "rebalance" the advantages of renting versus owning face many challenges, not the least of which is the difficulty in changing the allocation of homeownership advantages across thousands of local communities. The reality is that, for many moderate- and middle-income homeowners, the benefits of homeownership—many of which are not financial—will remain considerable.

The spatial concentration of a great deal of rental housing in higher-poverty and less desirable neighborhoods is a powerful force that shapes household preferences for ownership. In many U.S. suburban communities, especially those with better schools, affordable rental housing is scarce. These patterns are supported and reinforced by a long history of exclusionary zoning and housing policies in many middle- and upper-income suburban communities (Rothwell and Massey 2009). Renter households are at least twice as likely to live in inner cities as owner-occupied households, and the difference is even greater among lower-income renters and owners (Joint Center for Housing Studies 2006). Homeownership can provide access to a greater variety of neighborhood locations, including access to better schools and amenities. The scarce rental subsidies that do exist are often directed toward multifamily rental buildings. Therefore, those seeking detached, single-family rental housing may face even fewer affordable options in good neighborhoods.

Evidence on the Benefits of Affordable Homeownership to Families and Neighborhoods

Chapter 2 discussed many of the costs of foreclosure and distressed housing, and showed that the mortgage crisis hit many minority and lower-income communities particularly hard. Reading that chapter alone, one might conclude that the downside risks of homeownership—especially for people of color or modest means—are too great, and that renting is usually the wiser choice. Moreover, policymakers might come to the conclusion that such risks should mean that federal policy should actively discourage homeownership among low- and moderate-income households. Such conclusions ignore the substantial evidence that many modest-income homeowners have benefitted from homeownership. The key is to create affordable and sustainable options for homeownership that will reduce the downside risks of homeownership and avoid the boom-bust volatility that makes lower- and middle-income homeowners and neighborhoods vulnerable to foreclosure and large losses in home equity.

Chris Herbert and his colleagues at the Joint Center for Housing Studies reviewed the literature and found that, even in light of the mortgage crisis, homeownership offers low- and moderate-income families substantial opportunities for wealth building (Herbert, McCue, and Sanchez-Moyano 2013). Over many decades, homeownership provides such families with a vehicle to gain wealth. Homeownership offers families an opportunity to engage in a forced-savings plan that also provides for leveraging any gains in property values by a factor of five or more. This is not to dismiss the real downside risks of homeownership, and the significant economic, social, and personal costs of foreclosure. Households who need a great deal of residential mobility, or who cannot obtain mortgages at fair and reasonable terms, are likely to find that renting is more desirable than owning. However, to base long-term policy decisions solely on the problems created by irresponsible, high-cost lending ignores the benefits that homeownership provides in the context of a more responsible lending environment and less volatile housing markets.

Many critics of homeownership make the misguided assumption that the wealth gains of homeownership occur only in the context of high levels of housing-market appreciation. In fact, many of the gains in wealth made by strong price appreciation are wiped away by subsequent declines (Herbert, McCue, and Sanchez-Moyano 2013). Rather, the savings aspect of homeownership drives much of the wealth gains, especially for low- and moderate-income homeowners. Some argue that it may not be homeownership, per se, that directly causes the increased savings, and that homeownership is merely associated with higher savings rates. However, the fact that renters tend to save at substantially lower rates than homeowners strongly suggests that homeownership *enables* higher savings rates for many families. It may be that those choosing homeownership have other proclivities that push them toward higher savings rates, but homeownership may still be instrumental to increased savings. Without access to homeownership, many would not be able to engage in substantial amounts of saving, or benefit from financial leverage. Of course, if homeownership is financed at very high costs, because of risk-based or other high-cost financing, much of this savings advantage could evaporate.

For many families, homeownership has advantages beyond financial considerations, and the evidence suggests that these advantages are the most important factors in the desire to own a home. Rachel Drew (2013) analyzed a sample of over fourteen hundred respondents to the 2011 Fannie Mae National Housing Survey who were renters between the ages of twenty-five and sixty-four. Over 80 percent of these respondents expected to buy a home in the future. When asked why they would prefer to buy, they indicated which factors were "major reasons" to purchase a home. As shown in figure 5.2, the four most important reasons to buy were all nonfinancial reasons that involve location, access to good schools, the physical attributes of the home (e.g., space), and a sense of control, security, and stability. Financial reasons were secondary. Even in surveys before the housing crisis, these nonfinancial factors were ranked as more important than financial ones. Moreover, despite the tumult of the foreclosure crisis, prospective homeowners continued to believe that homeownership would provide them with a greater sense of control and stability than renting.

As indicated in figure 5.2, the top reason that many families prefer homeownership lies in its spatial association with "good places to raise children and provide them with a good education." The unfortunate reality is that exclusionary zoning and housing policies severely limit the number of rental units available in many places in metropolitan America. While these patterns may be changing at the margins, as modest amounts of suburban single-family housing are converted to rental housing in the aftermath of the crisis, there remain few rental options in many neighborhoods with strong schools and low crime rates. Homeownership can increase access to these commu-

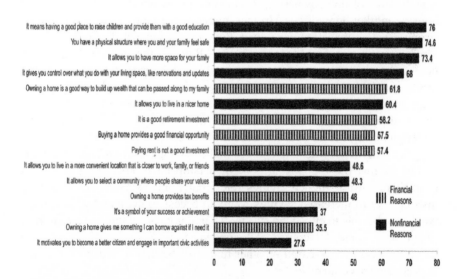

Figure 5.2.   Reasons Cited by Renters for Buying a Home in the Future, 2011.
Source: Prepared by author from data in Drew (2013), which utilized Fannie Mae National Housing Survey.

nities and expand housing choice among moderate-income families (Lee 2013). Thus, some of the effective benefits of homeownership are not due to tenure choice itself, but are enabled by greater access to communities where owner-occupied housing dominates the residential landscape. Encouraging suburban communities to build more nonluxury, family oriented rental housing is a worthy goal, but it is an uphill battle. Many suburbs—especially those with high-performing schools—continue to aim to minimize their supply of affordable family rental housing (Rothwell 2012). Therefore, maintaining access to affordable homeownership is crucial to providing fair housing opportunities in metropolitan America.

Recognizing the Reality of Local Housing Markets When Formulating U.S. Housing Policy

Homeownership can have social and economic benefits for some families. The evidence also suggests that higher homeownership rates can benefit neighborhoods (Rohe and Lindblad 2013). In fact, as larger institutional investors have purchased formerly foreclosed properties in the wake of the foreclosure crisis, they have identified higher homeownership rates as one characteristic of neighborhoods where they prefer to purchase homes for rentals (Immergluck and Law 2014). The stability associated with homeownership gives investors and renters confidence in the trajectory of a neighborhood.

None of this is to suggest that public policy should be focused more on providing affordable homeownership opportunities than on assisting renters. A balanced federal housing policy makes sense, and increasing rental support for low-income households remains a critical need in the United States. Efforts should be made to provide renters with greater tenant protections and more access to middle- and upper-income neighborhoods with strong school systems. However, it must be recognized that the political challenges here are immense, and improving the quality of rental options involves much more than increasing marginal levels of rental subsidy. Making quality, affordable rental housing much more widely available would require major policy changes in most local U.S. housing markets. Tenant-protection laws, including rent controls, security of tenure provisions, and exclusionary zoning, are largely embedded in state (and sometimes local) law. Changing such laws across hundreds of cities would be no simple feat.

In the meantime, many moderate- and middle-income households will continue to seek affordable, stable, owner-occupied housing. In the United States, the long-term, affordable, fixed-rate mortgage with a modest down payment has proven to be a critical vehicle for providing such housing. It has been particularly advantageous to moderate- and middle-income households in the United States for at least four reasons. First, it removes uncertainty from what is generally the largest single item in the household budget. Second, by reducing long-run mortgage costs and providing for stability of tenure, it fosters residential stability. Short-term loans create the need to refinance at a particular point in time, which increases the risks of forced sales or foreclosure, and can increase financing costs in the long run. Third, modest down payments allow households with limited wealth to save for other needs, including creating reserves for home repairs, auto repairs, education, and other critical needs. Down payments of 20 percent or more reduce the amount of savings that can be invested in other assets, and put more of the family's wealth at risk in the event of a major decline in housing value. Finally, homeownership offers households a mechanism to enter into what is effectively a highly disciplined, predictable savings plan, in which the build-up of equity can boost a family's financial assets. Even without high levels of property appreciation, the long-term, fixed-rate mortgage can provide a disciplined vehicle for savings that is hard to replicate through other means. Expecting moderate-income, or even many middle-income, families to have the discipline to regularly and routinely make contributions to a substantial savings program is often unrealistic.

In the long run, if access to safe and affordable mortgages with modest down-payment requirements is curtailed, many more moderate- and middle-income households will likely be forced to find housing in the private rental market, putting continued upward pressure on rents. Without a massive new federal commitment to funding affordable rental housing, which seems unlikely in the foreseeable future, these households will generally not qualify for rental subsidies. In most places in the United States, renters face a lightly regulated rental market that offers little protection against rapid rent increases or easy eviction or displacement. Given the spatial concentration of rental housing in most metropolitan areas, many families will find themselves constrained to renting in lower-income neighborhoods with low-quality schools and few amenities. Moreover, moderate-income families who want to put down roots in neighborhoods through homeownership are also likely to find many barriers, resulting in lower homeownership rates in low- and moderate-income neighborhoods than would be possible under fairer mortgage markets. A massive increase in federal funding of rental housing in the United States is not politically viable in the foreseeable future. Moreover, the weakness of tenant and fair-housing protections in most U.S. rental markets means that the rental market often has significant disadvantages compared to owner occupancy. In a climate of shrinking federal budgets and attacks on even existing levels of housing support, maintaining a strong federal role in housing finance will prove a critical tool for providing access to stable and affordable housing for a large segment of modest-income households.

THE FEDERAL ROLE IN CREDIT AND MORTGAGE MARKETS IN THE UNITED STATES

Since the late eighteenth century, there have been continual debates in the United States over the role of government in the formation, structure, and regulation of credit markets (Hoffman 2001; Immergluck 2004). This includes not only in mortgage and consumer credit markets but also in finance more broadly. Banks, savings and loans, and other lenders have generally relied on specialized, state, or federally issued charters that are clearly distinct from the more generic state charters or licenses under which most businesses operate. The granting of banking charters often comes with significant economic and societal obligations, including an obligation to—or duty to serve—a community, or set of communities. This obligation is based on a quid pro quo in which banks, savings and loans, mortgage companies, and other financial service providers are heavily dependent on a somewhat-tangled but critical web of federal and state infrastructure—including a regulatory system—without which they could not operate in a profitable and sustainable way.

Residential lenders are especially dependent on a strong system of government-enforced property rights, transparent and accountable property records and enforcement, zoning and land-use law, and transportation and public-safety services. These firms' assets are dependent on the sustaining value of the land and property that backs their loans and investments, which in turn depend on legal infrastructure and a bundle of public services delivered to a particular place. Thus, lenders and financiers derive value out of the public investments in all of these systems.

As Adam Levitin and Janneke Ratcliffe (2013) argue, public interventions, supports, subsidies (both direct and indirect), and infrastructure give the mortgage sector a particular "duty to serve." Even without such a duty, public involvement in these markets is needed to promote sound financial practices and avoid the boom-bust hypervolatility that accompanies lightly regulated, private financial markets. The period of generally stable mortgage markets that began in the 1930s, and lasted until the early 1990s, is perhaps the best example of how federal involvement in financial markets can reduce systemic risk, while improving access to credit in sustainable ways. The subprime booms of the late 1990s and middle 2000s provided the first real post–Great Depression experiment with largely private mortgage markets. Despite the lessons that should have been learned from contrasting these two periods, some continue to recommend heavily privatized mortgage markets. While a pervasive market-fundamentalist ideology has played a major role in such responses, so has a web of lobbying and political interests tied to the financialization of the economy since the 1970s, including the growth of securitization-driven financial products (Gotham 2009; Stiglitz 2012).

The emergence of S&Ls was supported by the licensing, regulation, and—in the twentieth century—subsidization and creation of public or quasi-public supportive institutions like Hoover's Federal Home Loan Banks (Immergluck 2004). Roosevelt's introduction of federal deposit insurance provided a critical federal backstop for S&Ls and banks, giving them access to low-cost deposits that then fueled their mortgage lending operations, as well as other lending. S&Ls, banks, and mortgage companies were able to utilize Federal Housing Administration (FHA) loans and, later, Veterans Administration loans, which together provided a major portion of housing credit during the middle decades of the twentieth century.

Adherents to a market-fundamentalist ideology sometimes argue that there is an "efficient" level of credit availability and that federal involvement in mortgage markets "distorts" this level. This simplistic argument ignores the fact that housing and housing finance are instrumental, primary goods that are critical to the production of other goods and services and strong determinants of the life chances of individuals and groups.

Even from within the neoclassical paradigm, financial markets—especially those involving real estate and housing—are wrapped up in the provision of public goods, quasi-public goods, and positive and negative spillover effects. Alexander Hamilton, an early champion of federal involvement in financial markets, realized that a financial infrastructure was a public good. Access to credit would bring all sorts of positive externalities to society. Much later, in the late 1920s, Herbert Hoover—hardly a radical—recognized that financial-industry participants left to their own devices often produced usurious credit for all but the wealthiest homebuyers, and shut out many who could, with access to affordable, longer-term, fully amortizing mortgages, easily afford to own their homes (Immergluck 2004).

From beyond the perspective of neoclassical economics, modern progressives and institutionalists often argue that distributional issues take on paramount importance in examining policies and market structures in the financial arena, especially when it comes to housing finance. Even if a deregulatory move might result in slightly less expensive credit for the average consumer, its benefits might not be worth the costs, especially if they impose serious harm on some segment of households. Saving the average homeowner a few dollars per year on her mortgage via a deregulatory action might be viewed as less important than enabling a segment of families to access sustainable, affordable homeownership and protecting them from financial predators.

Because access to responsible credit means access to future economic opportunity, the denial of such credit to members of certain communities is likely to mean more than the simple sum of losses to a set of random individuals. It means that these communities will have their prospects for economic advancement diminished.

The Federal Role in Promoting Stable, Responsible, and Fair Mortgage Markets

Since the 1930s, the federal government has been a major supporter of and participant in mortgage markets, using a variety of tools and interventions to support access to credit, especially for moderate- and middle-income homeowners. From at least the 1920s up until the early 1980s, the largest provider of mortgage credit in the United States was the S&L. Other forms of lenders were significant providers of residential credit, including individuals, savings banks, life insurance companies, mortgage companies, and commercial banks. Almost twenty years ago, Michael Lea (1996) defined three periods in the history of mortgage markets in the United States. The "Origins" period began in 1831 with the formation of the first-known S&L (called a "building and loan"), and ended in 1931, before the Depression-era federal interventions in the housing market. The Capra-esque "Wonderful Life" period began in the early 1930s and lasted until the early 1980s. Then came the "Brave New World" era, in which Fannie Mae and Freddie Mac began to grow as government-sponsored securitization markets. In addition to these earlier eras described by Lea, two later periods have since occurred: "Privatization," from roughly 1995 until 2007, and "Conservatorship," from 2008 to the present.

In the "Origins" period, the earliest S&Ls were membership-based nonprofit associations, which served as home-buying savers clubs and were modeled on Britain's "Friendly Societies." These S&Ls would issue shares through regular contributions from members, and as capital accumulated, it was offered to members as mortgages. These were local institutions, with members all living in the same area and many of them knowing each other. When S&Ls began to expand and offer deposit services to nonborrowers, depositors and borrowers were decoupled, so that losses from defaulting borrowers were spread over more depositors. By 1931, of the 12 million S&L members among 12,000 institutions, only 2 million had mortgages (Hoffman 2001, p. 154). Mutual savings banks were similar in form to the S&L, except that they were originally organized primarily for encouraging savings, not for making mortgages. Life insurance and mortgage companies also made mortgages by the late nineteenth century. These national-scale lenders utilized independent agents—essentially mortgage brokers—to originate loans.

Supported by increased regulation, S&Ls grew significantly in the early twentieth century. By 1930, S&Ls held about one-third of the outstanding home mortgages in the United States (Hoffman 2001, p. 155). S&Ls and savings banks together held about 45 percent of mortgage debt. There were significant differences in the nature of credit provided by different types of lenders. S&Ls provided longer-term loans with lower down payment ratios than banks or insurance companies. The average term of mortgages made by S&Ls in the 1920s was eleven years, versus six to eight years for those made by insurance companies and two to three years for those made by commercial banks (Lea 1996). Shorter term, lower-loan-to-value loans made by banks and insurance companies often required a second mortgage, and such lenders often charged very high additional fees (15–20 percent of principal) and high interest rates (Gries and Ford 1932, p. 28). These second mortgages were offered by "marginal participants" in the financial industry, which were often unregulated and operated in violation of state usury laws.

The 1930s saw the first direct federal involvement in U.S. mortgage markets. Herbert Hoover's Federal Home Loan Bank Act of 1932 created the Federal Home Loan Bank system to provide liquidity to and support the growth of S&Ls. Hoover and others saw the longer-term, lower down payment mortgage provided by S&Ls as a key tool in promoting homeownership and stimulating the housing market (Hoffman 2001). By providing S&Ls with access to additional capital for mortgages, the Home Loan Banks promoted the S&L-type loan with longer maturities and lower down payments. The Home Loan Bank system also responded to geographic credit imbalances. Because S&Ls were usually local institutions, growing areas often had an excess demand for mortgages, whereas older parts of the country tended to have an excess supply of savings and investment. In providing a national system of inter-S&L liquidity, the Home Loan Bank system allowed money to flow around the country through a new secondary market system (Hoffman 2001).

When Franklin Roosevelt was elected, he pushed for more aggressive interventions in the housing market. Congress passed the Home Owners Loan Act (HOLA) of 1933, which was aimed at pulling people out of foreclosure. It created the Home Owners Loan Corporation (HOLC), which purchased mortgages in default, extended the term of loans, and lowered monthly payments (Hoffman 2001). HOLA also created the federal S&L charter that helped establish S&Ls in places where few existed.

The National Housing Act of 1934, which created the Federal Housing Administration (FHA) mortgage-insurance program, marked the next major federal involvement in mortgage markets. It also extended federal deposit insurance to S&Ls (banks had their deposits insured in 1933), which was critical to bringing in more deposits, and thus lending capacity, into the industry. Deposit insurance for S&Ls effectively established a federal backstop for the S&L system that dominated mortgage markets for much of the twentieth century.

FHA mortgage insurance established the twenty- (and later thirty-) year, fully amortizing, fixed-rate mortgage with a 20 percent down payment as the dominant mortgage format for the rest of the twentieth century and beyond. The FHA led to the standardization of mortgages generally, setting the stage for the eventual expansion of secondary market activity and securitization that dominated mortgage markets from the 1980s onward. This standardization eventually enabled mass automation and vertical specialization in underwriting, processing, and servicing loans. The FHA increased the supply of mortgage credit and institutionalized a new set of underwriting criteria, making mortgages more affordable. From the 1930s to the 1940s, the average term for mortgages made by S&Ls increased from eleven to fifteen years, and S&Ls were not even the major users of FHA insurance (Lea 1996). Overall, the average loan-to-value for mortgages increased from less than 60 percent to 75 percent, and the bulk of loans became fully amortizing.

The impact of the FHA on the housing market was unparalleled. By 1937, FHA housing starts accounted for 45 percent of all housing starts in the United States (Jackson 1985). In 1950, the agency accounted for 35 percent of starts. Together with the newer Veterans Administration (VA) loans, the two programs accounted for 48 percent of starts. After World War II and the growth of the VA program, the FHA gradually declined in market share, until the late 1960s when Congress authorized a substantial expansion of FHA activity, including a major subsidized-loan component. In 1970, FHA loans still accounted for almost 30 percent of single-family loans (Immergluck 2004).

In 1938, the Federal National Mortgage Association (later known as Fannie Mae) was created as a government agency to buy and sell FHA-insured loans, and thus provide liquidity to FHA lenders (Goodman 2014). Then, in 1954, Fannie Mae was converted into a joint public-private corporation, although it was still effectively controlled by the government. In 1968, due in part to Vietnam-era budgetary pressures, the company was converted into a private, shareholder-owned, though "government-sponsored" corporation. Two years later, Fannie Mae was allowed to buy and sell mortgages that were not federally insured, Ginnie Mae was created to buy FHA and VA loans, and Freddie Mac was created as an affiliate of the Federal Home Loan Banks to purchase conventional mortgages from S&Ls. In 1989, Freddie Mac was reorganized into a government-sponsored, shareholder-owned private corporation similar to Fannie Mae (Goodman 2014). Ginnie Mae remained a government agency.

The government-sponsored enterprises (GSEs), led by Freddie Mac, soon moved to using securitization as a way to fund mortgages. The standardization and commoditization of mortgages facilitated by the FHA and the Home Loan Bank System provided the framework for the securitization systems within the GSEs. Fannie and Freddie were increasingly able to offer low-cost funding to mortgage originators due to their scale efficiencies and favorable government-sponsored status. Mortgage companies utilizing the GSEs did not need the brick-and-mortar and deposit-taking apparatus that an S&L required. Market share shifted from S&Ls to mortgage companies and other lenders funded via the growing GSEs (Immergluck 2004). Over time, investors perceived an implicit government guarantee on mortgage-backed securities issued by the two government-sponsored firms. Their securities were often referred to as "agency securities," which fueled the perception of federal backing. Later on, as the GSEs grew and became perceived as "too big to fail," the firms' general obligation debt became more attractive to investors, allowing the firms to raise capital at very low costs. This fueled the tendency of the firms to move back toward holding mortgages and other assets on their balance sheets, because funding loans and investments this way was more profitable than funding them through securitization (Goodman 2014). However, this also concentrated and increased the risk exposure of the two mortgage giants over the long run.

The development of the fourth phase of mortgage markets—the "Privatization" era—has already been described in chapter 1. The rise of private-label securitization (PLS) was fueled by deregulatory federal policy, as well as explicit support for the financial infrastructure required by PLS. PLS emerged as a serious force in the 1990s, fueling the first, smaller subprime lending boom in the late 1990s and then, after recovering from the Asian and Russian financial crises, grew strongly in the 2000s. The growth of PLS-funded mortgages quickly ate into the market share of the GSEs in the middle 2000s, putting pressure on the GSEs to lower credit-quality standards in order to preserve some of their market share (Financial Crisis Inquiry Commission 2011; Goodman 2014).

The current era of U.S. mortgage markets—best labeled "Conservatorship"—began in 2008 when the federal government placed the GSEs into conservatorship, and the FHA renewed its larger role in financing homeownership. Since 2009, the GSEs and the FHA have accounted for the bulk of U.S. mortgage finance, essentially excluding only the very large loans that exceeded their size limits. Under conservatorship, the GSEs were essentially governed by the dictates of the Federal Housing Finance Agency, their conservator and regulator. While conservatorship was intended in the 2008 Housing and Economic Recovery Act to be temporary, it has evolved into a long-term phase, which will last until federal policymakers can come to agreement on a "permanent" structure for the U.S. housing-finance system. As Laurie Goodman (2014) has written, however, it remains unclear when any such restructuring will take place.

In sum, beginning in the 1930s, there were two major circuits of institutional housing finance, both of which were heavily dependent on federal involvement. The deposit-based S&L circuit was supported by deposit insurance, a federal thrift charter and associated regulation, the Home Loan Bank system, and, to a lesser degree, by FHA and VA insurance and guarantee programs. Insurance companies, mortgage companies, and commercial banks, supported heavily by the FHA and the then-government-owned Fannie Mae, provided a second circuit of mortgage funding. The S&L circuit dominated until the 1980s, when the emerging GSEs began dominating secondary markets, and government-sponsored securitization grew rapidly. The market share of the deposit-based S&L and FHA circuits were eroded to the benefit of the newer GSE-based circuit, which increasingly served as the principal funding source for mortgage companies, banks, and even the surviving S&Ls. In all of these circuits, the public sector seeded, nurtured, and was largely responsible for the size and functioning of mortgage markets. Only with the rise of deregulation and private-label securitization in the 1990s and 2000s did a predominantly private segment of the mortgage market become more ascendant—particularly via funding and originating high-risk loans.

THE FUTURE OF HOUSING FINANCE IN THE UNITED STATES

Since 2008, the mortgage market, other than the "jumbo" segment that finances the most expensive homes, has been dominated by two circuits: (1) those mortgages insured by the FHA or guaranteed by the VA; and (2) those purchased by Fannie Mae or Freddie Mac. Very few mortgages have been funded by banks or S&Ls holding mortgages on their balance sheets, or by private-label securitization. Fannie Mae and Freddie Mac, in turn, have remained under strict government control through the conservatorship enabled by the Housing and Economic Recovery Act of 2008. While the numbers have varied, the GSEs, together with the FHA and the VA, have enabled approximately 85 to 90 percent of the mortgage market for lower, moderate, and middle-income homeowners. Only jumbo loans have been significantly funded through other channels, including portfolio lending by banks and S&Ls or via a trickle of private-label securitization that has remained available to only the most credit-worthy borrowers purchasing expensive homes.

In the immediate aftermath of placing the GSEs into conservatorship, policymakers began discussing the long-term future of secondary mortgage markets. Federal Reserve chairman Ben Bernanke and secretary of the treasury Henry Paulson laid out a range of general policy alternatives ranging from privatization to permanent nationalization (Mosser, Tracy, and Wright 2013). Then, in 2011, pursuant to the Dodd-Frank Act, the Obama Administration issued a memo reframing the debate over the future of the GSEs (U.S. Department of the Treasury and U.S. Department of Housing and Urban Development 2011). This time, the option of a public-sector-dominated model was absent. This memo, which was cited time and again in more detailed proposals, outlined three general policy alternatives: (1) a system of relatively unregulated private-label securitization with no access to explicit government insurance or guarantees; (2) a system that relied on private-label securitization but with access to a countercyclical government backstop mechanism in which federal involvement would be geared up only in times of severe market distress; and (3) a more continuous, subordinate government role implemented via some form of reinsurance of private-market risk in a system that relied mostly on private-sector-led securitization.

Since GSE conservatorship began, policymakers, think tanks, academics, and industry associations have offered more than two dozen more detailed plans to restructure the mortgage market (Griffith 2013). While there are many technical differences among these proposals, they can be broken down into two broad models. The first model is best called "Full Privatization" and resembles the first alternative in the Obama Administration's 2011 policy memo. In these proposals, the GSEs are replaced with a lightly regulated system of private-label securitization, similar to what dominated the subprime market during the subprime boom. Advocates of this model argue that private financial markets, left to themselves, are in the best position to efficiently deliver mortgage credit, and will provide for stable and sound mortgage markets without government involvement. According to advocates of such proposals, government involvement in mortgage markets—through affordable-housing objectives or other duty-to-serve obligations—will distort otherwise-efficient markets and lead to risky lending practices. Not surprisingly, many advocates of these sorts of proposals tend to lay the blame for the mortgage crisis on federal housing policy, excessive regulation, and generally too much federal involvement in housing finance (Panchuk 2013; Wallison, Pollack, and Pinto 2011).

Even for those who favor removing the role of government from markets in general, the privatization model has a fatal flaw. Realistically, the housing market is too big and too interwoven with the American economy to expect that the federal government will not intercede in the event of a major housing market collapse. The only two major national-scale housing market crises in modern history—the Great Depression and the more recent housing crisis—provide ample proof of this. In both of these events, the collapse of the housing and real estate economies drove the nation into severe economic crisis and federal interventions followed shortly afterward to "bail out" the private sector. In both cases, however, the government absorbed many of the losses without receiving the gains in the booming build-up to the crisis. As Phillip Swagel (2014), a former assistant secretary of the Treasury Department under President George W. Bush, points out, "A full private mortgage market might seem attractive on paper, but it ignores the political and financial reality that any future Congress and President will act to stabilize mortgage markets if Americans cannot obtain home loans." Privatization, more than any other prototype for restructuring mortgage markets, would lead to the privatization of gains and the socialization of losses in the housing sector. Moreover, advocates for this approach also tend to be advocates for minimal federal regulation of mortgage and financial markets more generally. The market fundamentalists who propose a lightly regulated, volatile system of privatized housing finance do so despite the fact that the public sector will absorb the costs of future busts. Such a system will also expose homeowners and neighborhoods to the same sort of yield-chasing, aggressive lenders financed via private-label securitization.

The most commonly proposed alternative to privatization is what some have called the hybrid model, but what I call here "Partial Privatization." This model is similar to the third option identified in the Obama Administration's 2011 memo. In these proposals, much of the infrastructure of securitization is owned and operated by private-sector entities that are regulated to some degree. These plans call for some federal role in the mortgage market beyond consumer regulation. This role generally involves providing a form of secondary guaranty or insurance of mortgage-backed securities issued by private investment banks. One form that this guaranty might take is federal mortgage bond insurance linked to private mortgage bond insurance. Typically, this insurance (or what might be thought of as reinsurance) would be issued on a guarantor basis, meaning that a private bond guarantor would guarantee a mortgage bond and the federal insurance would only kick in if the guarantor were no longer financially solvent. Generally, the private guarantor would need to hold between 5 to 10 percent of the total dollar amount of all mortgage bonds that it insured as capital. Other proposals would allow for bond-specific insurance or guarantees, and only require that the guarantor hold 5 to 10 percent of the particular mortgage bonds being insured. (Given the possibility of some mortgage bonds being considerably riskier than others, 5–10 percent capital on a per-deal basis is likely to be less robust than 5–10 percent on a guarantee firm's entire book of business.)

Some of these plans—including the most promising bipartisan proposals—would require that securitizations be conducted through a federally regulated "securitization platform," and access to federal insurance would require participating issuers of mortgage bonds to follow the standards of the platform. Some of these plans call for the platform to be owned by participating originating lenders in a cooperative structure, similar to how Federal Home Loan Banks are owned by their member banks and S&Ls. Private firms could still purchase and aggregate loans and ultimately issue the securities in most of these plans.

In most partial-privatization proposals, private-sector bond guarantors or insurers would drive much of the pricing of the underlying mortgages, since they would absorb most of the expected losses in noncatastrophic conditions. Such systems would likely lead to a much higher degree of "risk-based pricing" than was present in the traditional GSE circuit. In the traditional GSE system, the somewhat-higher expected losses of some borrowers were effectively cross-subsidized by others with lower expected losses. (The

GSEs, under conservatorship, have moved toward modest risk-based pricing; however, major cross-subsidization remains in the system.) This means that a broad range of mortgage borrowers received one standard mortgage rate. In the subprime market, which was funded by private-label securitization, borrowers assessed as higher risks were given much higher interest rates. (Moreover, mortgage brokers and originators often had additional incentives to layer on even higher costs to borrowers whenever possible.)

While risk-based pricing is based on the risk-return expectations of most private investors, it often leads to outcomes where those least able to afford higher interest rates are forced to pay them. Higher interest rates (or fees) then translate into higher monthly payments and a larger payment-to-income ratio, which in turn can increase delinquency and default rates, resulting in a vicious circle of weaker credit leading to higher-cost mortgages leading to even weaker credit. A one percentage-point increase in mortgage rates has been found to increase the rate of homeownership termination by 30 percent (Haurin and Rosenthal 2004). Additionally, higher mortgage costs reduce the financial benefits from homeownership and can substantially reduce the likelihood that owning makes more financial sense than renting for a particular household (Belsky, Retsinas, and Duda 2007; Herbert, McCue, and Sanchez-Moyano 2013).

Risk-based pricing can also foster highly segmented markets, in which certain groups of borrowers are steered toward higher-cost lenders, while other groups are steered toward lower-cost lenders (White 2009). Real estate agents or mortgage brokers might use race, income, or other characteristics as signals for credit quality and, perhaps in efforts to get a quick loan approval, steer borrowers toward higher-cost lenders.

Since the Obama Administration issued its 2011 memo on the future of the GSEs, there has been little discussion of a third option for restructuring housing finance—a permanent public option. In a public-option model, securitization markets would be more vertically integrated, similar to the way the private-sector GSEs operated before private-label securitization. One entity would purchase and/or aggregate mortgages from originating lenders, then bundle the mortgages into pools and issue securities backed by the loans in those pools. Contrary to the traditional GSE circuit, however, this entity would be a government-owned corporation with no private shareholders. This organization might contract out many of its day-to-day tasks to private contractors, but at the end of the day, the public organization would govern the primary aspects of the securitization process. The public option would allow the public sector to retain most of the profits derived from mortgage securitization, as well as accept the risk of catastrophic failure.

A stronger, more vertically integrated federal role in the secondary mortgage market, where a publicly owned institution provides the dominant channel for loan funding, would align the risk and rewards of housing finance better than the partial-privatization model, where the federal role is an indirect, catastrophic insurer of private mortgage-backed securities. In the public-option model, the public sector not only would assume the downside risks of a major housing-market failure—as it would in either the privatization or partial-privatization models—but would also reap a greater share of the upside revenues generated through the securitization process in better times. Moreover, by discouraging excessively risky activities, such a system is likely to lead to fewer mortgage crises.

Some advocates of partially or fully privatizing mortgage markets recognize the problems with the wild-west nature of the private-label securitization market of the 2000s. They suggest that newly constrained securitization markets and stronger consumer-protection laws will prevent the same irresponsible lending that private securitization fueled during the subprime boom (Bipartisan Policy Center 2013; Wartell 2011). Many also argue that the crisis has permanently changed investor behavior, resulting in less gullible investors. Stronger consumer-protection regulations will make it difficult for lenders to push high-risk products, and stronger regulations and more transparency in the securities markets will make it difficult to attract investment into irresponsible and excessively risky activities.

In this way, the privatization models hinge critically on the strength and permanence of the post-crisis regulatory reforms. They assume that the new consumer-protection laws will be vigorously implemented and not weakened over time by financial-sector lobbying and a fading public memory of the financial crisis. They assume that new regulations—some of which have turned out to be quite weak—will inhibit deceptive or irresponsible practices among various actors in the securitization process. Most partial-privatization proposals—including those contained in the 2013 Corker-Warner and 2014 Johnson-Crapo bills—depend critically on a new federal agency that issues insurance for mortgage-backed securities to be a strong regulator that avoids regulatory capture. The history of financial regulation, and the political power of the financial-services industry, suggests that consumer-protection or securities regulation may not be sufficient to restrain financial markets from reckless activity over the long run.

The public option would provide a heavily regulated, vertically integrated system of securitization supervised by a government-owned corporation through which all securitization is channeled. Such a model does not mean that all capital in the mortgage market would come from the public sector. Private investors would still be purchasing the mortgage-backed securities, which contain the bulk of the interest rate and prepayment risk. Moreover, risk sharing with the private sector could still occur by off-loading some of the back-end risk of the corporation onto the private sector through risk-sharing agreements or reinsurance. Some of these arrangements have already been developed under GSE conservatorship (Fannie Mae 2014a). The key is that the loan-funding channel—from the purchase and aggregation of recently originated mortgages to the issuing of securities backed by such mortgages—would run through the same organization. In the vertically dis-integrated private securitization stream of the 2000s, there were too many opportunities for various parties to pass off a sow's ear as a silk purse.

Why Has the Public Option Received So Little Consideration?

As of this writing, the public option has received little serious attention in the policy debates over the future of housing finance in the United States. Of the more than two dozen formal proposals identified for the restructuring of the GSEs—most of which were developed after the Obama Administration outlined its view of the alternatives—none resemble the public option described here (Griffith 2013). Most of these proposals were developed under the assumption that a public-sector-centered proposal was not politically viable. The failure to seriously consider a public option was tied to at least two major factors. The first was related to the political toxicity of Fannie Mae and Freddie Mac, and the persistence of the mistaken notion that federal housing policy—especially affordable housing policy—was at the heart of the subprime crisis. As long as many view the crisis as tied closely to federal interventions in the housing market, those favoring a small federal role in the mortgage market are at an advantage. Despite the overwhelming evidence that deregulation and increased privatization were the major factors driving the crisis, the market fundamentalists won many of the rhetorical and political battles. Well-funded conservative groups such as the American Enterprise Institute (AEI), as well as many in Congress, effectively maintained the myth that too much—rather than too little—government was the cause of the crisis. They have been particularly effective because of their ready access to an influential media outlet, the *Wall Street Journal*, to get out their message. As shown in chapter 1, the *Journal* published over forty articles by two key AEI staffers, Peter Wallison and Edward Pinto, during the height of the crisis. The bulk of these were commentary pieces that argued that the federal affordable-housing and community-reinvestment policies were a principal cause of the crisis. The *Journal* served as a highly influential amplifier for the AEI and its conservative allies.

A second factor worked to limit the range of policy alternatives to those that relied on private securitization as the core of a new mortgage-finance system. The modern structure of the financial-services industry and its close ties to policymakers, housing advocates, think tanks, and interest groups helped keep the debate centered on alternatives that built off the dominant, securitization-based financial infrastructure that had emerged over the last thirty years. Shortly after conservatorship in 2008, there were some discussions of a public-option model, or of fostering a "covered-bond" market of the sort used in other industrialized countries, in which banks hold mortgages on their balance sheets but then issue corporate bonds using mortgages to provide collateral for the bonds. However, as time went on, the very dense housing-finance policy network coalesced around a consensus that had two dominant characteristics: (1) a central goal of increasing the amount of private capital flowing into the mortgage market (as opposed to, say, a goal of providing access to safe and affordable mortgages for a wide spectrum of borrowers); and (2) a fundamental reliance on the apparatus of private securitization. Many of the financial economists, financial-services professionals, and even some nonprofit housing advocates that were part of this policy network had close ties to financial firms with vested interests in resurrecting a robust market in private-label mortgage-backed securities. Securitization, including private-label securitization, has been a major driver of the financialization of the economy over the last three decades (Gotham 2009). This financialization has had a political dimension too, as financial firms have been very aggressive in interacting with federal policymakers and their networks. Thus, the center of gravity in the mortgage-market policy network includes many individuals and organizations with interests and worldviews favoring the primacy of Wall Street institutions. If a public-option model were selected in the restructuring of the mortgage market, the opportunities for outsized profits and extreme levels of compensation would be curtailed.

The Costs and Inequities of Private-Sector-Dominated Mortgage Markets

A key aspect of the partial and full privatization proposals that has received little attention is the impact that such moves will have on the pricing of mortgages and, in particular, the substantial differences in mortgage costs that borrowers of different circumstances will face in the mortgage market. In the stable period of mortgage markets from the late 1930s to the middle 1990s, most borrowers paid essentially the same interest rates for their mortgages. FHA borrowers faced slightly higher mortgage costs due to a modest mortgage-insurance premium, as did borrowers with conventional loans who were required to obtain private mortgage insurance due to not putting at least 20 percent down when purchasing their homes. However, the effects of these charges on effective interest rates were quite modest. These mortgage markets, which were federally supported through deposit insurance, the FHA, and the GSEs, gave a wide spectrum of borrowers access to the same fundamental mortgage products, with only small differences in costs and terms. Those with somewhat-riskier credit profiles were effectively cross-subsidized by lower-risk borrowers. This kept interest rates relatively low for the borrowers with lower credit scores, which, in turn, provided them with reasonable monthly mortgage payments. Access to affordable, mainstream financing reduces mortgage risk and default rates, providing moderate- and middle-income homeowners with better chances to succeed as homeowners. Cross-subsidization broadens the risk pool in the system and makes for a less volatile and generally fairer mortgage market. As mortgage markets become more privatized, segmentation by risk becomes more likely, and borrowers with even moderately lower credit scores are likely to pay substantially higher mortgage rates. The ability of higher-cost lenders to steer some borrowers into mortgages that cost even more than risk-based pricing justifies can exacerbate mortgage-rate disparities even further.

Risk-based pricing is expected whenever private capital is asked to bear the bulk of the mortgage default risk. Attempts to cross-subsidize in private markets are difficult, because competing private capital will look to peel off the lowest-risk borrowers by offering them lower-priced mortgages. Risk-based pricing in mortgage markets also tends toward different groups of lenders specializing in different levels of risk, and a greater potential for steering certain groups of borrowers toward higher-cost lenders.

While the provision of federal catastrophic insurance would allow a partially privatized system to provide long-term, fixed-rate mortgages and lower the overall cost of mortgages compared to a fully privatized system, catastrophic insurance only addresses the "tail risk" in the mortgage market, which is usually triggered by a major housing-market collapse when private mortgage bond guarantors might be wiped out. Much of the more routine risk in mortgage markets would be assumed by private bond guarantors or some type of private credit enhancement. This is where significant differentials in mortgage pricing would arise, because the bond guarantors would charge more to insure pools of loans with riskier characteristics.

In 2013, the Bipartisan Policy Center's Housing Commission hired noted mortgage-securitization analyst Andrew Davidson & Co. to forecast the effects of restructuring mortgage secondary markets into a system of private-label securitization with access to a catastrophic federal guaranty of the sort employed in many of the partial-privatization proposals (Bipartisan Policy Center 2013). The company estimated different "annual credit charges" that would be entailed under various assumptions, including differences in credit scores and loan-to-value ratios, and how the private-sector insurance or credit enhancement was provided. The firm also created a set of scenarios assuming that loan-level private mortgage insurance was available in the event of mortgage default and foreclosure, as well as a set assuming that such insurance was not available. The latter was done because many mortgage insurers were not able to pay off on many insured loans during the mortgage crisis.

Figure 5.3 plots some of the key results of the Davidson & Co. analysis with the assumption that increases in interest rates due to the private bond guaranty would be similar to those generated by private-label securitization, in which subordinate tranches in mortgage-backed securities would absorb higher credit risks. It shows the premium, or increased interest rate, that borrowers would pay under different credit-score and loan-to-value levels, and with and without the availability of private mortgage insurance. The figure indicates a range (depending on whether private mortgage insurance was available) of interest-rate premiums that a borrower would face compared to a very low-risk reference case—a borrower with a very high credit (FICO) score of between 750 and 800, and a modest loan-to-value ratio of 80 to 85 percent, which suggests a substantial down payment of 15 to 20 percent.

As figure 5.3 indicates, a borrower with a credit score between 650 and 700 and a down payment of 5–10 percent is expected to face a mortgage with an interest rate between 1.3 and 2.4 percentage points higher than the very-high-credit-score, large-down-payment borrower. It is important to point out that these estimates assume only a small likelihood of a major decline in housing prices and, during a period of market distress, the higher-risk borrowers will likely see much higher interest-rate differentials. It is also important to recognize that a borrower with these characteristics—a credit score between 650 and 700 and a down payment between 5 and 10 percent—would generally not be considered a high-risk or subprime borrower. As Kent Colton and Michael Carliner from the Havard Joint Center for Housing Studies have pointed out, even a borrower with a 620 FICO score and a 5 percent down payment would have been considered a prime borrower prior to the

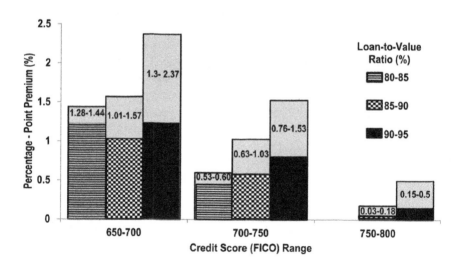

Figure 5.3. Interest-Rate Premiums Expected Under Partial Privatization.
Source: Prepared by author from data in Adam Davidson & Co., Inc. (2013), analysis prepared for the Bipartisan Policy Center (2013).

housing crisis (Colton and Carliner 2014). In 2000, well before the subprime home-purchase lending boom that began in 2003, over 25 percent of first-time mortgage borrowers had credit scores below 620 (Duke 2013).

These differences in mortgage costs are almost certain to have disparate impacts across homeowners of different racial and ethnic groups, and across different neighborhoods. In 2010, after the evaporation of the subprime market, the mean credit score of blacks receiving home purchase loans was 677, and the mean score for Hispanics was 701, while the mean for nonhispanic whites was 734 (Bhutta and Canner 2013). These thirty- to sixty-point differentials in mean credit scores means that many borrowers of color will receive higher-cost mortgages than white borrowers. Residential segregation means that these differences will also have a geographic effect, with minority neighborhoods facing substantially higher mortgage costs than white neighborhoods. These differences in mortgage costs are not trivial. For a $150,000 mortgage, each percentage point in higher interest rates will result in an increase in annual housing costs of over $1,000, and this does not include likely differences in mortgage-insurance premiums and other financing costs. Thus, a homeowner with a credit score just below 700 who put down a 5–10 percent down payment would expect to pay at least $1,300 to $2,370 more per year on a $150,000 mortgage than a borrower with a credit score above 750 who can afford a 15–20 percent down payment. In effect, risk-based pricing creates a penalty for those in the mortgage market with less wealth and less-than-stellar credit.

Other estimates on the interest-rate premiums that borrowers with less-than-stellar credit would face exceed the conservative estimates presented in figure 5.3. Fannie Mae prepared estimates for the Senate Banking Committee of the impact on mortgage rates for different types of borrowers from the proposed 2014 Johnson-Crapo bill. These projections suggest that a borrower with a credit score just under 700 and a down payment of less than 20 percent would face mortgage rates that were 0.9 to 2.7 percentage points higher than borrowers with credit scores above 740 and similar down payments (Fannie Mae 2014b). When considering differences in down payments as well as in credit scores, the potential differences in mortgage rates reached 3.5 percentage points.

Again, these large risk-based pricing differentials assume the presence of a federal guaranty against catastrophic risk. A full-privatization plan, which provides for no federal backstop, would entail even higher levels of interest-rate differentials that would cost modest-income borrowers even more.

AFFORDABLE, FAIR, AND STABLE MORTGAGE MARKETS
MAKE FOR STRONGER NEIGHBORHOODS AND CITIES

The high-risk, reckless mortgage markets of the early to mid-2000s did great harm to many neighborhoods and cities. The subprime and high-risk loan markets fueled highly speculative, irresponsible real estate investors and fraudsters looking to flip homes as fast as they could at inflated, unsustainable prices. They also fueled the construction of overly large homes in exurban locations far from jobs and without access to affordable transportation options. As a result, as described in chapter 2, inner-city neighborhoods, minority suburbs, and new fringe exurbs in many metropolitan areas were hit hard when the bubble burst and foreclosures surged. Overly aggressive, under-regulated lending leads to boom-bust housing markets not just at the metropolitan level, but also at the neighborhood level. They fuel irrational speculation as frothy appraisals fuel additional frothy appraisals, and investors flock to neighborhoods following word of quick flips that yield substantial profits despite little investment in the housing stock. Aggressive mortgage markets can fuel rapid price increases, especially in markets where housing supply cannot keep pace with the credit-induced demand, or fuel overbuilding in metro areas with more elastic housing supply (Chan, Haughwout, and Tracy 2014).

Notwithstanding the damage caused by reckless mortgage markets, returning to a mortgage market where 20 to 30 percent down payments are always required, and long-term, affordable, fixed-rate loans are not available would also be devastating to many cities and neighborhoods. Since the advent of the VA mortgage in the middle of the twentieth century, low down payments have successfully opened up credit access to a broad set of working- and middle-class families over many decades.

While low-down-payment mortgages, especially when used in combination with risky mortgage features such as high debt-to-income ratios, limited income documentation, or adjustable rates, can lead to higher risks of default, responsible low-down-payment mortgages can be originated at acceptable levels of risk (Quercia, Freeman, and Ratcliffe 2011; Reid and Quercia 2013). Moreover, requiring 20 percent or higher down payments from families with limited wealth can force them to put a much larger share of their savings into their house, making diversifying their assets all but impossible. Finally, lower down payments allow families without access to affluent friends or relatives to access homeownership. After all, requiring larger down payments is unlikely to constrain the homeownership fortunes of young families with affluent parents. However, it would have a significant effect on the options facing families from more modest circumstances.

Access to long-term, fixed-rate mortgages has also been critical to sustainable homeownership. Fixed-rate mortgages have consistently outperformed adjustable-rate mortgages in terms of default risk. The fixed-rate mortgage provides moderate and middle-income families with a predictable, stable form of forced savings that allows for easy and predictable budgeting.

Excessively tight mortgage markets will cut off many housing options for low- and moderate-income families. Many of these will be relegated to rental markets that are not very tenant-friendly. Even if families can afford to purchase a home, high down-payment requirements or risk-based pricing may severely limit their options, since they will not be able to afford the same home that they could with a lower down payment and lower-cost mortgage. By restricting the housing options of low- and moderate-income families, overly restrictive mortgage markets are also likely to lead to greater economic and racial segregation (Lee 2013).

The conclusion will review the key themes and findings of the book and outline a broad policy agenda. It will consider some of the expected realities of future policymaking options as well as longer-term, more fundamental lessons for producing sound, affordable, and fair housing markets in the United States.

Conclusions and the Way Forward

This book began by reviewing the causes of the great mortgage crisis of the 2000s. The crisis was proximately caused by a surge of subprime mortgage lending in the early to mid-2000s. The flood of subprime mortgages pushed up values in many housing markets and fueled explosive growth in home-building in others. By decoupling repayment ability from the underwriting process and by allowing for large-scale irresponsible lending, unsustainable price appreciation and development increased in many places. Mortgage lenders—and the housing industry—took advantage of what seemed to many to be perpetual home-price appreciation to peddle aggressive mortgage products. As long as prices continued to rise, fears of foreclosure were minimized, because borrowers could refinance or sell their homes. The instability of the subprime model was ignored by most industry and regulatory players, although ample warnings came from different quarters.

When home prices finally hit a ceiling in the hottest housing markets, and began their decline, foreclosures surged nationally, setting off a vicious cycle of price declines and foreclosures. Wholesale funders froze funding available to subprime lenders, and most of these lenders folded or shrank dramatically. Credit markets contracted quickly across the country, which in turn triggered price declines and housing distress in additional local markets. As housing prices fell and residential construction ground to a halt, the broader economy began hemorrhaging jobs. In 2008 and 2009, as the Great Recession roared, more people lost their jobs, and housing values continued to decline, many homeowners with prime mortgages became delinquent on their mortgages, leading to millions more foreclosures.

This surge in subprime lending in the early 2000s—which followed a smaller surge in the late 1990s—was fueled by capital flooding into a relatively new circuit of mortgage credit via private-label securitization (PLS).

This circuit took advantage of a decades-long structural shift to deregulated mortgage markets. Yield-hungry, risky capital has a habit of seeking out less regulated and more lucrative markets. The PLS circuit funneled reckless mortgages into vulnerable communities. From the 1930s up until the emergence of PLS, U.S. mortgage markets had generally flowed through three circuits. First, there was the FHA circuit, which involved mortgage companies, banks, and S&Ls making loans insured by the FHA and then usually selling them via the government agency Ginnie Mae (formerly through Fannie Mae). A second major institutional circuit of mortgage credit was deposit-based lending that flowed through S&Ls and (to some degree) commercial banks, which received federal deposit insurance to attract deposits and borrowed from the Federal Home Loan Banks to finance their mortgage activity. The third major circuit, which grew rapidly in the last quarter of the twentieth century, was the GSE-funded circuit, which connected relatively conservative investors to credit markets through a standardized, risk-limiting government-sponsored securitization channel.

In the 1990s and 2000s, a mortgage market circuit that attracted higher-risk capital emerged. Private-label securitization (PLS) markets took advantage of the growth of originate-to-distribute channels that had developed in the last quarter of the twentieth century. In the 1980s, federal legislation laid the groundwork for the weakening of state banking and mortgage regulation, and for the favorable regulatory climate and tax treatment for mortgage securitization. The relatively stable, standardized, and risk-limiting channel of securitization through the government-sponsored enterprises (GSEs), Fannie Mae and Freddie Mac, had grown rapidly in the 1980s and 1990s, as deposit-based lending by S&Ls declined sharply. S&Ls relied on more expansive brick-and-mortar and deposit-based funding, and suffered from the deregulatory moves of the 1980s that had allowed them to enter the commercial real estate market, with disastrous results. The growth of the GSE funding circuit fed the vertical dis-integration of the mortgage industry, and the growth of the originate-to-distribute model of lending. The number of mortgage brokers skyrocketed and mortgage companies increased their market share. Mortgage companies and brokers were less subject to regular supervision and regulation than S&Ls and banks. Increasingly, large commercial banking firms began running much of their mortgage-lending operations through affiliated, less-regulated mortgage companies. Mortgage companies were not regularly examined for compliance with antidiscrimination policies such as the federal Fair Housing Act, nor were they covered by the Community Reinvestment Act.

By the late 1980s and early 1990s, the mortgage market had become functionally dominated by originators that were lightly regulated and employed an originate-to-distribute model of mortgage lending. They would originate mortgages and then quickly sell them to the GSEs or, in the case of

FHA loans, to Ginnie Mae. However, these mortgages were highly standard-ized and risk-limited.

Not until PLS investors began to grow in the early to mid-1990s was there a significant appetite for higher-risk and subprime mortgages from a much broader array of originators. These higher-risk investors, in turn, fed a new supply of high-risk credit that spurred the formation of specialized, subprime lenders who needed little capital to begin lending. They could take advantage of the vast number of mortgage brokers that had sprouted up over the previ-ous two decades and the infrastructure of loan arrangers, wholesale lenders, and other pieces of securitization infrastructure that had developed. All that was needed were the Wall Street firms who would engineer the highly struc-tured mortgage-backed securities. With the advent of collateralized debt obli-gations, even more demand for higher-risk tranches of mortgage securities was synthesized and investor demand for subprime mortgage-backed secur-ities grew even more.

RESISTING FALSE NARRATIVES

Contrary to some persistent myths, the subprime boom was not the result of government housing policy or too much government involvement in the mortgage market. In fact, it was the result of the shrinking coverage of effective regulatory oversight of the mortgage market—which began in the early 1980s—and the growth of a new, almost-fully privatized channel of high-risk mortgage credit, which was funded by PLS sources. Yes, subprime lenders and their allies argued that increasing homeownership was a good thing, but they lobbied for privatization and less regulation—not for afford-able housing policies—as the means to that end. Instilling fear that greater regulation would dramatically restrict homeownership opportunities was their primary political defense against stronger regulation. This defense was largely successful in blocking effective federal legislation or rulemaking be-fore the crisis, and in convincing federal regulators to preempt state consu-mer-protection laws.

As detailed in chapter 1, a substantial body of research has now conclu-sively shown that neither the Community Reinvestment Act nor the Afford-able Housing Goals applied to the GSEs were contributors to the subprime boom and ensuing crisis. If anything, the timidity of these policies, and the fact that the CRA did not cover independent mortgage companies, may have made vulnerable populations and communities more vulnerable to lightly regulated subprime lenders and mortgage brokers. GSEs were foolish late-comers to the subprime party, and not among the primary instigators. Too little regulation was again the primary problem, with the GSEs' weak regula-tor failing to require them to maintain adequate capital and allowing them to buy higher-risk loans in 2006 and 2007 in order to preserve their share of the overall mortgage market. Holding subprime PLS on their balance sheets helped drive the firms into conservatorship, and their exposure to Alt-A and other exotic loans—combined with falling property values—eventually cost them billions in the short run. (In the end, the government's investment in the GSEs has been more than paid back, and was critical to preventing an even greater calamity in the housing market.)

THE COSTLY AND UNEVEN IMPACTS OF THE CRISIS

The mortgage crisis hit minority homeowners and minority neighborhoods particularly hard. It was not just low-income neighborhoods that were affected, but also many moderate-income, minority communities. Subprime lenders, after all, lent to many homeowners, so moderate-income neighborhoods with appreciable homeownership rates were choice targets. Because minority homeowners tended to have fewer financial assets like stocks and bonds, their homes generally accounted for a larger portion of their net worth. This, combined with their greater likelihood of receiving high-risk subprime loans, meant that when foreclosures surged and property values fell in neighborhoods with many subprime loans, minority families tended to experience much larger declines in wealth than white families. Younger families and families with children also suffered disproportionately, because they were more likely to have borrowed during the subprime boom than older and childless couples.

Despite the crisis often being portrayed in the media as a problem of either booming exurbs or distressed inner cities, the reality was more complicated and regionally contextualized. In metropolitan areas where housing prices soared during the boom and where foreclosures had been very low before the crisis, the locus of foreclosures did tend to be more suburban, especially in metropolitan areas with high central-city housing values. Many of these metropolitan areas were in California and Florida, as well as in Nevada and Arizona. The booming suburbs or exurbs that had been developed largely on the back of the subprime boom came crashing to a halt, and half-built subdivisions and "pipe farms" were left as symbols of irrational exuberance and deregulatory excess. In many other cities, however, a great deal of subprime lending—especially refinance lending—was concentrated in minority central-city or inner-suburban communities. This was a common scenario in slower-growth metros, where subprime lenders both had been the only game in town for many homeowners and had funded bouts of often highly speculative investment in small rental properties by landlords. Metropolitan areas falling into this category included Cleveland, Detroit, and Chicago. In some metropolitan areas, including Atlanta and Minneapolis, the subprime crisis was both exurban and urban; inner-city and newer sprawling suburban neighborhoods were both hit hard.

As the subprime crisis morphed into a broader mortgage crisis with many prime loans entering foreclosure, the intrametropolitan incidence of the crisis began to spread out. In the metropolitan areas where the crisis began mostly in central-city neighborhoods, it spread into the suburbs. Meanwhile, where the crisis began in the new exurbs, it spread into established suburbs that had been largely built and financed before the subprime boom.

The longer-term legacies of the subprime crisis are particularly clustered in low- and moderate-income and, especially, minority neighborhoods. More than five years after the crisis began, thousands of neighborhoods around the country have very high rates of underwater homeowners, and these communities are disproportionately minority neighborhoods.

Chapter 2 detailed the costs of foreclosure and demonstrated that they go far beyond the financial losses to the borrower and lender. The costs include effects on children's schooling, psychological and physical health, and the quality of neighborhood life. Foreclosure represents a shock to families, children, and neighborhoods that often results in forced residential and school mobility, emotional and psychological stress, declines in local home values, potential increases in vacant buildings, blight and crime, and fiscal stresses on local governments. Declining property values, in turn, can drag many homeowners underwater, so that their outstanding mortgages exceed their homes' values. This can dampen local spending and make it difficult for people to move in search of better employment options. Some of these broader impacts on regional and national economies are not the focus of this book, but have been discussed widely elsewhere (e.g., Mian and Sufi 2014).

The now-evident costs of mortgage distress and foreclosure, especially those that spill over onto neighborhoods, communities, and the broader economy, provide ample justification for regulating mortgage markets more carefully, and for providing greater protections for homeowners and communities. At the same time, it is important to recognize that policies that go overboard and make mortgage markets excessively risk-averse and restrictive pose their own set of problems, problems that are likely to disproportionately harm the same communities that bore the brunt of the crisis. If mortgages become overly restrictive or much less affordable in hard-hit neighborhoods, it will be even more difficult for them to recover. Any new mortgage-market architecture must prioritize equitable and affordable access to credit for all sorts of borrowers and neighborhoods.

FEDERAL EFFORTS TO REDUCE FORECLOSURES FELL SHORT, ESPECIALLY FOR THE HARDEST-HIT COMMUNITIES

The federal response to the foreclosure crisis was inadequate to address the scale of the problem and the vicious cycles catalyzed by mortgage distress. The response to the crisis improved over time, but because it took several years to become effective, the families and neighborhoods hit earliest during the crisis were generally not well served by the federal response. The crisis first hit those neighborhoods that had been at the center of the subprime lending boom—especially communities of color, both in cities and in sprawling exurbs. The timidity of the initial response also made it difficult to arrest the cycles of home-price declines, property distress, and credit withdrawal that fueled the spread and deepening of the crisis. This is not to argue that federal efforts were inconsequential or futile. Rather, the point is that these efforts came too slowly and with insufficient vigor to have large impacts on the most vulnerable communities and to contain the problem before it snowballed beyond the point where policy interventions could be more effective.

Until the middle of 2009, federal efforts were comprised mainly of modestly funded foreclosure-prevention counseling and voluntary, feel-good partnerships with the securitization and lending industries to increase loan modifications, many of which did not reduce mortgage payments even in the face of financial distress. Even after the Obama Administration began its Making Home Affordable initiative in 2009, these programs were slow to get started and took years to get up a real head of steam. More powerful and forceful actions would have been more successful in stemming the flow of foreclosures, thereby reducing their large spillover costs on families, on neighborhoods, and on the regional and national economies.

The legislation that funded the Troubled Asset Relief Program, the Emergency Economic Stabilization Act (EESA) of 2008, provided substantial funding for foreclosure prevention and relief efforts. However, the Bush Administration, while initiating efforts to address the problems of insolvent or financially distressed banks—including many of the largest financial institutions in the country—effectively ignored the provisions in EESA for aid to distressed homeowners. Not only was this unwise, but it also fueled public perception that EESA and other federal responses to the crisis were aimed at helping Wall Street interests rather than Main Street homeowners and regular citizens.

As President Obama came into office with stronger proposals for assisting homeowners, a perhaps less anticipated surge of public hostility rose against his proposals, led by ideological opponents to government intervention in the housing market. As news of a proposed plan to provide financial assistance to homeowners arrived, Rick Santelli, a floor-walker on CNBC's morning stock-market television show, went into his now-famous rant against "loser mortgages," in which he was able to stir up the wrath first of commodity traders and later, as the video went viral, millions of viewers who became instantly hostile to the notion of helping "undeserving" borrowers who had gotten into trouble with their mortgages. Santelli's call, during which he made reference to a need for a "Tea Party," fed into the growing antipathy from the right for the new president and the rapidly emerging Tea Party movement. Thus, as the Administration was attempting to rectify the complaint that billions were flowing to banks while homeowners received paltry sums for mortgage counseling, attempts to be more aggressive in helping homeowners met instant resistance from the political right.

Beyond hostility from those inspired by the Santelli rant, efforts to be more forceful in responding to the crisis also suffered from other forms of opposition. Many economists, including some within the Obama Administration, argued that strong efforts to assist borrowers could produce moral hazard effects, in which borrowers intentionally stop paying their mortgages in order to qualify for federal assistance. However, there was no evidence that delinquencies would increase substantially due to aggressive loan modifications. Moreover, any modest moral-hazard effect would likely have been an acceptable cost given the much larger reduction in foreclosures that a more forceful policy response could produce. An excessive fear of moral hazard was perhaps most evident in the Administration's failure to push hard for bankruptcy reform, under which judges would have been allowed to modify home loans via the bankruptcy process. While bankruptcy reform was originally touted as a "stick" to complement the carrots of incentive payments to services and investors for modifying mortgages, this stick never came to be. In this and many other, smaller details, the design of the Making Home Affordable program—as well as other aspects of the Administration's response to the crisis—effectively kowtowed to the priorities and preferences of the financial-services industry.

The most successful component of the direct federal response to the foreclosure crisis was the Home Affordable Refinance Program (HARP), especially what became known as HARP 2.0, which involved a set of changes to the original HARP initiative. When lenders complained of too great of a risk that they might have to buy back loans from the GSEs, the program guidelines were changed to reduce the chances of such repurchases and to allow lenders to refinance loans with substantially higher loan-to-value ratios. After these changes went into effect in late 2011, HARP activity increased markedly. However, HARP required borrowers to be current on their loans, and so did not help many of the most distressed borrowers. From a macroeconomic perspective, the program made a great deal of sense, because it allowed homeowners to lower their mortgage costs significantly, freeing up household funds for local spending. Moreover, it likely prevented a good number of foreclosures because it effectively reduced payment-to-income ratios, making it easier for households to make their monthly mortgage payments. However, it was of little use to most seriously distressed homeowners, who were behind on their payments.

More broadly, other federal interventions in the housing market were important. The rapid escalation of FHA lending was critical to keeping credit flowing, especially to first-time homebuyers unable to afford large down payments. The FHA also refinanced millions of homeowners who had received overpriced subprime loans, likely reducing foreclosures among these borrowers. From 2006 to 2009, the FHA went from an agency that originated fewer than 5 percent of home-purchase loans to one funding over 40 percent of home-purchase loans and an even higher percentage of loans for first-time homebuyers, minority homebuyers, and buyers in minority neighborhoods (Immergluck 2011; Schwartz 2014). Without the presence of an invigorated FHA, the mortgage crisis would certainly have been far worse. Efforts to keep interest rates low via quantitative easing by the Federal Reserve also proved to be important. By purchasing billions of GSE mortgage-backed securities on a monthly basis, the Fed kept mortgage rates low. This reduced the incidence of interest-rate shock among homeowners with adjustable-rate loans and provided affordable rates throughout the housing economy. This measure, however, disproportionately benefitted affluent homeowners who could readily refinance large loans into these low rates.

THE REGULATORY RESPONSE CONTINUES TO PLAY OUT

As detailed in chapter 4, the mortgage crisis and the ensuing policy debate culminated in the passage of the most influential regulatory reform legislation in decades, the Dodd-Frank Act. Dodd-Frank was a sweeping piece of legislation intended to deal with many different aspects of the mortgage and financial crises. Arguably, Dodd-Frank went furthest in terms of revamping and strengthening the consumer-protection infrastructure in mortgage and credit markets. It turned over rule-making for consumer-protection laws to a new agency, the Consumer Financial Protection Bureau (CFPB), led by a director appointed by the president. Previously, the Federal Reserve and other more bank-friendly regulators were given principal charge for these duties. The CFPB agency is currently funded through an independent portion of the Federal Reserve's budget so that it is insulated from annual appropriation battles in Congress.

Dodd-Frank also included many improvements in specific consumer-protection regulations, including instituting ability-to-repay standards and holding lenders accountable for using such standards in their underwriting. Questionable practices such as yield-spread premiums and prepayment penalties, while not completely banned, were made more difficult to include in most mortgages. In the end, while not a perfect law, the statute was considered a major step forward by consumer-protection advocates—a quantum leap from a regulatory model based on confusing and ineffective disclosure documents to one based on stronger proscriptive rules.

Dodd-Frank was less effective on other fronts. While it did put in place procedures for increased regulation—and the potential winding down—of "too-big-to-fail" institutions, it remains to be seen how effective these will be at preventing or reducing the magnitude of future bailouts. The law did little to improve regulation of the credit-rating agencies that were so clearly implicated in the subprime debacle. While increased transparency in securities markets was a significant aim of the legislation, it remains unclear how effective its measures will be. One key problem is that key regulators, including the Securities and Exchange Commission and the Commodities Futures Trading Commission, have not been given the financial independence and the broader authority that was given to the CFPB.

The real shortcoming of Dodd-Frank is its reversibility. While the legislation was designed to insulate the CFPB from annual appropriations battles, this has not deterred the agency's congressional foes from attempting first to kill the agency, and then to harass it via dozens of legislative proposals aimed at reversing its rulemaking or weakening the agency overall. Other components of Dodd-Frank must be implemented by agencies that have less insulation from Congress, including the Commodities Futures Trading Commission, which has been charged with regulating the vast derivatives market but has been given far too little capacity to do so. In the end, only fundamental shifts in the larger political system will produce a more robust, sustainable regulatory system that cannot be critically weakened as balances of power shift in Washington and memories of the crisis fade.

RECOGNIZING HOUSING FINANCE AS A CRITICAL DRIVER OF URBAN FUTURES

Despite a long history of housing finance influencing—and sometimes driving—urban form in the United States, discussions of mortgage markets and the public role in these markets often fail to recognize such impacts. Especially since the crisis, housing finance is often treated only as an issue of macroeconomic stability (which it is), rather than a driving force behind the housing options available to families and communities, the conditions and stability of our neighborhoods, and the fundamental shape of our metropolitan areas. At least since the early twentieth century, the structure of housing-finance markets in the United States has been a major driver of metropolitan sprawl, residential segregation, and the quality of housing conditions—especially for our most vulnerable citizens. Policy debates in this arena, however, often seem to ignore the critical spatial and public ramifications that the structure, regulation, and nature of housing finance has for our neighborhoods and cities, as well as for individual households and financial markets.

Debates about desirable levels of homeownership in the country are often conducted on highly individualistic, and sometimes strictly financial, terms about whether ownership has benefits for households. These are important issues to consider. However, homeownership has implications well beyond the individual, and even issues facing individual families are often much more about the place in which they can live than about the simple financial calculus of an investor. Homeownership may bring with it a stability and sense of control that some families desire. (Conversely, affordable rental options can bring with them greater flexibility that other families may prefer.) Spatially, greater access to homeownership may increase opportunities for modest-income families to live in stronger school districts and may offer a wider selection of single-family homes than the rental market does. It can facilitate decreased levels of racial segregation, as more minority families are able to live in a wider set of neighborhoods and localities. Moreover, access to homeownership can strengthen modest-income neighborhoods, by giving families a stronger stake in their neighborhood and protecting against escalating rents due to gentrification.

Shifting dramatically back to a housing system in which homeownership is available primarily to upper-middle-class and high-income families would have serious impacts on the nature of metropolitan America that go beyond restricted opportunities for building financial assets. It would restrict housing options—including access to more desirable neighborhoods and good school districts—and reduce homeownership rates in many moderate- and even middle-income neighborhoods. In places where tenant protections are scarce, more families would be subject to sudden increases in rent, irresponsible landlords, and easy eviction.

As income and wealth inequality persist in the United States, some will argue that homeownership should only be available to more affluent households, so that lower- and middle-income households might remain more mobile to reflect the more contingent and tenuous nature of such families. There is certainly an argument for increasing the provision of affordable, quality rental housing for low- and moderate-income families. However, many families will prefer, and benefit from, affordable homeownership options, and these should be preserved. The bottom line is one that should appeal to conservatives and liberals alike: policy should be aimed at preserving both affordable and stable rental and ownership options for all families for whom such options make sense. Rental options will often remain the most viable for low-income families, unless very deep subsidies for homeownership are available. However, for many moderate- and middle-income families, ownership can remain a good option if housing-finance markets are accessible, affordable, and risk-limiting. Very large down payments, a paucity of long-term fixed-rate mortgages, very stringent credit-score requirements, and steep risk-based pricing premiums will push many families who should have access to homeownership into the rental market.

A major privatization of mortgage markets will lead to highly segmented mortgage markets where higher-cost lenders specialize in lending to higher-risk borrowers, which will include many less affluent households and families of color. These lenders will be funded with higher-cost capital that will translate into more expensive mortgages with less advantageous terms. Higher interest rates may encourage many borrowers to take out adjustable-rate loans that promise lower costs in the short run at the risk of much higher rates later on. Therefore, risk-based pricing in mortgages can encourage higher-cost and higher-risk lending to be concentrated in precisely the sorts of borrower groups and communities that are least able to absorb economic shocks. The greater segmentation of the mortgage market will also make it more difficult to regulate higher-risk lenders and to maintain the safety and soundness of the overall market. The improved financial regulatory system enabled by Dodd-Frank should help control for abusive or reckless activity, but over time, the rigor of consumer-protection regulation may be weakened by industry lobbying and by a fading public memory of the crisis. Moreover, broader shifts in centers of political power could weaken consumer and financial regulation.

PRESCRIPTIONS FOR POLICYMAKERS

Given what we now know about the crisis, the response to the crisis, and the broader history of U.S. mortgage markets, what are the key policy principles to focus on when considering the future of housing finance in the United States? These principles should be applied to both fundamental and more detailed issues of housing-finance architecture and regulation. While many of the major issues will continue to involve debates at the federal level, there are ways that state and local policymakers can play a role in making housing finance—and housing markets generally—more fair, affordable, and sound.

A Renewed Call for Fairness in Housing Finance

Despite the fact that modest-income neighborhoods and communities of color bore the brunt of the mortgage and housing crisis, policymakers have given short-shrift to issues of fairness in recent debates over the future of housing finance and regulation. The Dodd-Frank Act, while laudable in many respects, did little to address the continued tendencies of mortgage markets to become segmented by race, class, and geography. Lawmakers took a pass on modernizing and expanding the Community Reinvestment Act

(CRA) and, after protests from banks, did not end up moving CRA enforcement to the CFPB. Dodd-Frank provides for some improvements to the Home Mortgage Disclosure Act (HMDA), which can help communities and regulators ferret out discrimination, but much of the new data will be difficult to utilize, especially by community groups. Moreover, while Dodd-Frank gave authority to the CFPB to propose a larger expansion of HMDA than what was directly specified in the statute, prospects of getting such changes through the rulemaking process are weak. One of the hallmarks of the last major federal bailout, the savings and loan rescue, was a set of changes to HMDA and CRA that reinvigorated both laws, and empowered local communities with access to increased and improved data. It remains to be seen whether Dodd-Frank will leave such a legacy.

Some continue to lay blame for the crisis on fair-lending and community-reinvestment policies that were in place decades before the crisis. Since the crisis, arguments that a new housing-finance system should include a duty to serve distressed or underserved markets have largely fallen on deaf ears. Given the generally hostile climate to affordable housing in Washington, it is understandable that some housing advocates have settled for modest set-aside funds for affordable housing in lieu of any real assurances that a new financial architecture will not exacerbate racially and geographically segmented markets. Additionally, the Washington consensus on housing-finance reform—among most Democrats as well as Republicans—has focused more on a primary goal of "bringing more private capital into the mortgage market" rather than providing for fair and affordable housing markets. If such a consensus is successful, the former goal will likely win out over the latter. Capital would once again get its way with little regard for homeowners or neighborhoods.

Housing advocates, mayors, governors, and others must recognize the long-term damage that will be done by unfair, volatile, and highly segmented mortgage and housing markets. To do this, the implications of a return to highly privatized and lightly regulated housing-finance markets must be made clear. Policies favoring such a future are likely to lead to suppressed local homeownership rates, weaker housing options, more bouts of housing vacancy and abandonment, increased economic and racial segregation, and upward pressure on local rents.

Preventing the Next Mortgage Crisis

To prevent a continuing cycle of boom-and-bust mortgage and housing markets, policymakers must avoid the mistakes of the past. To create a robust, stable housing market that is less likely to bring down the national and global economies, the United States needs to recognize the tendencies of privatized and lightly regulated markets to feed unsustainable housing-market activity.

Housing-price appreciation and construction should not be driven by lending patterns that feed unsustainable cycles, in which relaxed underwriting leads to rising prices that in turn lead to more relaxation in underwriting standards. Such cycles, when they hit the slightest hiccup, are prone to reverse quickly into vicious cycles of price declines, foreclosures, and lender contraction.

At the same time, extremely restrictive mortgage markets can themselves create a longer-term cycle of declining homeownership opportunities leading to decreased economic opportunity and then to further declines in homeownership. A balanced mortgage system is driven by empirical evidence on what constitutes sustainable underwriting and regulation. It also requires a strong federal presence in the provision of conventional mortgages and a backup system for lending to those with limited wealth and decent, but not stellar, credit scores. This backup system, which now principally takes the form of the Federal Housing Administration, is also critical to providing a countercyclical backstop to the overall housing-finance system, protecting against rapid declines in mortgage availability.

One of the greatest long-term challenges to ensuring greater stability and fairness in housing finance is the ability to maintain a strong system of regulation after memories of the financial crisis fade. On the consumer-protection side, a much stronger regulatory infrastructure has been put in place since 2010, although there is continual—perhaps constant—pressure to weaken the CFPB and new rules authorized by the Dodd-Frank Act. On the securities and safety-and-soundness side, less progress has been made. Mobilizing political support for stronger securities regulation has proven more challenging than mobilizing support for consumer-protection measures. Unfortunately, these topics have less tangible appeal to congressmen, community groups, and the general public.

A Federal Agenda for Fair and Stable Housing Markets

A federal agenda for fair, affordable, and stable mortgage and housing markets should include at least six major components:

1. Provide for a major federal role in mortgage markets, including the continued cross-subsidization of the broader market, so that any risk-based pricing remains marginal and modest-down-payment, long-term, fixed-rate mortgages are widely accessible as the dominant form of mortgage finance. Any partially privatized, hybrid system of secondary markets should include a meaningful duty-to-serve requirement for all private players, so that the responsibility to serve less affluent markets is not left solely to the FHA, or only to certain participants in the mortgage market.

2. Maintain a strong FHA with the ability to support a substantial portion of the overall mortgage market, especially during times of economic and housing-market distress, much as the agency did during the sub-prime crisis. Moreover, policymakers should recognize that the FHA absorbed many of the costs of the subprime crisis by refinancing millions of homeowners during the crisis. Therefore, a one-time major recapitalization of the FHA insurance fund should be undertaken to compensate the agency for the major losses it absorbed from the housing market due to reckless private-sector behavior. This one-time re-capitalization might come from funds flowing to the treasury from the GSEs, which are now reaping the gains of a stronger housing market. This will also keep FHA insurance premiums reasonable and not encourage the marginalization of FHA programs.

3. Modernize and reinvigorate fair-lending and community-reinvestment laws and their enforcement. In part due to their being unfairly blamed by some for causing the mortgage crisis, the environment for fair-lending and community-reinvestment laws in Washington has not been a good one. Debates over the future of housing finance and the initial implementation of the Dodd-Frank Act have left enforcement of CRA and fair-lending laws marginalized to the point where the laws seem to be afterthoughts. The vigor that was brought to these laws in the late 1980s and early 1990s needs to be renewed. The laws—especially the CRA—also need to be modernized to correspond to a world in which mortgage companies have become dominant forces in the market. CRA should cover all originators of mortgages. Fair-lending exams should be made public in the way that CRA exams are. HMDA data should include a wide variety of credit-related data so that it can become a useful tool for enforcing CRA and fair-lending laws, and for determining the credit needs of particular communities.

4. Improve and strengthen the regulation of capital markets. Foremost on this list is to improve the regulation of the credit-rating agencies. The paucity of substantive regulation of the rating firms was among the greatest failures of the Dodd-Frank Act. The SEC must be much less intimidated by the ratings firms. Moreover, specific legislation to re-vamp the assignment of credit-rating agencies to move away from the traditional issuer-pays model remains an important policy goal.

5. Provide for a strong federal role in financing affordable rental housing. The experience of the financial crisis demonstrated the importance of the FHA and the GSEs in financing rental housing. Without these sources, loans for rental housing would have essentially dried

up. The need for affordable multifamily rental housing will only continue to grow, especially if mortgage markets remain relatively tight and wages remain generally stagnant or even decline. Federally supported multifamily finance must also do a better job at serving smaller multifamily buildings more effectively.

6. Provide much greater levels of subsidy for affordable rental housing, as well as affordable homeownership. Major cutbacks in the federal HOME program, long waitlists for Housing Choice Vouchers, growing numbers of low- and moderate-income families, and rising market rents all combine to create a much greater need for new forms of subsidy for affordable housing. While low-income renters have the greatest need for direct subsidies, one-time subsidies to modest-income homebuyers can be a cost-effective way to provide long-term affordable housing. Down-payment assistance grants, of the sort often funded by the HOME program through state and local government, can be effective tools for opening homeownership opportunities. In addition, these programs can be used to fund more durable affordable-housing options such as community land trusts, limited-equity cooperatives, and deed-restricted housing, which can stretch the value of the subsidy across many more years and families. One potential source of funding for such initiatives are monies that would be generated from small charges on the mortgage-backed securities flowing through a new housing-finance secondary market structure, such as that proposed in the Senate's Johnson-Crapo housing-finance reform bill of 2014.

A Policy Agenda for State and Local Governments

While the broad structures of housing finance will continue to be driven by federal policy, state and local policymakers can have important impacts on housing finance and affordable housing. A state and local agenda for fair, affordable, and stable mortgage and housing markets should include at least five components:

1. Increase funding for affordable housing, including both low-income rental housing and funding for down-payment assistance for affordable homeownership. Some funding should be designated for more durable forms of homeownership, including community land trusts, limited-equity cooperatives, and deed-restricted housing, especially in higher-cost markets, or areas subject to potential gentrification pressure. Funding can come from affordable-housing trust funds, which in turn are often funded via real estate transfer taxes, tax increment fi-

nancing set-asides, inclusionary zoning in-lieu fees, and other sources. While funding from general revenue funds tends to be scarce, stronger cases must be made for funding affordable housing as a fundamental component of maintaining safe and accessible neighborhoods.

2. Enforce federal and state consumer-protection laws. The Dodd-Frank Act provides for states adopting and enforcing consumer-protection ordinances that are more stringent than federal regulations. If foes of federal regulation are successful in rolling back federal protections, state legislative action in this arena will become more important.

3. Adopt strong fair-housing and fair-lending statutes and enforce such laws vigorously, enhancing the efforts of federal regulators. State governments should work with nonprofit fair-housing agencies to ensure that local governments are affirmatively furthering fair housing in accordance with the federal Fair Housing Act and attendant regulations. Where single-family rental housing increases in suburban communities, special attention should be paid to ensure that local suburban municipalities do not unfairly discourage conversion of owner-occupied properties into rental properties. At the same time, local governments should be allowed to adopt reasonable housing-maintenance and blight-prevention ordinances and enforce such laws in a reasonable and unbiased way.

4. Institute "linked-deposit" or "responsible-banking" programs, in which state and local governments steer government business, including deposits, financial-service contracts, bond underwriting, and other business to banks that exhibit duty-to-serve practices and avoid irresponsible financial activities. Linked-deposit programs have been used by some state and local governments over the last few decades.

5. Hold lenders and property owners responsible for derelict properties. The community and public costs of derelict properties must be internalized to property owners and responsible mortgagees. Systems of fines and penalties that are levied on derelict properties must be enforceable so that such penalties have teeth. In particular, cities must be able to take control of—and sometimes acquire—derelict properties to rehabilitate or repurpose them in a responsible manner.

The United States stands at a crossroads. It can revert back to the boom-bust housing markets that left many families and neighborhoods devastated by foreclosures, rapid declines in housing prices, job losses, and other related problems. Alternatively, it can move toward sound and fair mortgage and housing markets based on principles of prudential regulation, a concern for fairness and equity, and the importance of housing to neighborhood and family stability and opportunity. Our cities have been scarred by the great mortgage crisis of the 2000s. Since the crisis, the nation has made real strides, especially in terms of improving consumer-protection regulation. However, there is much work to be done on shaping the future of housing finance and housing markets. How this work evolves will lead us down one path or the other. My hope is that this book helps illuminate the wiser path.

Bibliography

Aalbers, M. 2009. "Why the Community Reinvestment Act Cannot Be Blamed for the Subprime Crisis." *City and Community* 8: 346–350.

Abrams, C. 1955. *Forbidden Neighbors: A Study of Prejudice in Housing*. New York: Harper
and Brothers.

Adams, E., and P. Chase-Lansdale. 2002. "Home Sweet Home(s): Parental Separations, Residential Moves, and Adjustment in Low-Income Adolescent Girls." *Development Psychology*
38: 792–805.

Agarwal, S., E. Benmelech, N. Bergman, and A. Seru. 2012, December. "Did the Community
Reinvestment Act (CRA) Lead to Risky Lending?" National Bureau of Economic Research
Working Paper No. 18609.

Agarwal, S., G. Amromin, I. Ben-David, S. Chomsisengphet, and D. Evanoff. 2010, October.
"Market-Based Loss Mitigation Practices for Troubled Mortgages Following the Financial
Crisis." Working Paper WP 2011-3. Chicago: Federal Reserve Bank of Chicago.

Agarwal, S., and I. Ben-David. 2012, October 8. "Do Loan Officers' Incentives Lead to Lax
Lending Standards?" Fisher College of Business Working Paper No. 2012-03-007.

Agarwal, S., I. Ben-David, G. Amromin, S. Chomsisengphet, and D. Evanoff. 2013, October 3.
"Predatory Lending and the Subprime Crisis." Fisher College of Business Working Paper
No. 2012-03-008.

Agnello, L., and L. Schuknecht. 2011. "Booms and Busts in Housing Markets: Determinants
and Implications." *Journal of Housing Economics* 20: 171–190.

Alexander, F. 2011, June. *Land Banks and Landbanking*. Flint, MI: Center for Community
Progress.

Alexander, K., D. Entwisle, and S. Dauber. 1996. "Children in Motion: School Transfers and
Elementary School Performance." *Journal of Educational Research* 90: 3–12.

Allen, R. 2013. "Postforeclosure Mobility for Households with Children in Public Schools."
Urban Affairs Review 49: 111–140.

Alley, D., J. Lloyd, J. Pagan, C. Pollack, M. Shardell, and C. Cannuscio. 2011. *American
Journal of Public Health* 101: 2293–2298.

American Securitization Forum. 2007, December 6. "Streamlined Foreclosure and Loss Avoid-
ance Framework for Securitized Subprime Adjustable Rate Mortgage Loans." Retrieved
January 15, 2009, at http://americansecuritization.com/uploadedFiles/FinalASFStatemen-
tonStreamlined ServicingProcedures.pdf.

Andrew Davison & Co. Inc. 2013, February. "Modeling the Impact of Housing Finance Reform on Mortgage Rates." Paper prepared for the Bipartisan Policy Center Housing Commission. New York: Andrew Davison & Co. Inc.

Andrews, D., A. Sanchez, A. Johansson. 2011, January 25. "Housing Markets and Structural Policies in OECD Countries." OECD Economics Department Working Paper No. 836.

Andrews, E. 2007, December 18. "Fed and Regulators Shrugged as the Subprime Crisis Spread." *New York Times*. Retrieved June 20, 2008, at http://www.nytimes.com/2007/12/18/business/18subprime.html.

Apgar, W., A. Bendimerad, and R. Essene. 2007. "Mortgage Market Channels and Fair Lending: An Analysis of HMDA Data." Cambridge: Harvard University Joint Center for Housing Studies.

Apgar, W., A. Calder, and G. Fauth. 2004, March 9. "Credit, Capital and Communities: The Implications of the Changing Mortgage Banking Industry for Community-Based Organizations." Cambridge: Joint Center for Housing Studies of Harvard University.

Apgar, W., and A. Fishbein. 2004, May. "The Changing Industrial Organization of Housing Finance and the Changing Role of Community-Based Organizations." Cambridge: Joint Center for Housing Studies of Harvard University.

Apgar, W., and M. Duda. 2005, May. "Collateral Damage: The Municipal Impact of Today's Mortgage Foreclosure Boom." Minneapolis: Homeownership Preservation Foundation.

Applebaum, B. 2011, July 18. "Former Ohio Attorney General to Head New Consumer Agency." *New York Times*, p. B1.

Arnio, A., Baumer, E., and K. Wolff. 2012. "The Contemporary Foreclosure Crisis and U.S. Crime Rates." *Social Science Research* 41: 1598–1614.

Ashcraft, A., P. Goldsmith-Pinkham, and J. Vickery. 2010, May. "MBS Ratings and the Mortgage Credit Boom." Federal Reserve Bank of New York Staff Report No. 449.

Ashcraft, A., and T. Schuermann. 2008, March. "Understanding the Securitization of Subprime Mortgage Credit." Federal Reserve Bank of New York. Staff Report No. 318.

Ashton, P. 2009. "An Appetite for Yield: The Anatomy of the Subprime Mortgage Crisis." *Environment and Planning A* 41: 1420–1441.

Avery, R., and K. Brevoort. 2011. "The Subprime Crisis: Is Government Housing Policy to Blame?" Federal Reserve Board of Governors Finance and Economics Discussion Series Working Paper 2011-36.

Avery, R., K. Brevoort, and G. Canner. 2007, December. "The 2006 HMDA Data." *Federal Reserve Bulletin*, pp. A73–A79.

Bair, S. 2013. *Bull by the Horns: Fighting to Save Main Street from Wall Street and Wall Street from Itself.* New York: The Free Press.

Baker, D. 2009. *Plunder and Blunder: The Rise and Fall of the Bubble Economy.* San Francisco: Berrett-Koehler.

Barakova, I., P. Calem, and S. Wachter. 2012. *Financing Constraints to Homeownership in Relation to the Pre-2008 Housing Market Boom.* Philadelphia: University of Pennsylvania.

BasePoint Analytics. 2006. "A Study on Mortgage Fraud and the Impacts of a Changing Financial Climate." Unpublished white paper. Carlsbad, CA: BasePoint Analytics.

Bean, B. 2008, Summer. "Enhancing Transparency in the Structured Finance Market." *FDIC Supervisory Insights* 5(1), 4–11.

Been, V., I. Ellen, A. Schwartz, L. Steifel, and M. Weinstein. 2011. "Does Losing Your Home Mean Losing Your School?: Effects of Foreclosures on the School Mobility of Children." *Regional Science and Urban Economics* 41: 407–414.

Belsky, E., N. Retsinas, and M. Duda. 2007. "The Financial Returns to Low-Income Homeownership." In *Chasing the American Dream*, edited by W. Rohe and H. Watson, 191–212. Ithaca: Cornell University Press.

Bernanke, B., C. Bertaut, L. Pounder-DeMarco, and S. Kamin. 2011. "International Capital Flows and the Returns to Safe Assets in the United States, 2003–2007." International Finance Discussion Paper No. 1014. Washington, DC: Board of Governors of the Federal Reserve System.

Better Markets. 2012, September 15. "The Cost of the Wall Street–Caused Financial Collapse and Ongoing Economic Crisis Is More than $12.8 Trillion." New York: Better Markets.

Better Markets. 2014, August 27. "SEC's Rule on Credit Rating Agencies Is a Big Improvement, but It Must Still End the Egregious Conflicts of Interest." Washington, DC: Better Markets.

Bhutta, N., and G. Canner. 2013, November. "Mortgage Market Conditions and Borrower Outcomes: Evidence from the 2012 HMDA Data and Matched HMDA–Credit Record Data." *Federal Reserve Bulletin* 99(4).

Binham, C., and D. Schaefer. 2013, September 24. "CFTC Chair Gary Gensler Warns on Fund Cuts to Policy Derivatives." *Financial Times.* Retrieved June 4, 2014, at http://www.ft.com/intl/cms/s/92d6e6bc-2390-11e3-b506-00144feab7de.html.

Bipartisan Policy Center. 2013, February. "Housing America's Future: New Directions for National Policy." Washington, DC: Bipartisan Policy Center.

Blackwell, R. 2003, January 31. "Second OTS Pre-emption: Predator Law in N.Y." *American Banker.*

Blinder, A. 2013. *After the Music Stopped: The Financial Crisis, the Response, and the Work Ahead.* New York: Penguin.

Bocian, D., W. Li, and K. Ernst. 2010. "Foreclosures by Race and Ethnicity: The Demographics of a Crisis." Durham, NC: Center for Responsible Lending.

Bostic, R., K. Engel, P. McCoy, A. Pennington-Cross, and S. Wachter. 2008. "State and Local Antipredatory Lending Laws: The Effect of Legal Enforcement Mechanisms." *Journal of Economics and Business* 60: 47–66.

Bradford, C. 1979. "Financing Home Ownership: The Federal Role in Neighborhood Decline." *Urban Affairs Quarterly* 14: 313–335.

Bradford, C. 2002. "Risk or Race? Racial Disparities and the Subprime Refinance Market." Washington, DC: Center for Community Change.

Bratt, R. 1976. "Federal Homeownership Policy and Home Finance: A Study of Program Operations and Impacts on the Consumer." PhD dissertation, Massachusetts Institute of Technology, Cambridge.

Braucher, J. 2010. "Humpty Dumpty and the Foreclosure Crisis: Lessons from the Lackluster First Year of the Home Affordable Modification Program." Arizona Legal Studies Discussion Paper No 09-37. Tuscon: University of Arizona.

Brevoort, K., and C. Cooper. 2010. "Foreclosure's Wake: The Credit Experiences of Individuals Following Foreclosure." Federal Reserve Board of Governors. Working Paper 2010-59.

Brooks, R., and R. Simon. 2007, December 3. "Subprime Debacle Traps Even Very Credit-Worthy: As Housing Boomed, Industry Pushed Loans to a Broader Market." *Wall Street Journal*, p. A1.

Buhl, T. 2009, March 6. "Tranche Warfare: MBS Investor Sues American Home over REO Sales." *Housing Wire.* Retrieved October 18, 2012. at http://www.housingwire.com/news/tranche-warfare-mbs-investor-sues-american-home-over-reo-sales.

Calculated Risk. 2011. "REO Inventory: Fannie, Freddie, FHA, PLS and FDIC through Q2 2011." Retrieved September 2, 2011, at http://cr4re.com/charts/charts.html?Delinquency#category=Delinquency& chart=REOInventoryQ22011.jpg.

Calem, P., J. Hershaff, and S. Wachter. 2010. "Neighborhood Patterns of Subprime Lending. Evidence from Disparate Cities." *Housing Policy Debate* 15: 603–622.

Calmes, J., S. Carter, J. Ellis, F. Hossain, and A. McLean. 2008. "On the Issues: Financial Regulation." *New York Times.* Retrieved February 22, 2010, at http://elections.nytimes.com/2008/president/issues/regulation.html.

Campbell, J., S. Giglio, and P. Pathak. 2011. "Forced Sales and House Prices." *American Economic Review* 101: 2108–2131.

Canner, G., and N. Bhutta. 2008. "Staff Analysis of the Relationship between the CRA and the Subprime Crisis." Division of Research and Statistics. Board of Governors of the Federal Reserve.

Carrick-Hagenbarth, J., and G. Epstein. 2012. "Dangerous Interconnectedness: Economists' Conflicts of Interest, Ideology, and Financial Crisis." *Cambridge Journal of Economics* 36: 43–63.

Chaddock, G. R. 2011, March 11. "House Looks to Cut $62 Billion for Distressed Homeowners, Properties." *Christian Science Monitor.* Retrieved August 29, 2011, at http://www.csmonitor.com/USA/Politics/2011/0311/House-looks-to-cut-62-billion-for-distressed-homeowners-properties.

Chan, S., A. Haughwout, and J. Tracy. 2014, May 29. "How Mortgage Finance Affects the Urban Landscape." Paper presented at the American Real Estate and Urban Economics Association 42nd Annual National Conference, Washington, DC.

Chernick, H., A. Langley, and A. Reschovsky. 2011. "The Impact of the Great Recession and the Housing Crisis on the Financing of America's Largest Cities." *Regional Science and Urban Economics* 41(4): 372–381.

Collins, M. 2012, March 21. "FHA 'Short Refi' Program Gets an Extension." *National Mortgage News.* Retrieved April 3, 2012, at http://www.nationalmortgagenews.com/dailybriefing/2010_563/fha-short-refi-program-1029524-1.html?zkPrintable=true.

Colton, K. 2002, July. "Housing Finance in the United States: The Transformation of the U.S. Housing Finance System." Working Paper W02-5. Cambridge: Joint Center for Housing Studies, Harvard University.

Consumer Financial Protection Bureau. 2013, January 10. "Summary of the Ability-to-Repay and Qualified Mortgage Rule and the Concurrent Proposal." Retrieved June 2, 2014, at http://files.consumerfinance.gov/f/201301_cfpb_ability-to-repay-summary.pdf.

Consumer Financial Protection Bureau. 2014. "Small Business Review Panel for Home Mortgage Disclosure Act Rulemaking Outline of Proposals Under Consideration and Alternatives Considered." Retrieved June 4, 2014, at http://files.consumerfinance.gov/f/201402_cfpb_hmda_outline-of-proposals.pdf.

Cordell, L., Y. Huang, and M. Williams. 2012. "Collateral Damage: Sizing and Assessing the Subprime CDO Crisis." Working Paper 11-30/R. Philadelphia: Federal Reserve Bank of Philadelphia.

Cortright, J. 2008. "Driven to the Brink: How the Gas Price Spike Popped the Housing Bubble and Devalued the Suburbs." Washington, DC: CEOs for Cities.

Coulton, C., B. Theodos, and M. Turner. 2009. "Family Mobility and Neighborhood Change: New Evidence and Implications for Community Initiatives." Washington, DC: The Urban Institute.

Coulton, C., M. Schramm, and A. Hirsch. 2008, December. "Beyond REO: Property Transfers at Extremely Distressed Prices in Cuyahoga County, 2005–2008." Cleveland, OH: Center on Urban Poverty and Community Development, Case Western University.

Coulton, K., and M. Carliner. 2014, February 14. "The Impact of Housing Finance Reform on Mortgage Rates, Home Buyers and the Economy." Paper prepared for Leading Builders of America. Washington, DC: Leading Builders of America.

Courchane, M. 2007. "The Pricing of Home Mortgage Loans for Minority Borrowers: How Much of the APR Differential Can We Explain?" *Journal of Real Estate Research* 29: 365–392.

Cui, L. 2010, November 1. "Foreclosure, Vacancy and Crime." Retrieved April 17, 2015, at http://ssrn.com/abstract=1773706 or http://dx.doi.org/10.2139/ssrn.1773706.

Currie, J., and E. Tekin. 2011. "Is the Foreclosure Crisis Making us Sick?" National Bureau of Economic Research Working Paper.

Danermark, B., and M. Ekstrom. 1990. "Relocation and Health Effects on the Elderly: A Commented Research Review." *Journal of Sociology and Social Welfare* 17: 25–49.

Dastrup, S., and J. Betts. 2012, January 11. "Elementary Education Outcomes and Stress at Home: Evidence at Mortgage Default in San Diego." Unpublished manuscript.

Davenport, T. 2003, April 9. "Why OCC May Tread Lightly on Georgia Law." *American Banker.*

Davis, R. 2008. "I'm Always for Less Regulation: McCain's Economic Thinking." *Wall Street Journal.* Retrieved February 2, 2010, at http://online.wsj.com/article/SB120431596193503527.html?mod=Leader-US#printMode.

Dayen, D. 2014, August 28. "Remember This Moment When the Next Financial Crisis Strikes: The SEC Could Have Fixed Our Broken Rating Agencies. It Whiffed." *New Republic.* Retrieved September 1, 2014, at http://www.newrepublic.com/article/119256/rating-agency-regulations-why-secs-new-rules-wont-fix-them.

Ding, L., R. Quercia, W. Lei, and J. Ratcliffe. 2011. "Risky Borrowers or Risky Mortgages? Disaggregating Effects Using Propensity Scoring Models." *Journal of Real Estate Research* 33: 245–277.

Downs. A. 2007, April. "A Niagara of Capital into Real Estate Markets." Speech to the Berkeley Real Estate Advisory Council, Pebble Beach, CA. Retrieved June 10, 2008, at http://www.anthonydowns.com/niagaracapital.html.

Dreier, P., S. Bhatti, R. Call, A. Schwartz, and G. Squires. 2014. "Underwater America: How the So-Called Housing Recovery Is Bypassing Many American Communities." Berkeley: Haas Institute for a Fair and Inclusive Society at the University of California, Berkeley.

Drew, R. 2014, May. "Believing in Homeownership: Behavioral Drivers of Housing Tenure Decisions." Working Paper W14-3. Cambridge: Joint Center for Housing Studies, Harvard University.

Drum, K. 2010, January/February. "Capital City." *Mother Jones.* Retrieved January 14, 2014, at http://motherjones.com/politics/2010/01/wall-street-big-finance-lobbyists.

Dudley, W. 2012, January 6. "Housing and the Economic Recovery. Remarks at the New Jersey Bankers Association Economic Forum." Newark. Retrieved January 30, 2012, at http://m.newyorkfed.org/newsevents/speeches/2012/dud120106.html.

Duke, E. 2011. "Speech at the Federal Reserve Board Policy Forum: The Housing Market Going Forward: Lessons Learned from the Recent Crisis." Washington, DC. Retrieved September 1, 2011, at http://www.federalreserve.gov/newsevents/ speech/duke20110901a.htm.

Duke, E. 2013, May 9. "A View from the Federal Reserve Board: The Mortgage Market and Housing Conditions." Presentation to the Housing Policy Executive Council. Washington, DC. Retrieved June 29, 2014, at http://www.federalreserve.gov/newsevents/speech/duke20130509a.pdf.

Ellen, I., J. Lacoe, and C. Sharygin. 2013. "Do Foreclosures Cause Crime?" *Journal of Urban Economics* 74: 59–70.

Engel, K., and P. McCoy. 2011. *The Subprime Virus: Reckless Credit, Regulatory Failure, and Next Steps.* New York: Oxford University Press.

Ernst, K., D. Bocian, and W. Li. 2008. "Steered Wrong: Brokers, Borrowers, and Subprime Loans." Durham, NC: Center for Responsible Lending.

Faber, J. 2013. "Racial Dynamics of Subprime Mortgage Lending at the Peak." *Housing Policy Debate* 23: 328–349.

Fang, L. 2013, October 23. "The Scholars Who Shill for Wall Street." *The Nation.* Retrieved January 14, 2014, at http://www.thenation.com/article/176809/scholars-who-shill-wall-street.

Fannie Mae. 2011, August 5. "Fannie Mae Second Quarter Credit Supplement." Retrieved September 2, 2011, at http://www.fanniemae.com/ir/pdf/sec/2011/q2credit_summary.pdf.

Fannie Mae. 2014a. "Connecticut Avenue Securities (C-deals)." Retrieved July 3, 2014, at http://www.fanniemae.com/portal/funding-the-market/credit-risk/conn-ave.html.

Fannie Mae. 2014b, April 16. "Summary of Issues: Johnson/Crapo Discussion Draft." Fannie Mae memorandum.

Farrell, M. 2008, July 25. "Housing Crisis Hits Exurbs Hard." *Christian Science Monitor.* Retrieved November 19, 2009, at http://www.csmonitor.com/2008/0725/p03s02-usec.html.

Federal Deposit Insurance Corporation. 2008, November 20. "FDIC Loss Sharing Proposal to Promote Affordable Loan Modifications." Washington, DC: Federal Deposit Insurance Corporation. Retrieved August 18, 2011, at http://www.fdic.gov/ consumers/loans/loanmod.

Federal Housing Finance Agency. 2012a. "Foreclosure Prevention & Refinance Report." Fourth Quarter 2011.

Federal Housing Finance Agency. 2012b, June. "Refinance Report."

Federal Reserve Board of Governors. 2013, August 28. "Agencies Revise Proposed Risk Retention Rule." Retrieved June 2, 2014, at http://www.federalreserve.gov/newsevents/press/bcreg/20130828a.htm.

Fields, F., F. Justa, K. Libman, and S. Saegert. 2007, Summer. "American Nightmare." *Shelterforce* 150. Retrieved February 12, 2014, at http://www.nhi.org/online/issues/150/american-nightmare.html.

Financial Crisis Inquiry Commission. 2011, January. *Financial crisis inquiry report.* Retrieved August 21, 2012, at http://www.gpo.gov/fdsys/pkg/GPO-FCIC/pdf/GPO-FCIC.pdf.

Fitch Ratings. 2009, May 26. "U.S. RMBS Servicers' Loss Mitigation and Modification Efforts." New York: Fitch Ratings.

Fitch Ratings. 2012, July 9. "Fitch on AG Settlement: More Clarity, Not Much Change Yet for U.S. RMBS." New York: Fitch Ratings.

Foote, C., K. Gerardi, and P. Willen. 2013, August 1. "Government Policy and the Crisis: The Case of the Community Reinvestment Act." Retrieved January 14, 2014, at http://realestateresearch.frbatlanta.org/rer/2013/08/government-policy-and-crisis-case-of-community-reinvestment-act-.html.

Frame, W. 2010. "Estimating the Effects of Mortgage Foreclosures on Nearby Property Values: A Critical Review of the Literature." *Federal Reserve Bank of Atlanta Economic Review* 95: 1–10.

Furletti, M. 2002, June. "An Overview and History of Credit Reporting." Philadelphia: Federal Reserve Bank of Philadelphia.

Gagnon, J., M. Raskin, J. Remache, and B. Sack. 2011. "The Financial Market Effects of the Federal Reserve's Large Scale Asset Purchases." *The International Journal of Central Banking* 7: 3–44.

Geisst, C. 1990. *Visionary Capitalism. Financial Markets and the American Dream in the Twentieth Century.* New York: Praeger.

Gerardi , K., C. Foote, and P. Willen. 2010, September. "Reasonable People Did Disagree: Optimism and Pessimism About the U.S. Housing Market Before the Crash." Federal Reserve Bank of Boston Public Policy Discussion Paper No. 10-5.

Golding, E., R. Green, and D. McManus. 2008, February. "Imperfect Information and the Housing Finance Crisis." UCC 08-6. Cambridge: Harvard University Joint Center for Housing Studies.

Goodman, L. 2014, June 2. "Housing Finance Reform: A Realistic Assessment." Paper Presented at Lincoln Institute of Land Policy's Annual Conference, Cambridge, MA.

Gotham, K. F. 2009. "Creating Liquidity out of Spatial Fixity: The Secondary Circuit of Capital and the Subprime Mortgage Crisis." *International Journal of Urban and Regional Research* 33: 355–371.

Government Accountability Office. 2013, January 16. "Financial Crisis Losses and Potential Impacts of the Dodd-Frank Act." GAO-13-180. Washington, DC: Government Accountability Office.

Green, R., and S. Wachter. 2007. "The Housing Finance Revolution." Prepared for the 31st Economic Policy Symposium: Housing, Housing Finance and Monetary Policy. Kansas City: Federal Reserve Bank of Kansas City.

Griffith, J. 2013, July. "The $5 Trillion Question: What Should We Do with Fannie Mae and Freddie Mac? Comparison of 26 Plans to Reform Fannie Mae and Freddie Mac." Washington, DC: Center for American Progress.

Gruenstein-Bocian, D., K. Ernst, and W. Li. 2008. "Race, Ethnicity, and Subprime Home Loan Pricing." *Journal of Economics and Business* 60: 110–124.

Gruenstein-Bocian, D., W. Li, C. Reid, and R. Quercia. 2011. "Lost Ground, 2011: Disparaties in Mortgage Lending and Foreclosures." Washington, DC: Center for Responsible Lending.

Gruenstein-Bocian, D., W. Li, and K. Ernst. 2010, June 18. "Foreclosures by Race and Ethnicity: The Demographics of a Crisis." Washington, DC: Center for Responsible Lending.

Gyourko, J. 2009, November 13. "Five Myths about Homeownership." *Washington Post Online.* Retrieved July 2, 2014, at http://www.washingtonpost.com/wp-dyn/content/article/2009/11/13/AR2009111302214.html.

Hamilton, J., and J. Pachkowski. 2011, August. "The Consumer Financial Protection Bureau: Governance, Structure and Funding Issues." Wolters Kluwer Law & Business Briefing.

Hancock, D., and W. Passmore. 2010. "Did the Federal Reserve's MBS Purchase Program Lower Mortgage Rates?" Washington, DC: Federal Reserve Board of Governors. Retrieved August 19, 2014, at http://www.federalreserve.gov/pubs/feds/2011/201101/201101pap.pdf.

Harding, J., E. Rosenblatt, and V. Yao. 2009. "The Contagion Effect of Foreclosed Properties." *Journal of Urban Economics* 66: 164–178.

Hartwig, R., and C. Wilkinson. 2003, June. "The Use of Credit Information in Personal Lines Insurance Underwriting." New York: Insurance Information Institute.

Haughwout, A., D. Lee, J. Tracy, and W. van der Klaauw. 2011, September. "Real Estate Investors, the Leverage Cycle, and the Housing Crisis." Federal Reserve Bank of New York Staff Report no. 514.

Haurin, D., and S. Rosenthal. 2004, December. "The Sustainability of Homeownership: Factors Affecting the Duration of Homeownership and Rental Spells." Washington, DC: U.S. Department of Housing and Urban Development Office of Research and Policy Development.

Hayes, R. A. 1995. *The Federal Government and Urban Housing: Ideology and Change in Public Policy*, 2nd edition. Albany: State University of New York Press.

Helper, R. 1969. *Racial Policies and Practices of Real Estate Brokers*. Minneapolis: University of Minnesota Press.

Henserling, J. 2014, January 28. "Chairman Henserling's Opening Statement at Hearing on Consumer Financial Protection Bureau." House Financial Services Committee. Retrieved May 27, 2014, at http://financialservices.house.gov/news/documentsingle.aspx?DocumentID=367901.

Herbert, C., D. McCue, and R. Sanchez-Moyano. 2013, September. "Is Homeownership Still and Effective Means of Building Wealth for Low-Income and Minority Households? (Was It Ever?)." HBTL-06. Cambridge: Joint Center for Housing Studies at Harvard University.

Hernandez-Murillo, R., A. Ghent, and M. Owyang. 2012, August. "Did Affordable Housing Legislation Contribute to the Subprime Securities Boom?" Federal Reserve Bank of St. Louis. Working Paper 2012-005B.

Herszenhorn, D. 2010. "House-Senate Talks Drop New Credit-Rating Rules." *New York Times*. Retrieved June 4, 2014, at http://www.nytimes.com/2010/06/16/business/16regulate.html.

Hexter, K., and M. Schnoke. 2011. "Responding to Foreclosures in Cuyahoga County, 2010 Evaluation Report January 1, 2010 through December 31, 2010." *Urban Publications*, paper 452. Retrieved February 7, 2014, at http://engagedscholarship.csuohio.edu/urban_facpub/452.

Hillier, A. 2001. "Redlining and the Home Owners' Loan Corporation." Paper presented at the Fall Colloquium Series, University of Pennsylvania Population Studies Center.

Hiltzik, M. 2011, June 28. "Homeowners Deserve More than Halfhearted Mortgage Relief." *Los Angeles Times*. Retrieved August 23, 2011, at http://articles.latimes.com/2011/jun/28/business/la-fi-hiltzik-20110628.

Hoffman, S. 2001. *Politics and Banking: Ideas, Public Policy, and the Creation of Financial Institutions*. Baltimore: The Johns Hopkins University Press.

Hope Now Alliance. 2007. "Hope Now Alliance Created To Help Distressed Homeowners." Press release. Retrieved August 23, 2011, at http://www.fsround.org/media/pdfs/AllianceRelease.pdf.

Hoskins, S. 2014, January 9. "The Ability-to-Repay Rule: Possible Effects of the Qualified Mortgage Definition on Credit Availability and Other Selected Issues." Congressional Research Service, 7-5700.

Housingwire. 2014, May 21. "House Republicans Struggle to Control CFPB." Housingwire. Retrieved June 6, 2014, at http://www.housingwire.com/articles/30081-house-republicans-struggle-to-control-cfpb.

Howard, T. 2013. *Mortgage Wars: Inside Fannie Mae, Big-Money Politics, and the Collapse of the American Dream*. New York: McGraw Hill.

Immergluck, D. 2004a. *Credit to the Community: Community Reinvestment and Fair Lending Policy in the United States*. Armonk: M.E. Sharpe.

Immergluck, D. 2004b. "Hypersegmentation and Exclusion in Financial Services in the U.S.: The Effects on Low-Income And Minority Neighborhoods." *Social Policy Journal* 3: 25–44.

Immergluck, D. 2009. *Foreclosed: High-Risk Lending, Deregulation, and the Undermining of America's Mortgage Market*. Ithaca: Cornell University Press.

Immergluck, D. 2010a. "The Accumulation of Lender-Owned Homes During the U.S. Mortgage Crisis: Examining Metropolitan REO Inventories." *Housing Policy Debate* 20: 619–645.

Immergluck, D. 2010b. "Neighborhoods in the Wake of the Debacle: Intrametropolitan Patterns of Foreclosed Properties." *Urban Affairs Review* 46: 3–36.

Immergluck, D. 2010c, October 20. "State Foreclosure Mitigation Strategies: A Comparison of Round 1 and 2 Hardest Hit Fund Plans in States with Nonjudicial Foreclosure Processes." Retrieved November 1, 2010, at http://ssrn.com/abstract=1695217.

Immergluck, D. 2011. "From Minor to Major Player: The Geography of FHA Lending During the U.S. Mortgage Crisis." *Journal of Urban Affairs* 33: 1–20.

Immergluck, D. 2012. "Distressed and Dumped: Market Dynamics of Low-Value, Foreclosed Properties During the Advent of The Federal Neighborhood Stabilization Program." *Journal of Planning Education and Research* 32: 48–61.

Immergluck, D., and G. Smith. 2006a. "The External Costs of Foreclosure: The Impact of Single-Family Mortgage Foreclosures on Property Values." *Housing Policy Debate* 17: 57–79.

Immergluck, D., and G. Smith. 2006b. "The Impact of Single-Family Mortgage Foreclosures on Crime." *Housing Studies* 21: 851–866.

Immergluck, D., and J. Law. 2014. "Investing in Crisis: The Methods, Strategies, and Expectations of Investors in Single-Family Foreclosed Homes in Distressed Neighborhoods." *Housing Policy Debate* 24: 568–593.

Immergluck, D., and M. Wiles. 1999. *Two Steps Back: The Dual Mortgage Market, Predatory Lending and the Undoing of Community Development.* Chicago: Woodstock Institute.

Irwin, N., and A. Paley. 2008, October 24. "Greenspan Says He Was Wrong on Regulation: Lawmakers Blast Former Fed Chairman." *Washington Post*, p. A01.

Jacobides, M. 2005. "Industry Change through Vertical Disintegration. How and Why Markets Emerged in Mortgage Banking." *Academy of Management Journal* 48: 465–498.

Johnson, S. 2011, October 9. "Too Big to Fail Not Fixed Despite Dodd-Frank: Simon Johnson." *Bloomberg Business Week.* Retrieved June 4, 2014, at http://www.bloombergview.com/articles/2011-10-10/too-big-to-fail-not-fixed-despite-dodd-frank-commentary-by-simon-johnson.

Johnson, S. 2014, January 2. "The Rich Country Trap." *New York Times.* Retrieved January 14, 2014, at http://economix.blogs.nytimes.com/2014/01/02/the-rich-country-trap.

Joint Center for Housing Studies. 2006. "America's Rental Housing: Homes for a Diverse Nation." Cambridge, MA: Joint Center for Housing Studies at Harvard University.

Joint Center for Housing Studies. 2013, July. "State of the Nation's Housing." Cambridge, MA: Joint Center for Housing Studies at Harvard University.

Joint Economic Committee. 2007, June 5. "Momentum Builds For Schumer's Call For Additional Federal Funds to Avert Subprime Foreclosure Crisis." Press release. Washington, DC: Joint Economic Committee of the U.S. Congress.

Kaper, S. 2010a. "Cruel 'Joke': Consumer Protection to the Fed?" *American Banker.* Retrieved March 4, 2010, at http://www.americanbanker.com/issues/175_41/cruel-joke-consumer-protection-to-the-fed-1015378-1.html?zkPrintable=true.

Kaper, S. 2010b. "Failure to Cover Nonbanks Seen as Key Flaw of New Consumer Unit." *American Banker.* Retrieved March 4, 2010, at http://www.americanbanker.com/issues/175_42/failure-to-cover-non banks-a-flaw-1015412-1.html?zkPrintable=true.

Kashkari, N. 2012, April 27. "Why Few Homeowners Have Been Rescued." *Washington Post.* Retrieved May 2, 2012, at http://www.washingtonpost.com/opinions/why-homeowner-bail-out-plans-dont-work/2012/04/27/gIQAhpIImT_story.html.

Kemeny, J. 2006. "Corporatism and Housing Regimes." *Housing, Theory and Society* 23: 1–18.

Keys, B., T. Mukherjee, A. Seru, and V. Vig. 2010. "Did Securitization Lead to Lax Screening? Evidence from Subprime Loans." *Quarterly Journal of Economics* 125: 307–362.

Kiel, P., and O. Pierce. 2010. "Homeowner Questionnaire Shows Banks Violating Government Program Rules." *Propublica.* Retrieved August 22, 2011, at http://www.propublica.org/article/homeowner-questionnaire-shows-banks-violating-govt-program-rules.

Kim-Sung, K., and S. Hermanson. 2005, January. "Experiences of Older Refinance Mortgage Loan Borrowers: Broker- and Lender-Originated Loans." Washington, DC: AARP Public Policy Institute.

Kingsley, G., and K. Pettit. 2009. "High-Cost and Investor Mortgages: Neighborhood Patterns." Washington, DC: Urban Institute. Retrieved August 3, 2013, at http://www.urban.org/publications/411941.html.

Kirsch, L., and R. Mayer. 2013. *Financial Justice: The People's Campaign to Stop Lender Abuse*. New York: Praeger.

Kocieniewski, D. 2013, December 27. "Academics Who Defend Wall Street Reap Reward." *New York Times*. Retrieved January 14, 2014, at http://www.nytimes.com/2013/12/28/business/academics-who-defend-wall-st-reap-reward.html.

Konczal, M. 2012, December 12. "What Does the New Community Reinvestment Act (CRA) Paper Tell Us?" Roosevelt Institute. Retrieved January 14, 2014, at http://www.nextnewdeal.net/rortybomb/what-does-new-community-reinvestment-act-cra-paper-tell-us.

Korte, G. 2010, July 28. "Clock Ticking for Foreclosure Aid: Local Governments Must Use $1B in Federal Funds." *USA Today*, p. 1A.

Kranish, M., and F. Stockman. 2008, September 18. "Amid Turmoil, McCain Turns to Regulation." *Boston Globe*. Retrieved February 2, 2010, at http://www.boston.com/news/nation/articles/2008/09/18/amid_turmoil_mccain_turns_to_regulation?mode=PF.

Krugman, P. 2009, September 2. "How Did Economists Get It So Wrong?" *New York Times Magazine*. Retrieved January 11, 2014, at http://www.nytimes.com/2009/09/06/magazine/06Economic-t.html?pagewanted=all.

Krugman, P. 2010, December 20. "When Zombies Win." *New York Times*, p. 29.

Lambie-Hanson, L. 2013, March 15. "When Does Delinquency Result in Neglect? Mortgage Distress and Property Maintenance." Federal Reserve Bank of Boston Public Policy Discussion Paper 13-1.

Lea, M. 1996. "Innovation and the Cost of Mortgage Credit: A Historical Perspective." *Housing Policy Debate* 7: 147–174.

Leach, J. 2000, May 24. "Statement of Chairman of the Banking and Financial Services Committee, Hearings on Predatory Lending Practices." U.S. House of Representatives, Committee on Banking and Financial Services.

Lee, Y. S. 2013. "The Impact of High-Leverage Home Loans on Racial/Ethnic Segregation Among Homebuyers in the Mortgage Boom." PhD dissertation. Atlanta: Georgia Institute of Technology. Retrieved January 11, 2014, at https://smartech.gatech.edu/handle/1853/47672.

Lehnert, A., and M. Grover. 2008, May. "New Data Analysis Helps Identify Future Foreclosure Trouble Spots." *Community Dividend*. Federal Reserve Bank of Minneapolis. Retrieved March 19, 2009, at http://www.minneapolisfed.org/publication_papers_pub_display.cfm?id=2453.

Leinberger, C. 2008, March. "The Next Slum?" *Atlantic Monthly*. Retrieved March 12, 2009, at http://www.theatlantic.com/doc/200803/subprime.

Leonard, T., and J. Murdoch. 2009. "The Neighborhood Effects of Foreclosure." *Journal of Geographical Systems* 11(4): 317–332.

Levitin, A., and J. Goodman. 2008, February 6. "The Effect Of Bankruptcy Strip-Down on Mortgage Markets." Georgetown University Law Center, Research Paper No. 1087816.

Levitin, A., and J. Ratcliffe. 2013, October. "Rethinking Duties to Serve in Housing Finance." HBTL-12. Cambridge: Joint Center for Housing Studies at Harvard University.

Levitin, A., and S. Wachter. 2013. "Why Housing?" *Housing Policy Debate* 23: 5–27.

Levitin, A., and T. Twomey. 2011, Winter. "Mortgage Servicing." *Yale Journal on Regulation* 28(1): 1–90.

Lillis, M. 2009, July 16. "Obama Administration Abandons Cramdown." *Washington Independent*. Retrieved August 15, 2011, at http://washingtonindependent.com/51486/obama-administration-abandons-cramdown.

Lin, Z., E. Rosenblatt, and V. Yao. 2009. "Spillover Effects of Foreclosures on Neighborhood Property Values." *Journal of Real Estate Finance and Economics* 38(4): 387–407.

Lipton, E., and S. Labaton. 2008, November 16. "A Deregulator Looks Back, Unswayed." *New York Times*. Retrieved February 27, 2010, at http://www.nytimes.com/2008/11/17/business/economy/17gramm.html?pagewanted=all.

Lucy, W. 2010, February. "Foreclosing the Dream. An Excerpt." *Planning Magazine*, pp. 34–37.

Mallach, A. 2009, February. *Saving America's Struggling Communities: Defining the Federal Role in Addressing the Secondary Impacts of the Foreclosure Crisis*. Washington, DC: Brookings Institution. Retrieved August 29, 2011, at http://www.brookings.edu/topics/ financial-markets.aspx.

Mayer, C., E. Morrison, T. Piskorski, and A. Gupta. 2011, May. "Mortgage Modification and Strategic Behavior: Evidence from a Legal Settlement with Countrywide." Columbia Law and Economics Working Paper No. 404.

Mayer, C., and K. Pence. 2008, June. "Subprime Mortgages: What, Where, and to Whom?" National Bureau of Economic Research Working Paper No. 14083.

Mayer, N., P. Tatian, K. Temkin, and C. Calhoun. 2010, September. "National Foreclosure Mitigation Counseling Program Evaluation: Preliminary Analysis of Program Effects." Washington, DC: Urban Institute.

McCoy, P., and E. Renuart. 2008, February. "The Legal Infrastructure of Subprime and Nontraditional Home Mortgages." UCC08-5. Cambridge: Joint Center for Housing Studies at Harvard University.

Mian, A., and A. Sufi. 2008. "The Consequences of Mortgage Credit Expansion: Evidence from the 2007 Mortgage Default Crisis." Working Paper. National Bureau of Economic Research.

Mian, A., and A. Sufi. 2014. *House of Debt: How They (and You) Caused the Great Recession, and How We Can Prevent It from Happening Again*. Chicago: University of Chicago Press.

Mikelbank, B. 2008. "Spatial Analysis of the Impact of Vacant, Abandoned, and Foreclosed Properties." Federal Reserve Bank of Cleveland Office of Community Affairs Working Paper.

Min, D. 2013, June 12. "Beyond GSEs: Examples of Successful Housing Finance Models Without Explicit Government Guarantees." Testimony before the U.S. House of Representatives Committee on Financial Services.

Moody's Corporation. 2004. *2003 Annual Report*. New York: Moody's Corporation.

Moody's Corporation. 2008. *2007 Annual Report*. New York: Moody's Corporation.

Mortgage Bankers Association. 2011. "National Delinquency Survey: Facts." Retrieved August 23, 2011, at http://www.mbaa.org/files/Research/Flyers/NDSFAQ.pdf.

Mosser, P., J. Tracy, and J. Wright. 2013, October. "The Capital Structure and Governance of a Mortgage Securitization Utility." Federal Reserve Bank of New York Staff Report No. 644. New York: Federal Reserve Bank of New York.

Myrdal, G. 1944. *An American Dilemma: The Negro Problem and Modern Democracy*. New York: Harper and Row.

Nadauld, T., and S. Sherlund. 2009. "The Role of the Securitization Process in the Expansion of Subprime Credit." Federal Reserve Board of Governors, Finance and Economics Discussion Series 2009-28.

Nadauld, T., and S. Sherlund. 2013. "The Impact of Securitization on the Expansion of Subprime Credit." *Journal of Financial Economics* 107: 454–476.

National Consumer Law Center. 2009, September 11. "Homeowners Need Mandatory Loan Modifications and Expanded Access To Mediation; Current Programs Fall Short." Retrieved January 30, 2012, at http://www.nclc.org/images/pdf/foreclosure_mortgage/mortgage_servicing/loanmodificationonepage091109.pdf.

National Consumer Law Center. 2010, July/August. *NCLC Reports*. Retrieved June 4, 2014, at http://www.nclc.org/dodd-frank/nclc-rpts-ccu-jul-aug-2010-web.pdf.

Neumann, J. 2013, May 13. "Rating Firms Steer Clear of an Overhaul." *Wall Street Journal*, p. C-1.

Newberger, H. 2010. "Acquiring Privately Held REO Properties with Public Funds: The Case of The Neighborhood Stabilization Program." Washington, DC: Federal Reserve Board of Governors.

Newman, K. 2009. "Post-Industrial Widgets: Capital Flows and the Production of the Urban." *International Journal of Urban and Regional Research* 2: 314–331.

Nocera, J. 2008, October 2. "As Crisis Spread, Alarm Led to Action." *New York Times*. Retrieved October 2, 2008, at http://www.nytimes.com/2008/10/02/business/02crisis.htm.

Novick, B., K. Chavers, and A. Rosenblum. 2013, July. "Credit Rating Agencies: Reform, Don't Eliminate." *Blackrock Viewpoint*. Retrieved June 4, 2014, at https://www.blackrock.com/corporate/en-us/literature/whitepaper/viewpoint-credit-ratingagencies-reform-dont-eliminate.pdf.

Ong, P., and D. Pfeiffer. 2008, October. "Spatial Variation in Foreclosures in Los Angeles.' Unpublished manuscript.

O'Sullivan, E., and P. De Decker. 2007. "Regulating the Private Rental Housing Market in Europe." *European Journal of Homelessness* 1: 95–117.

O'Toole, R. 2008, February 17. "Land Use Regulation and the Credit Crisis." Retrieved January 14, 2014, at http://www.cato.org/blog/land-use-regulation-credit-crisis.

Panchuk, K. 2011. "House Republicans Push Back at Plan to Settle With Mortgage Servicers." Retrieved March 9, 2011, at http://www.housingwire.com/2011/03/09/house-republicans-push-back-at-plan-tosettle-with-mortgage-servicers.

Panchuk, K. 2013, September 4. "Hensarling in the House: Rep. Jeb Hensarling Pushes Housing Reform Center Stage." *HousingWire Magazine*. Retrieved July 8, 2014, at http://www.housingwire.com/articles/26684-henslaring-in-the-house.

Park. K. 2010, August. "Fannie, Freddie, and the Foreclosure Crisis." Chapel Hill: University of North Carolina Center for Community Capital.

Patterson, S., and D. Solomon. 2013, September 10. "Volcker Rule to Curb Bank Trading Proves Hard to Write." *Wall Street Journal*. Retrieved June 4, 2014, at http://online.wsj.com/news/articles/SB10001424127887323838204579000623890621830.

Paul, E. 2008. "Brownfields Redevelopment Toolbox for Disadvantaged Communities." Northeast-Midwest Institute. Retrieved July 28, 2010, at http://www.epa.gov/brownfields/pdf/bftoolbox_disadvantage_communities.pdf.

Pavlov, A., and S. Wachter. 2011. "Subprime Lending and Real Estate Prices." *Real Estate Economics* 38: 1–17.

Pennington-Cross, A., A. Yezer, and J. Nicholas. 2000. "Credit Risk and Mortgage Lending: Who Uses Subprime and Why?" Working Paper No. 00-03. Reston, VA: Research Institute for Housing America.

Percelay, B. 2007, September 20. "Predatory Borrowers." *Boston Globe*. Retrieved February 23, 2011, at http://www.boston.com/news/globe/editorial_opinion/oped/articles/2007/09/20/predatory_borrowers/.

Pfeiffer, F., S. Danziger, and R. Schoeni. 2013, April. "Wealth Disparities Before and After the Great Recession." National Poverty Center Working Paper Series #13-05.

Pinto, E. 2010, October 11. "Memorandum: Sizing Total Federal Government and Federal Agency Contributions to Subprime and Alt-A loans in U.S. First Mortgage Market as of 6.30.08." Washington, DC: American Enterprise Institute.

Pollack, C., and J. Lynch. 2009. "Health Status of People Undergoing Foreclosure in the Philadelphia Region." *American Journal of Public Health* 99: 1833–1839.

Popper, N. 2013, September 18. "S&P Bond Deals Are on the Rise since It Relaxed Rating Criteria." *New York Times*, p. B-1.

Powell, M., and A. Martin. 2011, March 30. "Foreclosure Aid Fell Short, and Is Fading." *New York Times*, p. A-1.

Prior, J. 2011, July 14. "Freddie Mac Authorizes HUD Unemployment Program." Retrieved August 22, 2011, at http://www.housingwire.com/2011/07/14/freddie-mac-authorizes-hud-unemployment-program.

Quercia, R., A. Freeman, and J. Ratcliffe. 2011. *Regaining the Dream: How to Renew the Promise of Homeownership for America's Working Families*. Washington, DC: Brookings Institution Press.

Quiggin , J. 2010. *Zombie Economics: How Dead Ideas Still Walk among Us*. Princeton, NJ: Princeton University Press.

Randall, M. 2011, July 7. "Questions on Warren's Role in Mortgage Talks Dominate Hearing." Dow Jones Newswires. Retrieved August 29, 2011, at http://www.foxbusiness.com/industries/2011/07/07/questions-on-warrens-role-in-mortgage-talks-dominate-hearing.

Randazzo, A. 2010, October. "Rethinking Homeownership: A Framework for 21st Century Housing Finance Reform." Policy Brief 93. Reason Foundation. Retrieved July 8, 2014, at http://reason.org/files/rethinking_fannie_mae_freddie_mac.pdf.

Reid, C., and E. Laderman. 2009, April 15. "The Untold Costs of Subprime Lending: Examining the Links among Higher-Priced Lending, Foreclosures, and Race in California." Paper presented at the Institute for Assets and Social Policy, Brandeis University.

Reid, C., and E. Laderman. 2011. "Constructive Credit: Revisiting the Performance of Community Reinvestment Act Lending during the Subprime Crisis." In *The American Mortgage System: Crisis and Reform*, edited by S. Wachter and M. Smith, 159–186. Philadelphia: University of Pennsylvania Press.

Reid, C., E. Seidman, M. Willis, L. Ding, J. Silver, and J. Ratcliffe. 2013, January. "Debunking the CRA Myth—Again." Chapel Hill: University of North Carolina Center for Community Capital.

Reid, C., and R. Quercia. 2013, September. "Risk, Access, and the QRM Reproposal." University of North Carolina Center for Community Capital.

Reynolds, A., C. Chen, and J. Herbers. 2009, June 29–30. "Evidence on Prevention." Presentation for the Workshop on the Impact of Mobility and Change on the Lives of Young Children, Schools, and Neighborhoods, the National Academies, Washington, DC.

Rodrik, D., and A. Subramanian. 2008, February 25. "We Must Curb International Flows of Capital." *Financial Times*. Retrieved April 30, 2014, at http://www.ft.com/cms/s/0/bee0b4b2-e3a5-11dc-8799-0000779fd2ac.html?nclick_check=1.

Rohe, W., and M. Lindblad. 2013, August. "Reexamining the Social Benefits of Homeownership after the Housing Crisis." HBTL-04. Cambridge: Joint Center for Housing Studies at Harvard University.

Rothwell, J. 2012, April. "Housing Costs, Zoning, and Access to High-Scoring Schools." Brookings Institution. Retrieved July 8 2014, at http://www.brookings.edu/~/media/research/files/papers/2012/4/19%20school%20inequality%20rothwell/0419_school_inequality_rothwell.pdf.

Rothwell, J., and D. Massey. 2009. "The Effect of Density Zoning on Racial Segregation in U.S. Urban Areas." *Urban Affairs Review* 44: 779–806.

Rumbold, A., L. Giles, M. Whitrow, E. Steele, C. Davies, M. Davies, and V. Moore. 2012. "The Effects of House Moves during Early Childhood on Child Mental Health at Age 9 Years." *BMC Public Health* 12(583).

Said, C., and K. Zito. 2007, December 7. "Bush's Plan for an Interest Rate Freeze Gets an Icy Response." *San Francisco Chronicle*. Retrieved August 23, 2008, at http://www.sfgate.com/cgi-bin/article.cgi?f=/c/a/2007/12/07/MNQCTPRVP.DTL.

Sandstrum, H., and S. Huerta. 2013. "The Negative Effects of Instability on Child Development: A Research Synthesis." Low-Income Working Families Discussion Paper 3. Washington, DC: Urban Institute.

Schafran, A., and J. Wegman. 2012. "Restructuring, Race, and Real Estate: Changing Home Values and the New California Metropolis, 1989–2010." *Urban Geography* 33: 630–654.

Scheessele, R. 2002. "Black and White Disparities in Subprime Mortgage Refinance Lending." Office of Policy Development and Research Working Paper. Washington, DC: U.S. Department of Housing and Urban Development.

Schlesinger, T. 2011. "The Shadow Financial Regulatory Commission." Amherst, MA: The Political Economy Research Institute. Retrieved January 26, 2011, at http://www.peri.umass.edu/shadow.

Schuetz, J., V. Been, and I. G. Ellen. 2008. "Neighborhood Effects of Concentrated Mortgage Foreclosures." *Journal of Housing Economics* 17: 306–319.

Schwartz, A. 2014. "The Essential if Problematic Role of FHA Mortgage Insurance." *Housing Policy Debate* 24: 666–669

Scott, K. 1977. "The Dual Banking System: Model of Competition in Regulation." *Stanford Law Review* 30: 1–49.

Securities and Exchange Commission. 2008, July 8. "Summary Report of Issues Identified in the Commission Staff's Examinations of Select Credit Rating Agencies." Washington, DC: Securities and Exchange Commission.

Sell, K., S. Zlotnik, K. Noonan, and D. Rubin. 2010. "The Recession and Housing Stability." Washington, DC: First Focus.

Shin, H. S. 2009. "Financial Intermediation and the Post-Crisis Financial System." Working Paper. Retrieved March 10, 2014, at http://www.princeton.edu/~hsshin/www/futurefinance.pdf.

Smith, M., and C. Hevener. 2011, December. "Subprime Lending over Time: The Role of Race." *Journal of Economics and Finance.* DOI 10.1007.s12197-011-9220-9.

Smith, R., and K. Ferryman. 2006. "Saying Goodbye: Relocating Seniors in the Hope VI Panel Study." Washington, DC: Urban Institute.

Society for Human Resource Management. 2012, July 19. "Background Checking—the Use of Credit Background Checks in Hiring Decisions." Alexandria, VA: Society for Human Resource Management.

Solomon, D., S. Sidel, and A. Luchetti. 2013, May 9. "Big Banks Push Back Against Tighter Rules." *Wall Street Journal.* Retrieved June 4, 2014, at http://online.wsj.com/news/articles/SB20001424127887324244304578471312603346762.

Special Investigator General for the Troubled Asset Relief Program (SIGTARP). 2011, July 28. "Quarterly Report to Congress." Retrieved August 1, 2011, at http://www.sigtarp.gov/reports/congress/2011/July2011_Quarterly_Report_to_Congress.pdf.

Special Investigator General for the Troubled Asset Relief Program (SIGTARP). 2012, April 12. "Factors Affecting Implementation of the Hardest Hit Fund Program." Retrieved May 18, 2012, at http://www.sigtarp.gov/Audit%20Reports/SIGTARP_HHF_Audit.pdf.

Starr, M. 2012. "Contributions of Economists to the Housing-Price Bubble." *Journal of Economic Issues* 46: 143–172.

Stiglitz, J. 2010. *Freefall: America, Free Markets, and the Sinking of the World Economy.* New York: Norton.

Stiglitz, J. 2012. *The Price of Inequality: How Today's Divided Society Endangers Our Future.* New York: Norton.

Stolberg, C. 2009, February 20. "Critique of Housing Plan Draws Quick White House Offensive." *New York Times.* Retrieved August 20, 2011, at http://www.nytimes.com/2009/02/21/us/politics/21obama.html.

Stucky, T., J. Ottensmann, and S. Payton. "The Effect of Foreclosures on Crime in Indianapolis, 2003–2008." *Social Science Quarterly* 93: 602–624.

Summers, L. 2009, January 15. "Letter of Larry Summers, Director-Designate National Economic Council to Senate and House Leadership." Retrieved January 18, 2009, at http://financialservices.house.gov/summers011509.pdf.

Swagel, P. 2014, April 18. "Mortgage Reform Is Worth the Small Extra Cost to Borrowers." *New York Times Economix.* Retrieved February 25, 2015, at http://economix.blogs.nytimes.com/2014/04/18/mortgage-reform-is-worth-the-small-extra-cost-to-borrowers/?_r=0.

Swarns, R. 2008, April 30. "Federal Mortgage Plan Falls Short." *New York Times.* Retrieved August 18, 2011, at http://www.nytimes.com/2008/04/30/business/30fha.html.

Tamny, J. 2008, October 30. "The Sanctification of Irresponsible Borrowers." *Real Clear Markets.* Retrieved February 23, 2011, at http://www.realclearmarkets.com/articles/2008/10/the_sanctification_of_irrespon.html.

Taylor, M., and B. Edwards. 2012. "Housing and Children's Wellbeing and Development: Evidence from a National Longitudinal Study." *Family Matters* 91.

Temple, J., and A. Reynolds. 1999. "School Mobility and Achievement: Longitudinal Findings from an Urban Cohort." *Journal of Social Psychology* 37: 355–377.

Thaler, R., and C. Sunstein. 2008. *Nudge: Improving Decisions about Health, Wealth, and Happiness.* New Haven: Yale University Press.

Thompson, D. 2009, October. "Why Servicers Foreclose When They Should Modify and Other Puzzles of Servicer Behavior." Washington, DC: National Consumer Law Center.

Timiraos, N. 2011, August 31. "An Accidental Housing Chief Embraces the Power of 'No'." *Wall Street Journal.* Retrieved September 2, 2011, at http://online.wsj.com/article/SB10001424053111904199404576538803284685440.html.

Timiraos, N. 2013, December 2. "Shift on Nonconforming Mortgages." *Wall Street Journal.* Retrieved June 6, 2014, at http://online.wsj.com/news/articles/SB10001424052702304 5794045792344820368l6774.

U.S. Chamber of Commerce. 2010. "Stop the CFPA." Retrieved March 1, 2010, at http://www.stopthecfpa.com.

U.S. Commission on Civil Rights. 1961. *Housing: 1961 Commission on Civil Rights Report, Book 4 .* Washington, DC: U.S. Government Printing Office.

U.S. Department of Housing and Urban Development. 2008. "Methodology for Allocation of $3.92 Billion of Emergency Assistance for the Redevelopment of Abandoned and Fore-closed Homes." Washington, DC: U.S. Department of Housing and Urban Development. Retrieved February 20, 2010, at http://www.hud.gov/offices/cpd/ communitydevelopment/ programs/neighborhoodspg/nspfa_methodology.pdf.

U.S. Department of Housing and Urban Development. 2010a. "Guidance for Tracking and Reporting the Use of NSP Funds: Obligations For Specific Activities." Washington, DC: U.S. Department of Housing and Urban Development. Retrieved August 31, 2011, at http://hudnsphelp.info/media/resources/NSPPolicyAlert_Obligations_4-23-10.pdf.

U.S. Department of Housing and Urban Development. 2010b, April 2. "Guidance on the Impact Of New Definitions for NSP-Eligible Properties." Retrieved September 13, 2011, at http://hudnsphelp.info/media/resources/ImpactOfNewDefinitions.pdf.

U.S. Department of Housing and Urban Development. 2010c. "HUD Secretary Announces National First Look Program to Help Communities Stabilize Neighborhoods Hard-Hit By Foreclosure." Retrieved September 3, 2011, at http://portal.hud.gov/hudportal/HUD?src=/ press/press_releases_media_advisories/2010/HUD No.10-187.

U.S. Department of Housing and Urban Development. 2010d, January. "Report to Congress on the Root Causes of the Foreclosure Crisis."

U.S. Department of Housing and Urban Development. 2011a, January. "FHA Single-Family Operations." Retrieved August 22, 2011, at http://www.hud.gov/offices/hsg/rmra/oe/rpts/ ooe/ ol2011.pdf.

U.S. Department of Housing and Urban Development. 2011b. "The Facts about the Neighbor-hood Stabilization Program." Retrieved September 1, 2011, at http://blog.hud.gov/2011/03/ 15/facts-neighborhood-stabilization-program.

U.S. Department of Housing and Urban Development and U.S. Department of Treasury. 2014, January. "The Obama Administration's Efforts to Stabilize the Housing Market and Help American Homeowners."

U.S. Department of the Treasury. 2009a, June 17. "A New Foundation: Rebuilding Financial Supervision and Regulation." Retrieved August 2, 2009, at http://www.financialstability. gov/docs/regs/FinalReport_web.pdf.

U.S. Department of the Treasury. 2009b, March 4. "Making Home Affordable: Updated De-tailed Program Description." Retrieved August 19, 2011, at http://www.treasury.gov/press-center/press-releases/Documents/housing_fact_sheet.pdf.

U.S. Department of the Treasury. 2010a. "Departmental Offices—FY 2011 Congressional Justification." Retrieved May 3, 2010, at http://www.ustreas.gov/offices/management/bud-get/ budget-documents/cj/2011/DO%20CJ%20508.pdf.

U.S. Department of the Treasury. 2010b, September 16. "Making Home Affordable." Unpub-lished presentation.

U.S. Department of the Treasury. 2011a, August 5. "Making Home Affordable Program Perfor-mance Report through June 2011." Retrieved August 29, 2011, at http://www.treasury.gov/ initiatives/financial-stability/results/MHA-Reports/Documents/ June%202011%20MHA%20Report%20FINAL.PDF.

U.S. Department of the Treasury. 2011b, June 9. "Obama Administration Releases May Hous-ing Scorecard Featuring New Making Home Affordable Servicer Assessments, Regional Spotlight on Phoenix Housing Data." Retrieved August 31, 2011, at http:// www.treasury.gov/press-center/press-releases/Pages/tg1205.aspx.

U.S. Department of the Treasury. 2012, April. "Making Home Affordable Program Perfor-mance Report through March 2012." Retrieved May 19, 2012, at http://www.treasury.gov/

initiatives/financial-stability/results/MHA-Reports/Documents/
Mar%202012%20MHA%20Report%20Final.pdf.

U.S. Department of the Treasury. 2013. "Hardest Hit Fund Third Quarter 2013 Performance Summary."

U. S. Department of the Treasury and U.S. Department of Housing and Urban Development. 2000. "Curbing Predatory Home Mortgage Lending." Washington, DC: U.S. Department of Treasury and U.S. Department of Housing and Urban Development.

U.S. Department of the Treasury and U.S. Department of Housing and Urban Development, 2011, February. "Reforming America's Housing Finance Market." Washington, DC: U.S. Department of the Treasury and U.S. Department of Housing and Urban Development. Retrieved February 18, 2011, at http://www.treasury.gov/initiatives/Documents/Reforming%20America%27s%20Housing%20Finance%20Market.pdf.

U.S. General Accounting Office. 2004, January. "Consumer Protection: Federal and State Agencies Face Challenges in Combating Predatory Lending." GAO-04-280.

U.S. Government Accountability Office. 2010, December. "Neighborhood Stabilization Program: HUD and Grantees Are Taking Actions to Ensure Program Compliance but Data on Program Outputs Could Be Improved." GAO-11-48.

U.S. Government Accountability Office. 2011, May. "Survey of Housing Counselors about HAMP." GAO-11-376-R.

U.S. Government Accountability Office. 2012, June. "Foreclosure Mitigation: Agencies Could Improve Effectiveness of Federal Efforts with Additional Data Collection and Analysis." GAO-12-296.

U.S. House of Representatives. 2008, July 30. "H.R. 3221 Housing and Economic Recovery Act." Retrieved September 12, 2011, at http://www.govtrack.us/congress/bill.xpd?bill=h110-3221.

U.S. House of Representatives. 2009. "H.R.1. American Recovery and Reinvestment Act of 2009, Title XII, Community Development Fund." Retrieved March 17, 2009, at http://thomas.loc.gov/cgi-bin/query/z?c111:H.R.1.enr.

U.S. House of Representatives. 2010. "H.R. 4173. Dodd-Frank Wall Street Reform and Consumer Protection Act." Retrieved September 1, 2011, at http://docs.house.gov/rules/finserv/111_hr4173_finsrvcr.pdf.

U.S. House of Representatives. 2012, October 6. "The Obama Administration's Response to the Housing Crisis. Hearing before the Subcommittee on Insurance, Housing and Community Opportunity of the Committee on Financial Services, U.S. House of Representatives." Serial no. 112-69.

U.S. Securities and Exchange Commission. 2010a, April 16. "SEC Charges Goldman Sachs with Fraud in Structuring and Marketing of CDO Tied to Subprime Mortgages." Retrieved April 24, 2010, at http://www.sec.gov/news/press/2010/2010-59.htm.

U.S. Securities and Exchange Commission. 2010b, November 23. "Response of the Office of Chief Counsel Division of Corporation Finance, Re: Ford Motor Credit Company LLC, Regulation AB Item 1120." Retrieved June 2, 2014, at http://www.sec.gov/divisions/corpfin/cf-noaction/2010/ford072210-1120.htm.

U.S. Securities and Exchange Commission. 2014, August 27. "SEC Adopts Credit Rating Agency Reform Rules." Retrieved September 1, 2014, at http://www.sec.gov/News/PressRelease/Detail/PressRelease/1370542776658.

U.S. Senate. 2007, October 3. "Senate Bill 2136: Helping Families Save Their Homes in Bankruptcy Act of 2007." Retrieved September 3, 2011, at http://www.opencongress.org/bill/110-s2136/text.

Villafranco, J., and K. McPartland. 2010, December. "New Agency, New Authority: What You Need to Know About the Consumer Financial Protection Bureau." Kelley Drye. Retrieved June 6, 2014, at http://www.kelleydrye.com/publications/articles/1423.

Wallison, P. 2011, January 27. "Financial Crisis Inquiry Report: Dissenting Report." Washington, DC: Financial Crisis Inquiry Commission.

Wallison, P., A. Pollock, and E. Pinto. 2011, January 20. "Taking the Government out of Housing Finance: Principles for Reforming the Housing Finance Market." Washington, DC: American Enterprise Institute.

Warren, E. 2007, Summer. "Unsafe at Any Rate." *Democracy*. Retrieved January 2, 2008, at http://www.democracyjournal.org/article.php?ID=6528.

Warsh, K. 2007. "Market Liquidity: Definitions and Implications." Speech at the Institute of International Bankers Annual Washington Conference, Washington, DC. Federal Reserve Board of Governors. Retrieved May 5, 2014, at http://www.federalreserve.gov/newsevents/speech/warsh20070305a.htm.

Wartell. S. 2011, February 9. "GSE Reform: Immediate Steps to Protect Taxpayers and End the Bailout." Testimony before the House Committee on Financial Services. Washington, DC: Center for American Progress. Retrieved July 2, 2014, at http://www.americanprogressaction.org/issues/housing/report/2011/02/09/8999/gse-reform-immediate-steps-to-protect-taxpayers-and-end-the-bailout.

Weise, K. 2010, December 17. "Fannie and Freddie's Regulator Opposes Reducing Mortgages for Struggling Homeowners." *Propublica*. Retrieved August 29, 2011, at http://www.propublica.org/article/fannie-and-freddies-govt-regulator-opposes-reducing-mortgages-for-strugglin.

Weiss, N., D. Getter, M. Jickling, M. Keightley, and E. Murphy. 2008, August 19. "Housing and Economic Recovery Act of 2008." Congressional Research Service, order code RL34623. Retrieved January 2, 2009, at http://assets.opencrs.com/rpts/RL34623_20080819.pdf.

Wheaton, W., and G. Nechayev. 2008. "The 1998–2005 Housing Bubble and the Current Correction. What's Different This Time?" *Journal of Real Estate Research* 30: 1–26.

White, A. 2009. "Deleveraging the American Homeowner: The Failure of 2008 Voluntary Mortgage Contract Modifications." *Connecticut Law Review* 41: 1107. Retrieved April 17, 2015, at http://ssrn.com/abstract=1325534.

White, A. 2011. "Foreclosures and Modifications—Securitized Mortgage Data through May 25, 2011." Retrieved September 2, 2011, at http://www.valpo.edu/law/faculty/awhite/data/index.php.

White, A. M. 2009. "Borrowing While Black: Applying Fair Lending Laws to Risk-Based Mortgage Pricing." *South Carolina Law Review* 60(3). Retrieved April 17, 2015, at http://ssrn.com/abstract=1507289.

Whitehouse, M. 2007, May 30. "Subprime Aftermath: Losing the Family Home. Mortgages Bolstered Detroit's Middle Class—Until Money Ran Out." *Wall Street Journal*, p. A-1.

Williams, S., G. Galster, and N. Verma. 2013. "Home Foreclosures and Neighborhood Crime Dynamics." *Housing Studies*. DOI 10.1080/02673037.2013.803041.

Woodstock Institute. 2008, September 23. "First Half 2008 Foreclosure Filings." Chicago: Woodstock Institute. Retrieved February 7, 2014, at http://www.woodstockinst.org/sites/default/files/documents/foreclosurefilings_1H08_woodstock.pdf.

Woodstock Institute. 2011, February 9. "Last Quarter 2010 Foreclosure Filings." Chicago: Woodstock Institute. Retrieved February 7, 2014, at http://www.woodstockinst.org/sites/default/files/documents/foreclosurefactsheet_4Q10_woodstock_0.pdf.

Wyly, E., and C. Ponder. 2011. "Gender, Age, and Race in Subprime America." *Housing Policy Debate* 21: 529–564.

Zandi, M. 2012, May 12. "The Politics of Forgiving Mortgage Debt." *Washington Post*.

Ziol-Guest, K., and A. Kalil. 2013, April 20. "Long-Run Impact of Childhood Housing Instability on Adult Achievement." Paper presented at the meeting of the Society for Research in Child Development, Seattle, WA.

Ziol-Guest, K., and C. McKenna. 2013. "Early Childhood Housing Instability and School Readiness." *Child Development* 85: 103–113.

Notes

INTRODUCTION

1. Better Markets, "The Cost of the Wall Street-Caused Financial Collapse and Ongoing Economic Crisis Is More than $12.8 Trillion," *Better Markets*, September 15, 2012. Available online at http://bettermarkets.com/sites/default/files/Cost%20Of%20The%20Crisis_2.pdf (accessed April 15, 2015). Government Accountability Office, "Financial Crisis Losses and Potential Impacts of the Dodd-Frank Act," GAO-13-180 (Washington, DC: Government Accountability Office, January 16, 2013).

1. REVISITING THE ORIGINS OF THE SUBPRIME CRISIS

1. As of December 20, 2013, Worldcat, a leading bibliographic search engine of books in libraries around the world, listed over seven hundred books listing the key words *subprime crisis*, *mortgage crisis*, or *foreclosure crisis* and that were published between 2008 and 2013. When limiting the search to books appearing in at least five listed libraries, the number of books still exceeded 250. A Google Scholar search of *foreclosure crisis* between 2008 and 2013 yields over thirty-six hundred articles and books. A similar search on *mortgage crisis* yielded over fourteen thousand articles and books, as did a search on *subprime crisis*.

2. The CRA places an obligation on commercial banks to serve the credit needs of their communities. The law provides for regulators defining "assessment areas" for each institution but does not prescribe any specific amount of lending, but banks are expected to offer their loans to all parts of their assessment area and not exclude lower-income neighborhoods or borrowers. The Federal Housing Enterprises Safety and Soundness Act of 1992, among other things, established a system of formal affordable housing goals for the GSEs that were proposed and implemented by the GSE's mission regulator, the U.S. Department of Housing and Urban Development.

3. In the United States, the dominant credit-scoring system—the Fair Isaac Corporation or "FICO" score—ranges from 300 to 850. Traditionally, individuals with credit scores above 720 are considered to have very strong credit, with scores between 620 and 680 considered somewhat marginal, and scores below 620 classified as "subprime" in nature. Credit scores are based on payment history, amounts owed, length of credit history, the amount of recent credit activities, and types of credit (Fair Isaac Corporation 2010).

3. THE FEDERAL GOVERNMENT TO THE RESCUE?

1. *Note:* Lightly shaded boxes indicate foreclosure prevention policies; darker boxes are mitigation policies. Dashed, white boxes are external events; dashed, shaded boxes are policies likely to have significant indirect effects on foreclosures. ARRA= American Recovery and Reinvestment Act; HERA=Housing and Economic Recovery Act; FHA= Federal Housing Administration; NSP=Neighborhood Stabilization Program; 2MP= Second Mortgage Modification Program; HARP=Housing Affordable Refinance Program; HHF= Hardest Hit Fund; EHLP=Emergency Home Loan Program; PRA=Principal Reduction Alternative; HAFA=Housing Affordable Foreclosure Alternatives; GSE=Government sponsored enterprises; UP= Home Affordable Unemployment Program; Dodd-Frank = Dodd-Frank Wall Street Reform and Consumer Protection Act.

2. Loan modifications received by NFMC clients receiving loan modifications resulted in substantially lower loan payments than would have been received without counseling. The Urban Institute researchers estimate that NFMC clients receiving loan modifications in the first two program years reduced their mortgage payments by $267 per month more than they would have without NFMC counseling. The sustainability of modifications was also greater for NFMC clients than for other borrowers.

3. Twelve-month redefault rates would be expected to be substantially higher than these rates.

4. By allowing homeowners to refinance into lower-cost mortgages, HARP would also result in providing borrowers with more disposable income. Thus the program also had a goal of stimulating the economy more broadly. Arguably, this goal became more important as the economic crisis worsened.

5. In the first step of the modification, the loan servicer rolls any unpaid interest and fees into the outstanding loan balance. Then, the servicer reduces the interest rate on the loan down to as low as 2 percent (with half of the loss in interest being absorbed by the federal government). If the 31 percent monthly debt-to-income ratio has still not been reached, the term of the loan can be extended to as long as forty years. If the 31 percent ratio has still not been reached, the servicer, at its option (and sometimes requiring the permission of the lender/investor), can defer the due date of some of the principal on the loan (called "forbearance").

6. White (2011) collected data from private-label mortgage backed securities that show loss severity rates ranging from 40 to over 80 percent with a median of approximately 64 percent. Fannie Mae's quarterly reporting shows that REO sale prices as a share of unpaid principal balances averaged approximately 56 percent in 2009 and 2010 (Fannie Mae 2011). Because unpaid principal balance does not include interest and fees, loss-severity ratios will be greater than 44 percent on such loans, and most likely approach something on the order of 50 percent.

7. A short sale occurs when a borrower sells her house for less than the amount owned on the outstanding mortgage(s) and the lender(s) agrees to release the mortgage on the property for this amount. Deeds-in-lieu of foreclosure occur when borrowers sign over their property to the lender in exchange for the mortgage being released.

8. Changes to the PRA program in 2012 made sizable increases to the incentives for principal reductions, essentially tripling them. This increase may affect the future participation of the GSEs in the PRA program, although as of May 2012, the FHFA continues its policy of not participating in the program.

9. Requirements for starting trials changed significantly in June 2010 because full verification of income was not required uniformly before this date. As a result, conversions to permanent modifications increased significantly after this date (U.S. Department of Treasury 2011a).

10. There is considerable debate over how pooling and servicing agreements and the structures of private-label securitization structures impede substantial loan modifications. Thompson (2009) is among those who argue that securitization is not a significant impediment to modification, while Levitin and Twomey (2011) argue that securitization structures can effectively impede modifications. Moreover, Agarwal et al. (2010) find that securitized loans are significantly and substantially less likely to be modified than loans held in portfolio.

11. The eighteen-month deadline to obligate NSP 1 funds did not mean that all funds had to be expended within that timeframe. According to HUD regulations, *obligation* means "the amounts of orders placed, contracts awarded, goods and services received, and similar transactions during a given period that will require payment by the grantee (or subrecipient) during the same or a future period" (U.S. Department of Housing and Urban Development 2010b). Obligations must be for specific NSP activities that can be linked to a specific address or household. Thus, a subcontract to a third party that would later purchase specific properties would not be considered an obligation.

12. One source of national estimates of foreclosed properties is the financial blog Calculated Risk (2011), which relies on estimates from the housing economist Tom Lawler and have been generally consistent with some other estimates. Calculated Risk's estimates include properties owned by the GSEs, HUD/FHA, private-label securities, and FDIC-insured banks. Properties owned by credit unions, non-FDIC-insured lenders, and some smaller federal agencies are not included. Thus Calculated Risk estimates that the data represent "at least 90 percent" of all foreclosed properties. To account for the incomplete coverage, I multiply the Calculated Risk totals by 1.11 to come up with the range.

13. As NSP 1 was being implemented in the spring of 2010, the definitions of *foreclosed* and *abandoned* properties were broadened to make the funds more flexible and responsive. For example, the definition of *foreclosed properties* was broadened to include properties for which a mortgage is more than sixty days delinquent as well as tax-delinquent properties (U.S. Department of Housing and Urban Development 2010c).

Index

About the Author

Dan Immergluck is professor in the School of City and Regional Planning at Georgia Tech in Atlanta, where he teaches and conducts research on housing, real estate, mortgage finance, and community- and economic-development topics. He is the author of three previous books, more than four dozen scholarly articles, numerous book chapters and encyclopedia entries, and scores of applied-research and policy reports. Dr. Immergluck has worked with federal, state, and local governments, foundations, and nonprofit organizations on a wide variety of projects. He has testified several times before Congress, as well as before the Federal Reserve Board and a variety of state and local legislative bodies. Professor Immergluck has served as a visiting scholar at the Federal Reserve Bank of Atlanta and as a senior fellow with the Center for Community Progress. He is an associate editor of the *Journal of the American Planning Association* and sits on the editorial boards of four journals. He has been quoted frequently in national media, including the *Wall Street Journal*, the *New York Times*, the *Washington Post, Bloomberg-Business Week,* National Public Radio, and other outlets.